*SLASH
RANCH
HOUNDS*

SLASH

High-Lonesome Books

SILVER CITY, NM

G. W. "Dub" Evans

RANCH HOUNDS

Publisher's Preface Copyright © 2003 by M.H. Salmon

ISBN-13: 978-0-944383-64-3 (hardcover)
ISBN-10: 0-944383-64-5 (hardcover)
ISBN-13: 978-0-944383-87-2 (softcover)
ISBN-10: 0-944383-87-4 (softcover)

First Edition Copyright © 1951

University of New Mexico Press
Albuquerque, NM

~ ~ ~ ~ ~ ~ ~ ~ ~ ~ ~

Reprint Edition
First Printing 2003
Second Printing 2010

High-Lonesome Books
P.O. Box 878
Silver City, NM 88062

To

my father
the late G. W. EVANS;
my brother, LEE EVANS,
who has ridden with me
on more hunts than
has any other man;
and to my friends,
JUDGE C. M. BOTTS;
and the late
J. W. KIRKPATRICK
—good sportsmen all
and good companions,
whose love of good
hounds exceeds that
of any other men
I have known

I DEDICATE THIS BOOK

A PREFACE FROM THE PUBLISHER

A Land for Hounds, Hunters, and Lovers of the Wild

Rising out of a sea of grass, scrub, and a lot of dust during the current drought, the Gila National Forest of southwest New Mexico is an anomaly in an otherwise arid land. Here are pine and oak and aspen, trout streams, and high peaks separated by a maze of impossible canyons. If it weren't so big—3.3 million acres—it would seem out of place.

At its core are the Gila and Aldo Leopold Wilderness areas, some 800,000 acres of roadless terrain, off limits to motor vehicles, chain saws, and development. And just to the east in Arizona, separated by an invisible state line but connected by an unbroken geography, is the Blue Range Primitive Area, another 200,000 acres of wild country. Over the many years this territory of big predators and lost canyons has produced an unparalleled storyline of hounds and hunters.

Of course all of us are inclined to brag on our home or adopted state or range. Some other states may have larger forests or wilderness areas, or more game per square mile, or bigger bears and lions. Other ranges have produced great hounds and hunters too, but too often their pursuits are lost to history. But in the Gila Range of southwest New Mexico and southeast Arizona, history had fortune on its side, and writers and chroniclers of various talents came in pursuit of it. The chase got written up, and the characters, human and hound and beast, are etched in print for all time.

Consider the famous bear and lion men of this section: Ben Lilly; Montague Stevens; Clell and Dale Lee; Nat Straw; James "Bear" Moore; Frank Hibben; Will Evans; Dub Evans. Consider the books: *The Ben Lilly Legend* by J. Frank Dobie; *Ben Lilly's Tales* by Ben Lilly, Neil Carmony editor; *Meet Mr. Grizzly* by Montague Stevens; *Life of the Greatest Guide* by Dale Lee and Robert McCurdy; *Mogollón Mountain Man* (Nat Straw) by Carolyn O'Bagy Davis; *Hunting American Lions* and *Hunting American Bears* by Frank Hibben; *Hunting Grizzlies, Black Bear and Lion "Big Time" on the Old Ranches* by Will Evans, and *Slash Ranch Hounds* by Dub Evans. And the famous hounds: Lilly's "Crook" and "Tip;" Steven's "Sleuth;" the Lee Brothers "Blue" and "Pilot;" Hibben's "Pancho," "Sissy," and "Drive;" and "Brownie" (actually there were several "Brownies") of the Evans family.

Everyone has their favorite among hound books (mine is *Meet Mr. Grizzly*) but *Slash Ranch Hounds* is certainly among the best in any section. It is very strong on the intricate workings of hounds in pursuit of scent. While not a "how-to" book, any houndman can benefit from Evan's training tips and hunting techniques, most told within the context of stories. And Dub Evans was simply a good writer, who could render an exciting chase that we can feel today without the need for tall tales and exaggerations. From long experience following the hounds horseback in wild country, he knew that an honest recall of actual events was the best story of all.

And now that we're into the 21st century, what's left of this country that produced all these stirring events, races between hound and quarry, and books of hunting history? Surprisingly, quite a bit. The Wilderness and Primitive areas are still roadless, and even outside of wilderness, much of the terrain is remote, sees few visitors, and will tax any man afoot or horseback. Black bear and lion are relatively abundant, and still legal game for hunter and hound. The grizzly is gone, but the wolf is coming back.

Dub Evans of course would be astounded that anyone would favor the return of the wolf. He devotes an entire chapter in *Slash Ranch Hounds* to the critter's extirpation in the Southwest. While he could accommodate some black bear and lion on his ranch, the extermination of the wolf he could only describe as "good riddance." And rumors of the grizzly's return would not please him either, for he and his family worked hard to kill among the vary last "big bears" in this state and in Texas. The cattleman had their reasons for wanting the wolf and grizzly gone. Yet something of the wild went out of the wilderness with their demise.

We here at High-Lonesome Books want to be part of keeping the history alive, in print and in the field. We have hounds ourselves, coursing hounds to be sure, but like you we thrill to the chase. We're pleased that *Slash Ranch Hounds* is now on our list of published books, joining *Meet Mr. Grizzly* and a number of the other hounds and hunting books listed above. We favor a wild Gila, big enough for bears and lions and their legal pursuit by hounds. Big enough for wolves and "big bears" too, and cows and cowboys. As predators long gone come back, a new history is being written (see our book *The Wolf in the Southwest* by David Brown). Wolves will one day be legal game in the West; now there's a challenge for hound and hunter! Whether houndman or cowboy, mule packer or backpacker, fly fisher or birdwatcher with granola in your daypack, the Gila Range is still the country for lovers of the wild.

M.H. Dutch Salmon
High-Lonesome Books
Silver City, New Mexico
September 2003

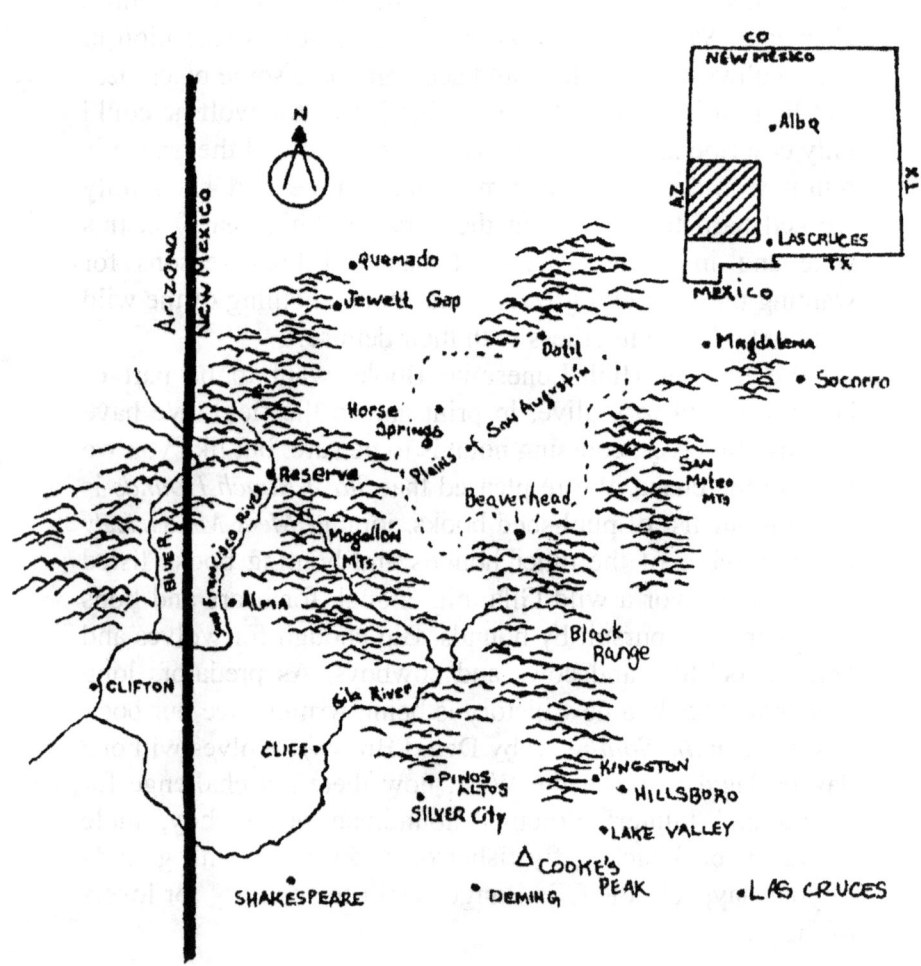

FOREWORD

Those of us who have had the distinct privilege of being with Dub Evans and his hounds in the wilderness recognize that this book is not fiction, though to the uninitiated, parts of it will read like fiction—or even stranger.

Dub is one of the closest observers I ever knew. He can "read sign" like an Indian tracker. And, better still, he has the faculty of pointing out to the novice all the interesting things he sees, and explaining the mysterious ways of Nature which he has learned first hand. This book will give the reader an inkling of what I mean. But it will be only an inkling, for no man could put on paper a substitute for an actual experience with the author and his hounds.

And those hounds! Developed through generations for the hunting of big game, they display intelligence, wisdom, courage, and patience almost beyond belief. The author is a successful rancher and a leader in public and religious affairs; but, next to his family, I believe his first love is for his hounds. And the reader will love them, too, before the book is finished.

C. M. Botts

Albuquerque, New Mexico
October 9th, 1951

CONTENTS

		PAGE
	INTRODUCTION	1
CHAPTER		
I	THE VERSATILITY OF A HOUND	13
II	THE MYSTERY OF SCENT	24
III	DOUBLING BACK	36
IV	DEER, ANTELOPE, AND BEAR	50
V	CHARACTERISTICS OF LIONS	63
VI	MT. TAYLOR LION HUNT	74
VII	WOLF CUNNING	81
VIII	WHEN BELL CAME AFTER SCOTTY	91
IX	UNUSUAL HUNTS	98
	TWO COMBINATION HUNTS	98
	LION KILLED WITH BARE HANDS	104
X	LION MARKERS (By J. Frank Dobie)	107
XI	HUNTING LIONS WITH A LASSO (By Dr. Henry M. Calvin)	123
XII	"GET AWAY FROM THAT BEAR"	136
XIII	TWO TAYLOR CREEK MALES	142
XIV	MORE UNUSUAL HUNTS	148
	HUNTING LIONS AT SEVENTY-FIVE	148
	HOUNDS THAT HUNT ALONE	151
	LION HUNT IN THE NIGHT	154

SLASH RANCH HOUNDS

CHAPTER		PAGE
XV	OLD MAN GRIZZLY	159
XVI	FIVE LION HUNTS	167
	HORSE-KILLING LIONS	167
	LION KITTENS	170
	A FAMILY HUNT	174
	ONE MORE CHANCE	176
	FASTEST HUNT ON RECORD	178
XVII	OLD FIVE-TOE TOM	182
XVIII	TWO STOCK-KILLING BEAR	189
XIX	"TAKE YOUR TIME, BUT HURRY" (By Hoxie Thompson)	196
XX	"HOUND VITAMINS" (By Hoxie Thompson)	204
XXI	A NINE-FOOT LION	211
XXII	BEAR AND ANTELOPE HUNTS	214
XXIII	BLANCHE	224
XXIV	NO BAG LIMIT ON LOOKING	233
XXV	OLD BROWNIE	244

INTRODUCTION

My father, George W. Evans, had hunting hounds and hunted with them along the Nueces and Frio rivers, in east-central Texas, when he was a boy, and kept a strain of good hunting hounds throughout his lifetime. When he moved with his family and cattle into the Davis Mountains of west Texas in 1884, he brought his hounds along also. He located on Cherry Canyon in the heart of the Davis Mountains and used his hounds not only for pleasure but for the protection of his livestock.

The hounds contributed also, then as they have since, to the feeding of the family. Particularly in the fall of the year, when bear were fat on natural mast (mostly juniper berries, acorns, and piñon nuts), the hounds were used to hunt bear, and the fat from these mast-fed bear was rendered and used for cooking oil. The usual procedure was to put up enough bear oil while the bear were fat to last until fat bear were again available. Maybe this sounds like one of the hardships of frontier living, but it wasn't. There is no better shortening to be had anywhere for biscuits or pastry than bear oil. We use it to this day, and you would be surprised how many of the letters and telegrams we get, from people who have visited or hunted with us before, are worded, "Will arrive such-and-such a day. Have the bear-oil biscuits ready!" Biscuits shortened with good, well-rendered oil from a mast-fattened bear have a flavor not equaled by any other kind of biscuit, and people who have tried them always come back for more.

Will and Joe were the only children in the family at the time George and Kate Means Evans moved to west Texas; but as the years passed there was born to them a big family: Lee, G. W., Jr. ("Dub"), Rube, Ell, Paul, Grace (the only girl, now Mrs. Bill Cowden), and Graves.

As the boys of the family grew up and married and began to spread out it was necessary to buy ranches in other localities. In 1910, my mother's brother, John Z. Means, his two eldest sons (Sam and Huling), my brother Joe, and I formed a company called John Z. Means & Company. This company acquired ranches in Reeves, Winkler, Ward, Loving, and Culberson counties, centering on the Pecos River in west Texas. In 1916, we bought the Harry Martin ranch and cattle in Grant County, west of Silver City, New Mexico.

This would be as good a place as any, I suppose, to tell how the Slash brand came into the Evans family. One of the ranches acquired by John Z. Means & Company in 1910 was the Running W outfit purchased from Johnson Brothers, of Pecos, Texas. Sam Means and I went to Pecos to take charge of this outfit, Sam as manager and I as wagon boss. I was twenty-two years old at the time. This deal was made entirely on credit, even the $25,000 down payment being nothing more than a promissory note.

Although this outfit, which ran from ten to fifteen thousand cattle, was called the Running W, we were surprised to find that the prevalent running brand was a Slash ($\diagdown$) on the left shoulder running well down on the ribs, and a Slash ($\diagup$) on the left hip, each slash about twelve inches in length. We were very much impressed with this brand because it was so easy to put on and so easy to see. So, when the time came to tally the Johnson Brothers cattle out to the newly formed John Z. Means & Company, we used the same Slash brand on the opposite side.

INTRODUCTION

We have used the Slash brand ever since. Later, when buyers objected to having so much of the hide spoiled by those two long slashes on the shoulder and hip, I adopted (and still use) a much shorter slash on the left jaw and left thigh. I have been interested in the Slash brand since 1910, have been exclusive owner of the brand in its present form since 1943,* and never intend to let it go. It is still "easy to put on, easy to see."

Things went well at first, and John Z. Means & Company developed a substantial equity in the ranches and the 25,000 cattle on them. But the drouth of 1917 and 1918 upset all our plans, causing the loss of most of the vast herd of 15,000 cattle on our Texas ranches and leaving us with an enormously increased debt, due to expenses incurred for feed and additional pasturage in trying to save some of the cattle.

We weren't the only ones hurt, and no one who lived through that dry spell will ever forget it. Even the newspapers remember. The fourth July, 1951, issue of the San Angelo (Texas) *Standard Times* says:

If you'd been here in 1917 and 1918, when it didn't rain a drop for 19 months, the current drouth would look like a rainstorm . . . During that overwhelming drouth cattle died by thousands. You could ride a horse from one end of the North Concho to the other without gettting his feet wet. . . . It extended all over the Southwest, so there was nowhere to send cattle and most of them died. About two thousand people left, going anywhere they could. A lot of them went to Fort Worth and worked in the packing houses, slaughtering the cattle there wasn't enough grazing land to feed. It was really a three-year drouth . . . There was a little rain in 1916, but none in 1917 and 1918.

There's one thing the newspaper story doesn't tell; a thing I remember better than anything else except maybe our own troubles. Up to 1916, that country was thickly populated with quail and rabbits. After the drouth, there wasn't a quail to be found

---

* When Slash Ranch was sold to Adams and Estes in 1938, the old Slash brand with its long slashes went with the ranch and is still in use by the present owner, Roy Cleveland. My own short slashes, used one on the left jaw and one on the left thigh of the animal, are fairly accurately reproduced by the red "slashes" on the jacket of this book.

SLASH RANCH HOUNDS

anywhere, or hardly a rabbit. It's pretty hard times when quail and rabbits can't make a living, but that's the way it was in 1917 and 1918 in west Texas. The buzzards did fine. Everything and everybody else starved, moved out, or went broke.

Finally, in an effort to save some of the Pecos River herd, in 1917, we purchased the western half of the Red River Land and Cattle Company's V Cross T Ranch in western Socorro (now Catron) County, eighty-five miles southwest of Magdalena, New Mexico. This purchase included three thousand V Cross T cows already on the range, and we immediately shipped two thousand head more up from the drouth-stricken Texas ranches.

Sam Means took charge of the new Magdalena ranch, and we were just about set up there in time for the big snow of 1918 and 1919. When spring finally came, we had lost 2,500 more head of cattle. By this time, we had more debts than cows to pay them with.

Early in 1919, the Means and Evans families decided to divide the ranch properties belonging to the Company. This would not affect the original ranches in west Texas, belonging to John Z. Means and George W. Evans, Sr., these having always been operated separately from the Company holdings. In the division of properties, two new partnerships were formed: Means & Sons, who took over the Grant County ranch known as the H Bar Y; and Evans Brothers, who took over the Company-owned Texas ranches with the 2,500-head remnant of their original 15,000-head herd, and the Magdalena ranch with its remaining 2,500 cattle, all that were left after the snowstorm.

As soon as possible after the division, the Company-owned Texas ranches and cattle were sold and, in June, 1919, I moved to the Magdalena ranch with my wife, Beulah Gillett Evans, and two children, Pansy and G. W., III. Bob and Jim, the other two children making up our present family, were born in New Mexico.

My brother, Lee, was living in New Mexico, having bought

INTRODUCTION

the L Bar Ranch, on land grants from Gross-Kelly, in 1916. This ranch is located forty-five miles west of Albuquerque in the Mt. Taylor country. Lee and I had married sisters; Beulah, my wife, and Lou C., Lee's wife, were the daughters of Captain and Mrs. J. B. Gillett, one of the pioneer ranch families of west Texas.

The Magdalena ranch, known as the Slash, (later also referred to as Beaverhead) is located in the Gila country between the Black Range on the east and the Mogollons on the west. Two prongs of the Gila, the East Fork and the Middle Fork, head in this area. This being a natural habitat for bear and lion, the obvious procedure was to start a pack of hounds; and what was more natural than that the start of such a pack should come from the original pack in the Davis Mountains, out of the stock that had been so faithfully maintained by my father?

In fact, Sam Means had already started a pack of hounds. He had Alice, of the original Evans strain, and a Redbone hound by that name that had been given us by a Government hunter. I mated these hounds, and out of this mating came a litter of pups, two of which were Brownie and Bell. It was under the leadership of these two great hounds that my pack became nationally known.

This Brownie (see Illustration 1) was named after an outstanding hound owned and trained by my father in Texas, one of a pair of registered American foxhounds presented to my father by Mr. Sheldon and Mr. Payne of the Sheldon & Payne Arms Company, of El Paso. It was the custom then, in the early days of the Means and Evans families, to have annual hunts at which, at times, there would be as many as fifty hounds, combining the packs of the several ranchmen in the surrounding area. The practice was to put out one "strike" hound and keep all the others behind the horses until a trail was struck. It was no easy job to keep all those fresh hounds of the mixed packs at heel while my father's Brownie was out in front to make the strike, but there was no doubt about Brownie's fitness for the job. Although, during the rest of the year, our hounds, including Brownie, were used to catch foxes, cats, and panthers, I never knew Brownie to open up on anything but a bear while being used as a strike dog on a bear hunt. Of course, as soon as Brownie opened, there was no way of holding back the rest of the pack, and the grand race would be on.

Nothing is more exciting than a fast start on a bear trail in the early morning when the bear has left the feeding grounds and headed for a rough mountainside of a heavily wooded canyon to lay up. It is impossible to travel at a fast rate of speed through rough country in large groups, and as soon as the chase was started the party would break up into groups of two or three, all of them riding madly, trying to stay within hearing of the hounds. Inevitably some would be lost out of the race and would never know what happened until they got back to camp. Usually on such a hunt, when the kill has been made there is the blowing of the hunting horn or the firing of three well-spaced shots to call the hunters in.

So it was in memory of this great strike dog of my father's that I named my first Brownie; and, lest any reader get the idea that this Brownie lived forever, I had better explain here that there has been at least one Brownie in my pack ever since, all descendants, more or less directly, of that first offspring of Redbone and Alice. Various registered blood lines have entered into the development of what are now known as Slash Ranch hounds, but our hounds, themselves, have never been registered. Birth dates have never been kept, either, except more or less roughly in our memories. The name Brownie has been a sort of honorary title in my pack, given to pups that showed special promise. All of these things may be a little confusing to the reader, however clear it seems to us; and our use of such name-variations as "Old Brownie," "Little Brownie," etc., to distinguish one Brownie from another, may add to the confusion. But this needn't matter very much. All of the Brownies have been much alike in the major qualities that

INTRODUCTION

make a hunting hound. All have been great performers, and no bearer of the name has ever disappointed me. In fact, I think so much of the Brownies that I wanted to call this book "The Brownies"; but people persuaded me that the name has too many other meanings.

All of the hunts in the early days in Texas were on a non-commercial basis; but after moving to New Mexico I was raising a family that had to be clothed, fed, and educated and, since the drouth and storms had left Evans Brothers heavily in debt, it was a natural sideline to make use of the horses, pack equipment, and hounds and to charge a fee for the hunts. It helped pay living expenses for a growing family, leaving all the money from cattle sales to pay off our vast debt more quickly.

Most of these hunts were made on our own range, and at times when they could be either combined with or sandwiched in between ranch work that had to be done. When we would move out from headquarters on a hunt I would usually take along three cowboys. One would act as guide for the hunters while the other two would scatter salt, ride fences, or brand calves that had been missed in the regular "works."* I realized fully that the only way the outfit could be paid out was to take the best possible care of the ranch and cattle at all times, and I would never let a hunt interfere with the regular ranch work. I was manager and part owner of the Evans Brothers ranch, a big mountain outfit with from three to five thousand cattle, from 1919 to 1938; and, during part of that time, from 1930 to 1943, I was also operating, developing, part owner and manager of Augustine Plains Ranches, Inc., where we were running three or four thousand cattle. The hunts were made only at such times as I could get away from the pressing duties of running the two ranches. Ours is and has always been

---

* Works: periodically, cattlemen systematically "work" their ranges, sending riders over the entire area to round up, inspect, doctor, brand—in a word take inventory of their stock. These periodic efforts are called "works."

a serious, successful, working cattle outfit, not in any sense merely a "dude ranch" for hunters.

A hunt in the big mountains without proper mounts would be a failure, but on a ranch of the size I was operating at the time these hunts were made, over a hundred head of saddle horses and from ten to twenty pack mules are required to mount and equip properly the number of hands necessary for branding and gathering cattle for shipping. Naturally, when this work was completed there were plenty of horses for the hunters to ride, as well as mules to pack the needed camp equipment.

There is one other thing that perhaps should be mentioned. I have always felt that men and horses and hounds alike deserve one day of rest out of seven, and we have always tried to plan our hunts so that Sunday would be a day of rest. But sometimes circumstances altered our plans. There were times when, for one reason or another, a hunt just couldn't be called off at sunset on Saturday; and there were times, a few, when the hounds struck a hot trail on a lazy Sunday ride intended only for sightseeing. There were times, too, when paying guests had only a limited number of days to spend with us and when it would not have been fair to them to refuse to hunt. My conscience has never hurt me over these occasions. In fact, I know of few better, less sinful ways to spend a Sunday than in the big mountains with horses and hounds and good companions, whether in camp or actually on the trail of a bear or lion. A man surely can't think any very mean or wicked thoughts in such surroundings, and even less so if he's busy keeping on top of a horse and in hearing of a running pack over rough country. A great writer once said that the woods were God's first temples; and, to me at least, the voice of a hunting pack is music equal to that of any organ.

I long for the ability to express just what I know and how I feel about the stability, loyalty, endurance, and complete honesty of a good hound. I have seen one work hour after hour, day

INTRODUCTION

after day, on the trail of a bear or lion and never once offer to take any of the ever-present tracks of other animals.

Some of the best lessons that I have learned in life I have learned from the faithful performance of a hound. On the trail there are times when it seems useless to continue and one is inclined to give up; but not so with a good hound. Many times I have seen a trail suddenly get better and both hound and hunter amply rewarded for the unusual effort of the hound in staying instead of quitting. In business I have seen some tough spots where it looked useless to continue, and have derived the courage to carry on by thinking of hunts I had made when things looked hopeless to me but where a good hound wouldn't quit even after I had tried to call him off.

The Evans Brothers company was liquidated in 1937 and 1938, delivering over 3,700 cattle. The Augustine Plains Ranches, Inc., owned, one-third each, by W. D. Johnson, Sr., W. D. Johnson, Jr., and myself, was divided in 1943, the Johnsons getting two-thirds of the ranch and cattle and the other third of each becoming my property. My third of the cattle numbered over twelve hundred head and my part of the ranch is known as the Montosa Ranch, which I still own and operate. My present headquarters is at Montosa Ranch, twelve miles west of Magdalena, New Mexico, on Highway 60, at the foot of Tres Montosas Peaks, with a beautiful view of the San Mateo Mountains to the south and of the Magdalena Mountains to the east. As a matter of fact, before the Montosa house was built, I went there and chose the site that would give it the best possible advantage of these views.

Slash Ranch lies about 75 miles southwest of Montosa, at the head of Beaver Creek. It is this location which gave the place its official name, Beaverhead, under which name its post office was established in 1922. For seven years, the Beaverhead post office was located at Slash Ranch headquarters.

Horse Camp is situated eighteen or twenty miles nearly due

west of Beaverhead, in a niche cut for it by special Federal dispensation into the edge of the Gila Wilderness. It is rough country between Beaverhead and Horse Camp, making the distance seem further than it really is; and when, as frequently happens, the hounds strike a varmint trail en route one way or the other, the trip may easily require a day.

One last word and then this Introduction is finished. We have never made it a practice to kill every animal we have treed, whether lion, bear, or cat. Hunting mostly on our own range, where our own calves run the major risk of any depredation these animals may do, we still feel that these beasts, too, have a place and a right to continue to live in reasonable numbers in these mountains; that they should not be hunted out of existence. About the lobo wolf we feel quite differently. These we have always tried to exterminate. But lion, bear, and wildcats come, in our minds, under a different category. Of course, most of the hunters we guide want trophies, and for them kills are made; and when an individual animal, bear or lion, becomes a known cattle-killer, naturally we hunt him down. But we, ourselves, hunt more for sport than for trophies; and when the hounds bark "treed" under an animal which has given them and us a sporting trail to follow, that animal may well be left alive to run again, for our delight, another day.

I want to make it plain that it is not my object to build up the lion population so it will be easier for me to get one for a paying guest hunter. Nothing could be further from the truth. I do, however, want to see some lions left because they belong here naturally, and when left alone will help to keep the deer population in balance with the food supply. In 1934, we had a severe drouth in the southwestern New Mexico area with which I am most familiar. This area—from the East Fork of the Gila across Jordan Mesa, the Green Fly and Cassidy areas, and on across Indian Creek and to Canyon Creek on the west—was heavily stocked

INTRODUCTION

with deer and in such a drouth a serious loss was inevitable. The reliable supply of deer food has remained meager since the drouth, and even with predators in the area under control, the deer population has never built back to anything like the numbers prior to 1934.

Livestock cannot be blamed for the non-recovery of deer feed, as, in 1937, all the cattle were removed from the Green Fly allotment and the allotment had complete non-use by livestock for four years. At this time, before restocking, an inspection was made by Bill Cole, forest ranger for the district, Loyd Wall, assistant supervisor from Silver City, and myself, and Mr. Wall reported that the unstocked area showed no appreciable improvement and recommended a doe season. An open season on does was declared for one season only, and since the area is only accessible by pack, very few does were taken off.

The area is still very lightly stocked with cattle, and the mesas are abundantly covered with grass, even constituting a fire hazard, but the stuff that deer live on is sick and there will never be a healthy deer population until it is reduced to a point below the carrying capacity and kept under control until the deer feed has recovered. I believe the forest officials want to exercise such controls but the organized sportsmen, because of unfamiliarity with all the facts, raise such a protest that nothing is done. If the lions and coyotes were left alone in the area, they would help some in keeping the deer population in balance, but they, too, are kept down and a sorry herd of deer remains on what used to be the very best hunting area.

Out of this herd of deer, which I estimate at five thousand, there are removed each year only about two hundred bucks, few of which are very good. If a cow man applied the same control to a cow herd this size, taking off a couple of hundred steers each year, he would soon go out of business because the surplus would grow until the feed supply was exhausted and then die off in great numbers, but would increase fast enough to keep the feed down.

There should be a doe season, and no predatory animal control until the area recovers. I believe there are no more than a half dozen lions in the whole area described, and there never was a better lion country.

I have made only one commercial lion hunt in the last ten years, and that was to keep a promise made earlier. I turn away lion hunters each year, and intend to continue to do so as long as conditions remain as they are. I have not only given up hunting, but, also, the raising of hounds for sale. It takes too long now to get a lion; in fact, there is no certainty of getting one at all. And until there is some other effort to make the deer herd fit the feed supply, the lion should be left alone to let nature keep things in balance as nearly as possible.

If this be treason to the conservationist, he'll have to make the most of it. We don't think it is treason. We think, from long observation, that the predator, kept under reasonable control, is needed to keep Nature's own balance in the woods they roam. And, whether that's right or wrong, we like to know there are still a few of them alive—to pit their wits against the Slash Ranch hounds!

CHAPTER I

THE VERSATILITY OF A HOUND

In the central part of the Slash Ranch range is Black Mountain, on which there is no permanent stock water; but all along the eastern foothills of Black Mountain and the western foothills of the Black Range, big springs break out and form Beaver Creek, which actually is the headwaters of the East Fork of the Gila River.

Leading off into Beaver Creek there are some rough, brushy points known as the Kemp Points, named after Ben Kemp, who homesteaded on Beaver Creek in 1904. Black Mountain is all rough and brushy, which, with permanent water in Beaver Creek, reached by stock via trails off Kemp Points, made an ideal setup for wild cattle.

In 1919, when I came to Beaverhead, then known as the old V Cross T headquarters, there were about four hundred of these wild cattle running in the Black Mountain area, most of them watering in Beaver Creek and the East Fork, which is formed by the junction of Beaver and Taylor creeks. Taylor Creek rises in the Black Range (not to be confused with Black Mountain).

Soon after I took over this property I had a visit from Cole

SLASH RANCH HOUNDS

Railston, manager of the Adobe Ranch, the eastern half of the Red River Land and Cattle Company's property, which they retained. They continued to use the V Cross T brand. Cole wanted to know what I intended to do with the wild cattle on Black Mountain. I simply told him that I wanted them cleaned out. They were all branded, and still belonged to Cole's outfit, and were so wild that none of them were tallied out to us.

It had been Cole's practice for many years to send a pack outfit back into Black Mountain to brand up the calves that had been missed in the regular works. These outfits usually consisted of about four top cowboys, each with a string of eight or ten good horses. Range branding is very difficult in rough country, and calves that are run onto, roped, branded, and turned loose in the same area never forget, and will run whenever they see a rider afterwards. As these wild cattle were running on our range, but bearing Cole's brand, I told him it should be his responsibility to gather them, and that if he didn't get them out in two years I would gather them for him.

He said that no one had ever been able to do anything about the wild cattle on Black Mountain. We reached an understanding to the effect that he had the privilege of sending an outfit into our part of the range any time he desired for the next two years, but every time they came on our side I was to have a man with them to see that our cattle were not choused,* and that when a bunch of our gentle cattle were used as a "hold-up," they were not to be unduly damaged.

A hold-up is a small bunch of gentle cattle that are moved around from place to place to be held in small clearings by a couple of men while other riders circle the surrounding country for wild cattle. If these riders jump a wild bunch they try to head them into the hold-up. Always when approaching the hold-up with the wild ones, the boys sound a warning so that the men

---
* Chouse: to stir up, annoy, or needlessly drive cattle.

THE VERSATILITY OF A HOUND

on watch will be on the alert and will ride around to the opposite side and try to stop the wild cattle in the hold-up.

Many times this works, but sometimes the wild cattle break right on through, and the only way to stop them in such cases is to rope them. The cowboy doing the roping usually tries to catch the ringleader, but even if he does, and there are several head in the bunch, the others will scatter and have to be hunted up at another time, with another trial at a hold-up.

The ones that are roped usually have to be tied to a tree and left there for two or three days until their will to run and fight is broken to where they can be kept in and driven with the gentle cattle. This is a very slow and expensive way to gather cattle. A limited few are gathered on days when the cowboys get all the breaks. At other times, none at all are gathered on one of these runs.

Cole moved four men into Black Mountain in the late summer of 1919, with A. B. (Cris) Criswell in charge. I was represented by J. B. Dearing. After a month or six weeks they had gathered less than twenty head of cattle, but had managed to put V Cross T on about all the wild calves not already branded. The same thing happened in 1920—the calves were branded, but no cattle taken out.

I made plans to take over the situation in the early spring of 1921. I was to furnish the outfit and Cole was to have a man or two with us. I had with me three regular riders: Sim Smith, J. B. Dearing, and Scotty; also my brothers, Joe and Lee Evans, and Huling Means. With Cole's two men, "Cris" Criswell and Pat Davis, I had nine of the best mountain hands to be found anywhere. I gathered and put on grain thirty of our best mountain horses. Cole's men brought their own mounts and so did Huling Means. Huling had a two-days' ride from his H Bar Y ranch through the Mogollons to get to Beaverhead.

The winter had been dry with little or no snow on Black

SLASH RANCH HOUNDS

Mountain summit, the elevation of which is 9,303 feet. All the cattle had to come to Beaverhead or the East Fork for water, but were so wild that they watered only at night. We were camped on Beaver Creek and kept our horses in a corral on plenty of good *vega* hay, and grain. We would have breakfast, mount out, and start up the cattle trails toward Black Mountain as soon as it was light enough to see. We had already tried all ordinary methods of handling these wild cattle. They simply could not be stopped in hold-ups and we knew that the only hope was to run down, rope, and tree-tame each individual animal. So, when we came in sight of the cattle, we would charge them, and each cowboy would rope and tie as many as he could. We would hunt and tie up cattle all the forenoon, and in the afternoon go around with a herd of gentle cattle and bring in all we could of those we had caught, placing them in a specially built "trap" on Beaver Creek.

Some were so wild and mean they would die before they would give up. The loss ran to about 10 per cent, but in the first ten days we caught and delivered to Cole 160 of the wildest cattle I ever handled, including a lot of full-grown steers. The next ten days yielded only about half as many; and as Joe, Lee, and Huling had business of their own to look after, these three left me when the first big runs were over.

We had made a good start, however, and kept right on after these wildest of the wild ones with our own outfit after the other men had to leave. We were hunting and running the cattle over an area of thirty or forty thousand acres of the roughest and brushiest country imaginable, and when we got down to about the last hundred it was so slow that the cost per head gathered was prohibitive. Not only was the work extremely hazardous, many getting falls during these wild races, but the extra load had begun to tell on both men and horses.

My father, who was living in Texas, came to New Mexico for

THE VERSATILITY OF A HOUND

a visit. When he heard of the trouble we were having cleaning up this remnant of wild cattle, he said if I would use a hound on them I would save a lot of time. I told him that I was afraid it would ruin my pack of hounds for bear and lions, as the wild cattle ran the same country as this game. He told me that he had used his very best hounds in hunting wild cattle in brush country along the Nueces River and in San Saba County, where he ranched as a young man, and that when bear-hunting time came, he would go back into the same country and use the same hounds to start bear that he had used to start wild cattle, and not once did they start a cow trail instead of a bear. I had, at the time, Brownie and Bell at the head of my small, and young, pack—these two out of Alice and Redbone.

I started out trying Brownie on wild cattle. He had been my main start-hound for bear and lions when but a little over a year old. We went into the high saddles of Black Mountain, where only the wild cattle ranged. When I found fresh cattle tracks I would get off my horse and follow the tracks on foot, encouraging Brownie to help me. In no time he was following the tracks, but not opening, as he would have done on a varmint trail. What a find this was! All we had to do was follow along, watch Brownie do the trailing, and look for cattle.

As soon as the cattle were jumped, Brownie would open and follow close behind them. We could make much better time following Brownie, since we did not have to look for tracks, and could even go around the worst places, where thick brush and rock piles made fast riding impossible.

One thing is certain, that if you crowd a wild cow close enough she will continue to hunt lower country. Black Mountain is completely surrounded by a mesa area which has gentle cattle using it on the 7,000- and 7,500-foot levels. By crowding wild cattle as Brownie would, they would run out onto these lower mesas, and, if we were close enough when an opening showed up, we usually could rope the animal. If there were several head in a bunch, we sometimes would catch several on one mesa, leave them tied to trees, then go back into the high country and do the same thing over again, if it were not too late in the day.

To "tie up a wild one," meant using a special piece of good, new rope six or seven feet long, prepared in advance and carried for this purpose. The animal, when roped, is pulled up to a sapling or young tree, usually not more than twelve inches in diameter, with no low forks, limbs, or underbrush. The tie-up rope is then thrown around the horns, using the middle of the rope, and tying a double cross knot in front of the horns; then the loose ends are brought around the tree, where a specially tied noose or slip-knot in one end is slipped over the other that has a double round knot. This can be done very quickly, and all the animal can do after the catch rope is removed is to go round and round the tree. After a day or two of this it is usually possible, by turning the wild one loose into a hold-up bunch, to drive it out of the mountains.

After a day or two of tying up, we would take a hold-up bunch and gather up the ones we had caught. We were not always able to stay within sight or hearing of Brownie on these races, and he very soon learned to come back for us if we got lost. As soon as we came within sight of him he would turn, and, traveling in a trot or lope, would lead us back to the trail, or to the animal if he had left it bayed in a thicket. On windy days and in very rough areas where we couldn't possibly stay within sight or hearing, I have seen Brownie come back to us many times.

After learning to use a hound for this work, not only did the practice become real sport but, until the last wild cow was caught off Black Mountain, we figured that Brownie saved us $2,000 per year labor cost on this work alone.

I never knew him to switch tracks. After he was on the trail of a certain animal the trail could lead through many other cattle tracks or even past other cattle, but he would keep after the

THE VERSATILITY OF A HOUND

original animal until it was brought to bay or run out into the open country.

Once, at headquarters, when the boys were breaking a young mule to work, the mule jerked loose with the blind-bridle and harness on, and before they could saddle up, was out of sight in a four-thousand-acre pasture with dense brush and rough headers. In the pasture were about one hundred saddle horses and a dozen or more mules. The boys hunted for the mule a couple of hours. They found many of the loose horses and mules, and decided the lost mule, dragging a rope, was wound up in the brush somewhere. I put Brownie on the track, and in a short time he led us to the mule, with the loose rope all tangled up in a thicket. Without Brownie's help we might have lost the animal.

Lee and I were riding in the Black Mountain country, once, looking for cattle. We separated and were to meet at a certain designated place. Lee didn't show up, and after waiting due time, I knew he had had trouble. I went to where I had seen him last, and had no difficulty in getting Brownie to take the trail of his horse. We followed it several miles and found Lee with a badly crippled horse which had hung his foot in a crack of rock and wrenched an ankle. We had to bring Lee in and send back for his saddle.

In the summer of 1924, we were camped for summer branding work at a permanent camp on the East Fork, where we kept a man the year round. This camp was about twelve miles south of headquarters. In addition to our own men, we had two or three men representing neighboring outfits. There was only one bunch of wild cattle left on Black Mountain at this time, consisting of a white-flanked cow with one horn turned down, another wild cow, and about a half dozen steers, ranging in age from three to six years. This bunch ranged on the southeast side of the mountain, and was closer to our location than to any of our other camps.

I proposed that we set aside one day to see what we could do

SLASH RANCH HOUNDS

with this wild bunch. This suited the cowboys fine, for most of them really love to run wild cattle. It is exciting work. I have trailed a bunch to the edge of a thicket, stopped to have a whispered consultation, tighten saddles, and get ready generally just before we were to jump them—and the hands of even the oldest and steadiest of the bunch would be shaking so they could hardly roll a cigarette.

There were nine of us who rode away from camp early in the morning, each mounted on his best wild-cow horse, and taking our second best mounts, which would be corraled high up in the mountains about the center of where the activity was to take place. We always let the hounds go with the branding outfit, as there are enough scraps for them to eat, but they are left tied and never allowed loose where we are working cattle. This time, however, we took Brownie, knowing what he would be worth to us on such a mission. With his help we soon found, and were in hot pursuit of, the last of the wild cattle. The cowboys became scattered and lost almost at once, but those of us who knew how to hunt with Brownie stayed on the tracks, making the best time we could. When we were unable to keep up he would come back for us, and we were working into lower country all the time.

Two or three of us were still together when we sighted the cattle, and were able to tie up three of the steers. We all got together at the corral for a remount, and, with Brownie, went back to pick up the trail where the cattle had first scattered. We kept this up until seven head had been tied up. The eighteen horses we had used were pretty well tired out, but when the last steer was caught Brownie was still going strong. Several of us carried water in canteens, just to have it for him when he got too hot. When this happened, as it did several times, especially in the afternoon, whoever had water, would dismount, push the top of his Stetson in and fill the top with water. Brownie would drink, cool off a minute, and, without encouragement, be on the trail

THE VERSATILITY OF A HOUND

again. The work of this well-trained hound was a revelation to the cowboys who had not seen a good hound work after wild cattle.

I want to call particular attention here to the amazing endurance of a hound. This was strikingly shown in Brownie's excellent work with wild cattle, but it is equally true (though often overlooked) in the work of hounds running down bear and lions. What hunters often overlook on such hunts is that, while the hounds may work for hours on a cold trail, traveling fast for many miles without water over the roughest kind of country, the animal they seek is either laying up (resting) or moving leisurely over trails of his own choosing until he is actually jumped; yet in spite of this, the hounds retain enough stamina and speed to crowd him so closely that he is forced to bay or tree. Knowing the speed a bear or lion can show in such a chase, this ability on the part of tired hounds has always seemed remarkable to me and I stress it here in case it may not be pointed up enough in my stories of the individual hunts.

About a year later, Sam Means came over for a visit, and not knowing where we could find a bear or lion, we decided to make a run for a four-year-old stag* which we knew to be in the general vicinity in which we had caught the seven head of wild cattle the year before. I had been telling Sam about working wild cattle with Brownie; and as Sam had always kept hounds, and really loved to hunt, he was eager to give it a trial.

We went into the very highest saddles on the southeast slope of Black Mountain, and soon picked up the track of the stag we were looking for.

Brownie followed the track as usual, but we found such rough going we were not always able to keep him in sight. This pleased

---

* Stag: in the language of cattlemen, an animal not castrated until after it has developed bull characteristics. Such an animal is apt to be bigger and far more vicious than a common steer.

Sam fine, and he got a great kick out of having Brownie come back for us when we couldn't keep up. We crowded the stag enough so that he began to hunt lower country. When he came out into the edge of a juniper-covered mesa east of the mountain, we sighted him and decided it was best to rope him while he was out in pretty good country. When we got within roping distance our horses were winded. Sam was the first to throw and his rope settled around the stag's horns, when the stag turned on Sam, whose horse ran over a thick-topped juniper bush a few feet high. The horse fell, but his front feet didn't clear the bush and hung in the top of it. Sam was caught with his leg under the horse and the horse couldn't get up. I had just missed a loop at the stag, and realizing that he would be on Sam in a second or two, I stepped off my horse, pulled a .30-30 rifle out of the scabbard, and took a quick shot at the animal's head. The shot went a fraction too high to kill, but the bullet made a clean cut of the rope between the horns. This turned him loose, and he came directly at me. My next shot was mighty quick and well placed, as it dropped the stag right at my feet. I immediately turned my attention to Sam. It was necessary to uncinch his saddle to get the horse off him. Neither was hurt, but it was a real pile-up.

The juniper brush was very thick at this place, and when the fracas was over my horse was nowhere in sight. I saddled Sam's horse, put Brownie on my horse's track, and he bayed the runaway in a thicket about a mile from the scene of the accident. By the time I got back Sam had the stag partly skinned. We finished skinning him, quartered him as best we could with only our pocketknives, and hung the meat in the shade. We then went on to D Bar where Sim Smith kept camp. We told Sim about the stag, and he, later, took a couple of pack mules and brought the meat in.

The chasing of runaway horses was still something new and

THE VERSATILITY OF A HOUND

different in tracking for Brownie, but, as in all other cases, he delivered the goods.

By the fall of 1923, with Brownie's help, all the wild cattle were cleaned out, and we secured the permission of the Forest Service to put in 1,264 young steers. Thus Brownie had enabled us to use a great grazing area which had been useless as long as it was occupied by the wild bunch.

With the profits on these new cattle added to what we were making on our others, we turned the tide for the first time since the drouth and depression, and began to make enough to pay running expenses and the interest on our staggering debt and have a little left over to apply on principal.

CHAPTER II

THE MYSTERY OF SCENT

In maintaining a pack of hounds, it is necessary to have a pup or pups in the pack, taking training. It is more difficult to teach a hound without the help of a trained one. It is natural for a hound to trail, but when hunting bear or lions, which are always scarce, there are always present many other tracks which should not be followed. A young hound naturally loves to run deer, coyotes, foxes, cats, badgers, and any number of other animals, and without the help of a trained hound to check these many trails, it is almost impossible to know when to scold or when to encourage the novice. Strange as it might seem, a trained hound doesn't always have to go to the pup to do the checking, but somehow knows from the way he works that the track is not good.

The most hopeless hound is one that has all the qualifications of a good one, works with the pack, does his share of picking up the trail, opens only when on scent, shares the confidence of the pack, and then gets off on another trail. Because of the help he has been the others will go to him, and time is wasted before the true ones find the error and pick up the right trail. This is not a common happening, but one which I never knew how to correct, and

THE MYSTERY OF SCENT

I have been compelled to get rid of a few otherwise good hounds that had this great fault.

There are hunters who claim to have had hounds that would not follow the back track, but I have never made such claim. If one is traveling in a certain direction, and comes to a track where the animal has been traveling in the opposite direction, it is natural for hounds to go in the direction they are going, which would be on the back track. If a track is picked up in the bottom of a canyon where the animal has crossed coming off the shady side and going up the side where the sun is shining, the back track is much easier to smell, and the hounds naturally take the wrong direction. If a trail is approached at right angles and the scent is fresh, with all scent conditions equal, it is rare that the back track is followed. The colder the trail, the more difficult it is for a hound to know which end to follow.

For some reason, an animal leaves more scent going downhill than when climbing. I have watched this where the ground was unfavorable for seeing tracks, and could tell which direction the animal was going by the difference in the way the hounds worked, even could be certain enough to turn around on the trail and was later proved to be right.

One of the most interesting things about a trained hound is the privilege of prowling a mountain range with such a hound along without seeing a track of any sort. The man who knows his hound can tell if there have been bear or lions in the area, which of the two has left the sign, and whether the sign is fresh or old. By watching and listening to a well-trained hound, it is easy to read the signs and know beyond doubt, without even seeing a track, just what has been prowling the woods.

Most start hounds bark differently on a bear trail than on a lion's. Usually there is enough difference to enable the hunter to tell which it is, but if uncertain from the voice alone, he can tell by watching where the trail leads. Bear and lions often use the same area, which is usually the roughest country in the vicinity, but they don't travel alike.

A lion or cat will step on top of every rock in its course. Whether this is just to keep its feet toughened or to keep from making tracks that can be seen, I do not know, but the direct contact that is made by stepping right on top of the rock makes it the very best place for a hound to put his nose to find the scent. I have seen smart hounds check the top of every rock or boulder along the trail, and make good time without trying to find the scent on the ground. He will also smell of any brush that happens to be on the course. I have seen hounds put their muzzles to the tip of a stiff twig that has scraped the animal's side or back, open with enthusiasm, and go forward with certainty. After following a cold lion trail for a day or two, the noses of the hounds will be red and raw from having closely checked the top of innumerable rocks.

Knowing that, at one time or another, all who have trailed bear or lions with hounds have had mystifying experiences, I will relate some of these experiences which I have had. But, because the pattern of scent is extremely varied, I have never been able to come to any positive conclusions, with the exception that I know a scent will hold much longer and can be followed more steadily without gaps, if the weather and ground surface is uniformly dry than if there has been recent moisture. This applies at elevations of from six to ten thousand feet and in the climate of the arid Southwest.

Some hunters seem to think moisture is an aid to trailing, but my experience has been that just the opposite is true. When the sun comes out on recently wet ground in this high altitude, the evaporation is so rapid that any scent which might have been present in the moisture seems to disappear at once, and the only places where there is enough scent for the hounds to follow are the shady spots. This means jumping from one shady spot to an-

THE MYSTERY OF SCENT

other, and the chances are that the trail will be lost completely if the animal turns back, or materially changes its course.

Another bad condition is to have a wet snow followed briefly by thawing weather, then a sudden freeze, forming a crust on top of the snow sufficient to support the animal. Bobcats or lions walk very lightly and can easily pass over such snow without breaking through, and there is very little scent left on the surface. It is much easier for a hound to carry a trail across dry, bare rock than across a glazed-over snow bank.

Soft snow holds scent better than most anything else, especially if several inches deep. Hounds can't tell one track from another by looking at it, but depend entirely on their noses. A good start hound will check any depression indicating tracks in the ground or snow, but will show no evidence of recognition until he has stuck his nose into it. Old, trained hounds checking very old tracks in deep snow will bury their heads almost completely in the snow, begin to wiggle their tails, and finally pull their heads out and give long drawn-out barks on lion tracks a month old.

Quality of the soil has something to do with holding scent. Clay surface seems especially bad if wet. Being very sticky, wet clay clings to the animal's feet and forms a coating which prevents scent from reaching the ground to enable the hound to follow, though the coating might not be visible on the animal's foot. Dry clay that is soft enough for an impression will hold scent that hounds can follow.

We were hunting in the Datil Mountains of New Mexico, where a lot of ground surface is covered with clay. The time of the year was June, and we were several miles from camp without finding any fresh lion sign. About midday there was a heavy thunder shower, sufficient for the water to run on the ground. Some of the hunters said if we could only find a lion trail made after the rain we would have a cinch. I didn't argue, because, knowing that mountain lions do most of their prowling at night,

SLASH RANCH HOUNDS

I thought it most unlikely that we would pick up a trail made in the afternoon. On the way to camp, with the hounds well out in front, feeling fresh and rested from the recent rain and cooling hail, they winded a scent, giving tongue with great enthusiasm. By the side of the trail, there was a pine tree with very dense foliage, heavy enough to keep the ground beneath practically dry during the storm. The scent on these dry needles was very strong, but try as they would, the hounds could not work the trail away from the tree. We stayed out of the way to give them every chance, but they simply couldn't get a lead off.

I left my horse in order to circle the tree on foot looking for lion tracks. I soon found one in the muddy clay, made since the rain and probably not more than an hour old. I called Brownie and showed him the track. He was trained to check any tracks that we pointed at, and no dog living loved the scent of lion better than Brownie. He put his nose right on the track, even pressed it into the ground, but there was not enough scent to register. I followed the fresh tracks for several hundred feet across an open flat and called the hounds for repeated checks, always with the same result.

Either there was enough clay stuck to the lion's feet to prevent the animal scent from passing through to the ground, or the sunshine had caused all scent to evaporate. The scent was so strong under the tree that the hounds went back to it many times, but never were able to follow this trail away from the tree in any direction. I have had other similar experiences, but this was the most striking.

Bobcats leave even less scent than mountain lions. The late Milt Craig and I were hunting lion in the Taylor Creek country, and as we were riding along close to the main top rim of the canyon I saw a bobcat cross a small header in front of us. Milt said, "If we can't find a lion, let's run a cat." We were not more than two minutes reaching the spot where I had seen the cat, but there

THE MYSTERY OF SCENT

was only enough scent for the hounds to open a few times; never enough to get a trail leading away from the spot. At other times, I have seen the same hounds follow, to a successful end, a bobcat trail that had been made several hours before.

Another time, Lee and I rode over to Horse Camp to see about water, as the summer was dry, with stock-water scarce. The round trip on horseback is thirty-six miles and, made in one day, doesn't leave much time for anything else. On our way to Horse Camp we detoured by way of upper Indian Creek. In this rough area, there usually is plenty of water which the cattle do not use until the water is dried up in more accessible places; but we found water low at Horse Camp and getting lower day by day. We decided we would return to Horse Camp in a few days to work on the spring there.

As we rode down Indian Creek we saw a fresh-looking track of a good-sized black, or brown, bear. Tracking conditions were good in the dry, soft dirt, and we followed the track down Indian Creek for several miles to a point where the bear climbed out of the canyon bottom, turning off at right angles. We discovered later that the bear was following the scent from a pile of cat and coyote carcasses which had been piled in a header by Scotty, from his winter's trapping.

On our return trip to Horse Camp four days later, we brought the hounds along, making the same detour by upper Indian Creek. As soon as the hounds reached the canyon they opened upon a trail and took off down the canyon at a fast gait. We rode after them, checking for bear tracks, but there was nothing but the track we had seen on our earlier trip. We followed at a lope because we were eager to see what would happen when the hounds reached the spot where the bear had turned to go to the cat and coyote carcasses. The trail was good enough for the hounds to pick up easily by circling if they ran past the place where the bear made the turn. They followed the trail right to the pile of carcasses and we called them off, as the bear was probably well into the Mogollons or the West Fork of the Gila by that time.

The following is a quotation from a letter written by Ernest Lee, of E. E. Lee & Brothers, big-game hunting guides, of Tucson, Arizona, about scent:

> Ever since we started hunting we have given a great deal of thought to scent, trailing conditions, a subject that has never been mastered by any hunter, in our opinion; so like you, we must base our judgment upon our own experiences. We hope you cover this as thoroughly as possible in your book as there are a great many angles to it.
>
> Yes, we have seen a pack of hounds fail to handle a lion trail which should have been fresh, or hot; and one of these packs trailed a lion, and did a good job of it, which I had killed seven days before with another pack of hounds; and I know it was this trail the hounds were following because they trailed her from where the other pack of hounds had jumped her. She had jumped from a number of trees before finally being killed, and this last pack of hounds trailed her to each tree until they reached the last one.

On the fifth day of May, 1925, we were cold-trailing a big male lion out of Taylor Creek. The trail was leading south across White Tail toward the good lion country of Cox, Hoyt, and Diamond creeks.

Our party consisted of Lee and Graves Evans, Bill Cowden, our brother-in-law; Bill's cousin, Elliott Cowden; and myself. It was too rough to follow behind the hounds across Whitetail and Cox canyons, so we stayed out on good ground as much as possible. When we topped out on the south side of Cox Canyon, we were a little ahead of the hounds, which we could hear coming about halfway down the hillside. The lion climbed out between us and the hounds and ran right into us. He went right on through the saddle in sight of us, making twenty-foot leaps as he ran.

We called the hounds off from below, thinking that we would save much time by putting them on the lion's fresh trail on top. The ground in the saddle over which we had seen the lion run, was real gravelly, with practically no vegetation. The hounds were

THE MYSTERY OF SCENT

pretty hot, but came to us on the run in response to our urgent call. Imagine our disappointment when they failed completely to pick up the trail where we had seen the lion only a few minutes before. We gave them every opportunity, but they acted as if there were no scent there.

By making a circle across the first canyon we found the lion trail where he had settled down to walk or trot, and from there the hounds followed the trail to where we came upon the lion on Hoyt Creek, lying on a ledge on some big rocks about fifty feet from us. As Elliott Cowden and Graves had not yet killed a lion, I proposed that they sit down, one on each side of me, and hold aim as I counted, and as I reached the count of three, for them both to shoot; then each could always say he had killed a lion. I counted "one-two," but before I said "three," Graves shot. He missed the lion, which raised up, broadside, making a perfect target for Elliott, but instead of shooting while he had this excellent chance, he lowered his gun, looked around and said, accusingly: "Graves, you shot before he said 'three.'" By that time the lion was out of sight, and we thought for a time we had lost him for good. We later located him on the bluff, and this time Elliott shot and killed his lion.

In June, 1928, Joe Evans and I were hunting on Black Mountain and found where a lion had killed a deer in the bottom of a canyon. The hounds trailed around the kill, making some circles, but each time would head back to the kill. On one of these circles they must have come close to where the lion was bedded, for, soon after, on the next circle when they went higher up on the mountain, they hit a much fresher trail indicating that the lion had moved out. The area was nice for riding; we were able to stay up with the hounds, and we thoroughly enjoyed watching them work. The trailing was slow and rapidly got worse. Within an hour we were on a cold trail, and the hounds were just taking it a track at a time. They couldn't "wind" the track even a few inches to one side—and they had to smell right in the track, or on the very rock where the lion put his foot. We didn't think the lion had been gone more than an hour; still we were making very poor time and the prospect of overtaking this lion was not good. We were close to the hounds and watching every move they made, when Blue, a young hound, trailed up to the base of a tree and tried to climb the tree, which was sloping enough for him to get a foothold. He seemed to be trying to smell higher than he could climb. Joe said: "Look up in the tree." The lion was up there just peacefully lying on a limb out of Blue's reach.

On some occasions I have cold-trailed bobcats and found them already treed, but this was the first time I had found a lion already treed without having been crowded any.

I have mentioned just a few cases when the scent seemed to go away very quickly; but I know of many such cases. On the other extreme, I have found lion trails that I knew to be five days old that were good enough for the hounds to follow, making pretty good time.

In 1949, while hunting deer along the rim of the Middle Fork on the east side of Indian Creek, I saw what looked like a fresh track of a big male lion, and followed it for some distance on foot. Five days later, after deer season was over, Lee came over for a hunt and I told him of seeing this lion track. We went farther east toward Jordan Canyon, where the hounds picked up the trail of a lion, and we had not followed it far before we saw that it was the track of a big male, heading west toward where I had seen the track five days before. We could hardly believe it could be the same trail, but it kept getting closer to this place. When we got within a half mile of the place where I had seen the track, I circled ahead of the hounds, going to the exact spot. I looked carefully to see if there were fresher tracks, but found none. My boot track and the lion track were easy to see, and there was no

THE MYSTERY OF SCENT

other track there. The hounds soon reached this very spot, and with hardly any hesitation, went right on with the trail.

In April, 1949, Benito, one of my hands, and I went to Horse Camp to do some riding. Ed Jeffers, of Springer, who keeps hounds and loves to hunt, said he might come down in a day or two to ride with us. He was going to bring his own horses and hounds and, as he had such a long way to come, he thought it might be advantageous if we could have some sign located by the time he reached us.

I sent Benito to look for sign. He had been gone but a short time when I saw him returning, riding fast, and I knew he had found what he was looking for. He said that he had found lion "markers," or "scrapes," and also the tracks of a big lion on the east side of Indian Creek, about two miles from the ranch. We went to the spot with the hounds that same afternoon. They readily took the trail, following it so rapidly that we couldn't keep up with them. The trail led down toward the Middle Fork, but stayed mostly on the east side of Indian Creek, passing through some extremely rough country. Just before sundown we were out on top on the east side of Indian Creek, where it empties into the river, at which point the trail led across the creek. It was impossible to get a horse across anywhere. We could see and hear the hounds as they worked up the opposite side from us and we knew they couldn't get out.

It was nearly dark, and we thought that when they reached the last high rim and couldn't get out, it would be a good time to call them off the trail. We tried this, but they were so eager to follow the lion that we had to leave them.

When we reached camp, Ed was already there. Said he got anxious and came on. I told him how lucky he was, that we already knew where there was a fresh lion trail.

My hounds came in some time in the night and we left early next morning, taking both packs down on the west side of Indian

Creek, so as to get the lion track on top of the bluff which the hounds could not climb the night before. We found the trail as soon as we reached the spot. It left the bluffs there, and was hard to follow across an open, grass-covered mesa, but got better when we reached the rough, brushy hillsides.

The trail led on west across some very rough country and finally across the Middle Fork and headed for the Mogollons. This was getting out of our territory and we quit the trail in the afternoon, thinking we might find the trail of another lion closer home. The next day we went east from Horse Camp to hunt on Black Mountain, and about two miles east of camp, on the main trail, the hounds picked up a lion trail. They had not followed it far until we saw the track, and found that they were working backward on the trail. We turned them around, and I told Ed that it looked just like the track we had been following for two days. We let the hounds follow it anyway and, sure enough, it led us to the very spot where Benito had found the track, and was the same trail we had followed before.

As stated earlier, when a hound is on a cold trail it is necessary to make contact by smelling right on the spot where the animal's foot or body touched, but when the trail is fresh and there is body scent in the air along the course, it is possible to follow the trail at full speed, and if there is some wind the hound might be even several yards from the track yet still be "on the beam," at full drive with head in air and rarely smelling the ground.

Some time ago, while on a hunt near Horse Camp with my brother, Lee; Dr. Shaw, of Miami, Florida; and Harvey Blair, of Wichita, Kansas, Harvey saw a bear while the hounds were at heel. We headed for the spot on the run but before we reached the exact spot the hounds picked up the scent and were away at full speed, opening with great enthusiasm. Harvey had his eye on Blue to be certain they were where he had seen the bear, and

THE MYSTERY OF SCENT

called to me, saying, "The bear crossed this opening twenty or thirty feet west of the course the hounds are following." I didn't even slow up, as I knew nothing could stop those hounds on a bear trail so fresh; still Harvey knew exactly where he had seen the bear cross. The bear was traveling north and there was a breeze from the west, so, instead of the hounds being directly over the track, they were well to the right, but well within the "scent channel," running full speed, weaving in and out, heads in the air, and really making time.

It is not clear just how wide this scent channel might be, but, with favorable atmosphere and especially after bear, which probably leave a stronger scent than other animals, I think that, for a brief period after the animal has passed, it might be a hundred feet wide. Many times while hunting with hounds, when approaching where a varmint has recently crossed, the hounds will wind the trail some distance away, proving that the scent channel is quite wide.

These actual experiences go to show that the hounds can sometimes follow a trail that is at least a week old. Then again, the same hounds, in the same general area, will be unable to follow successfully a lion trail not more than an hour old.

There is nothing so strange as the mystery of scent.

CHAPTER III

DOUBLING BACK

Only those who have trailed bobcats and lions have had the chance to observe the trick these animals have of doubling back on a trail; and only those who are really familiar with hunting hounds can truly appreciate the supreme development of hunting sense which enables really outstanding hounds to unravel such tangled trails.

Doubling back is distinctly a characteristic of the cat family; and whether it is done by instinct or by reasoning, I do not know. I only know that it happens, and relate here some of my own experiences in proof.

But first let me quote from a letter written to me by E. E. Lee on this subject. The Lees have had a world of experience in hunting Southwestern big game with hounds, and what they have to say about doubling back can certainly be classed as expert testimony. Of course, the fact that they speak highly of Slash Ranch hounds makes the letter no less interesting to me:

> You mention the habit that some lions have of doubling back on their own trails. . . . We believe lions do this more often than the average hunter thinks they do. Many times hunters tell us of some chase where the scent

DOUBLING BACK

of the trail just played out and the hounds never could work it any farther. Some of these hunters will mention that their hounds finally tried to take the back track, which these hunters considered a crazy stunt on the part of the hounds and stopped them from doing.

While quite a few lions do this, there are not too many hounds who have the ability to straighten out such trails; but we have owned and hunted with a number of hounds who were exceptionally good at figuring out just what a lion had done when it doubled back, and will say that some of the best we have ever owned, who lost little time on a double-back, were Slash Ranch hounds. We have hunted with a few other hounds who were extra good at this, but it is our opinion that more of your strain of hounds were good at this than any other strain we have hunted with. Two in particular were really good ones on such trails. These were Rat and Ruby, a pair you sold as young pups to Clarence Echols, of Cloverdale, New Mexico.

Ruby was a small black-and-tan female with a naturally crooked tail. Rat was a larger black-saddle-and-tan hound which we obtained from Clarence when he was about a year old and who went to work for us and made an extra good bear and lion hound. Ruby started working (for Clarence) when a young pup; but after one year's hunting, when she helped catch nine lions, Clarence's doctor told him his heart was bad and he had better quit hunting with hounds, so we bought Ruby. She was a good lion hound at eighteen months, an exceptionally fine and smart trailer on a crooked, mixed up trail. On double-backs, Ruby did not waste a minute but took the trail right back until she found where the lion had turned to one side. She would change the tone of her voice when she found this place.

Another Slash Ranch hound was Josie, a medium-sized black-and-tan we bought from Aaron Inman. She too was mighty good on a double-back trail.

Many lions we have trailed have done this doubling back on their own trails, sometimes more than once. The most times we counted on one chase was seven, for distances of from fifty yards to a quarter of a mile. . . . One time I watched a lion do this; and no doubt there were many other times they did it when the lion and the hounds were so far from us we did not know about it.

It is not unusual for a lion to double back on his or her trail just before taking a tree. This often causes good hounds to be very slow in locating the lion, especially when the tree is on a mountain side . . . with the wind or air current blowing up the mountain. This takes the body scent of the lion higher in the air so the hounds do not get it anywhere near the tree. We have known lions to pass under a big tree and go on for some distance . . . then double right back on their own trail and, without leaving the trail, jump and strike the tree twelve or fifteen feet from the ground, so that there is no turn-off from the trail. Under such circumstances, the best tree hounds have plenty of trouble locating the treed lion.

My own experiences bear out those of the Lees in every detail. There was a certain bobcat that ranged in the upper Indian Creek country that was trailed many times by my hounds. Judging by the size of his tracks, I figured he was a large male. I wondered why the hounds always lost this particular cat, and one day while they were after him I learned the reason.

The trail was fresh but the area was too rough for me to follow the hounds closely on horseback, so I worked around ahead of them and took a stand on a point where I had a good view of three or four rough hillsides. I could hear the hounds, hot on the cat's trail, coming in my direction. About that time I saw the cat running, straight across the canyon from me. While I was watching him, he went up a big tree. The hounds were not yet in sight, but were coming fast.

To my surprise, the cat didn't stay up the tree; he came down and went right back over his own trail away from the tree and toward the hounds, in spite of the fact that the hounds were getting close and making a lot of noise. The cat back-tracked about fifty yards, then turned off sharply at right angles and went over the top of the ridge into the next canyon.

About the time the cat went out of sight, the hounds reached the tree which he had climbed and left. The tree was tall and had a brushy top in which it would have been very difficult for the hounds to have seen the cat even if he had stayed there, and certainly they couldn't tell whether he was there or not. The scent must have been very strong on the base of the tree where the cat had gone up and down, and the hounds barked "treed" with complete confidence. I gave them time, waiting to see if they would straighten out the trail, but they were so sure that this was trail's end that they made no attempt to do it. I figured that cat had taught me something and had earned a reprieve, so I called the hounds off and made no effort to put them on the trail where the cat had climbed over the ridge.

The luckiest double-back I ever saw from my point of view, and the unluckiest from the standpoint of the lion, was on a hunt with Bud McGahey, of Borger, Texas. This was in February, 1929. I had heard reports of lion sign in the Magdalena Mountains, so when Bud McGahey came for a hunt, we went in and camped at the Water Canyon ranger station. The Kelly boys, who lived in Water Canyon, furnished us with horses and J. B. Kelly acted as our guide. J. B. Kelly is a fine horseman, raised in the mountains in which we were hunting, and he knew every trail even when all the trails were covered with snow and invisible to eyes not familiar with the country. But in spite of good mounts and good guidance, we spent ten days of hard riding without a strike. After covering the whole range pretty thoroughly, we were positive that there were no lions in that area at that time. The "lion sign" reported must have been dog tracks.

I felt very badly about not being able to start a lion for Bud and I told him that I had to take the hounds back to the ranch anyway, and, if he had time, we would continue the hunt a day or two at no extra cost to him. He said, "I wouldn't want to come to New Mexico and return without going to Beaverhead anyway." So we decided to go back to the ranch and hunt at least one more day.

We rode out from the ranch early next morning, going into the Taylor Creek country, in which was to occur, about four years later, the first encounter with the "Old Shot-tail" lion about which I'll tell later. We crossed Taylor Creek just below Big Rock, with Brownie hunting way out ahead of us. By the time we topped out on the south side of Taylor Creek the hounds were gone, so we rode east along the rim until we found where the hounds' tracks followed an old lion track, which we could see in the snow where it still lay on the north slopes.

SLASH RANCH HOUNDS

The hounds had made good time even on this old trail so long as it lay in snow, but they couldn't follow the scent where the snow had melted, so we soon overtook them. We knew the general course the lion was taking, so we cut ahead for the track and were able to pick it up every time we hit a snow-covered slope. We would then call the hounds to this new trail.

After a few miles of this kind of tracking the trail got better and the hounds were able to follow it from the scent left on the brush and rocks.

Late in the afternoon, as we were crossing a rough header of Hoyt Creek, the hounds jumped the lion. We were across the canyon from them, but we saw the lion go up through some cliffs with the hounds in hot pursuit. Our horses were tired by this time, but we made the best time possible in the direction the lion and hounds were going.

Before we reached the bottom of the canyon, Bud said, "I see the lion coming back, right where it went out a while ago!"

About this time, we heard the hounds coming, hot on the lion's trail. The rimrock here was broken and brushy and we lost sight of the lion, but we saw the hounds pile off the rim and down into the same place where they had first jumped the lion. Here they made a circle among the rocks and then headed up-slope again, going over the rim just where they had gone before.

Since Bud had seen the lion, we knew that the hounds were right in coming back down into the canyon, but we thought when we saw them go up and out again at the same point that they had become confused and were rerunning the old track. However, we went out of the canyon in the direction they had taken; and, by the time we had reached the rim of main Hoyt Creek, the hounds had crossed and were going up the other side. This had to be fresh trail, which indicated that this lion had laid not a double but a triple trail—going up once, coming back, and going up again on the same track.

DOUBLING BACK

The main Hoyt Creek Canyon is deep at this point and, with tired mounts, we figured we would be lucky if we made it down to the creek and out to the top on the other side before dark. We were hoping the lion would tree before reaching the far rim, and it seemed likely that this would happen, since the hounds were running fast on fresh scent and the mountain was high and steep.

But the lion was still laying a tangled trail, doubling back for short distances every time an opportunity offered. These switchbacks would slow the hounds just enough to give the lion a brief breathing spell, and the chase would go on.

We were feeling pretty low when they didn't either tree or turn back on the big mountainside; and, when the hounds went over the top and out of hearing to the east, it looked as if our hunt were over. There was nothing left for us to do but to get down into the canyon as soon as we could and try to get out on top again before dark, in the hope of hearing the hounds again. We started down, but it was slow going. The horses were very tired and the hillsides really steep.

We were still some distance from the bottom when we heard the hounds—coming back! When they came over the hill at a full run, it was exactly at the spot where they had topped out earlier, in the opposite direction. The lion was doubling back again; and, again, we saw her, running hard, not far ahead of the hounds. And this time, just before she reached the bottom of the canyon, she treed.

I was never gladder to see a lion treed! Poor Bud had hunted ten days without even a chase, and then to see this long day's ride end in failure would have been really bad. But this lion doubled back once too often, and Bud got his trophy. We had the lion killed and skinned by dark, and the mere fact that we had fourteen miles of rough country to ride in the dark to get home made little difference.

My only regret that night was that Bud's lion was a female,

small, and not much of a trophy in my estimation after all the work she had cost us. When we reached the ranch that night, one of the Lee brothers (mentioned earlier in this chapter, and elsewhere in this book) was there. He was hunting for the Government then, had come in to mail his report, and had with him the skin of a large male lion he had recently killed over on Diamond Creek. I told Bud that there might be a possibility of trading Lee out of that hide, exchanging the hide of the small female for that of the large male. But Bud said, "I wouldn't take a thousand dollars for the skin of *my* lion, or give fifteen cents for one I didn't kill myself."

Bud also killed an eagle and a coyote on that same hunt, both with unusual shots worth mentioning. On the way to Beaverhead, we saw an eagle on a post. I stopped the car, but, as Bud stepped out to shoot, the eagle took off. Bud fired anyway and hit the eagle in flight, dropping it dead. The shot at the coyote was almost as unusual. It was at very long range, and the ground was glazed with ice. Bud's shot went low, ricochetted, split into several pieces and one or more pieces hit the target. The coyote ran only a few more yards and then fell dead.

I have had many fine hunts with Bud McGahey. He never complained, not even after sixteen hard hours in the saddle at the end of eleven days of trophyless hunting. He believes as I do, that the way to success whether in hunting or in business is to keep staying.

Another instance of this trick of doubling back occurred on a hunt which included my good friend, Judge C. M. Botts, of Albuquerque. Any association with Judge Botts is bound to be memorable, but this hunt is memorable also for the fact that it gave us our first acquaintance with the lion we later came to know as "Old Shot-tail." Old Shot-tail was a female and this first hunt for her laid the foundation for our later feeling of respect, almost affection, for her. She was a real master of the art of laying tangled trails.

DOUBLING BACK

This hunt began with the killing of a calf on Tom Jones' ranch on Taylor Creek. Tom found the kill, which was unmistakably that of a lion, and we decided to take the pack into that area to see if we couldn't run down the killer. The last time I had seen Judge Botts, he had said he would join us on a hunt; so I telephoned him and asked him to come. He said he was too busy and talked some about business appointments, cases in court, and so on; but I told him things like that shouldn't be considered alongside a really important matter like a lion hunt, so he came.

We decided to go down to Tom Jones' Taylor Creek ranch and hunt from there, enjoying the hospitality of Tom and his wife, Nora. We sent our horses, horse feed, hounds, and feed for them on ahead in care of one of the ranch hands, and Judge Botts and I drove through in my car. Beaverhead ranger station is about a quarter of a mile north of our ranch headquarters and we invited Ranger Eddie Tucker and his wife, Louella, to join us; so they also sent horses down to the Jones ranch for their own use but spent the nights at the station, driving down early each morning in their car to join the hunt.

About twenty miles from Beaverhead the road passes the old Garcia ranch, where there is a well and windmill and some adobe houses. Camped there at this time were a foreman, named McKenny, and ten C. C. C. boys who were engaged in shooting porcupines. The boys were armed with .22 rifles for this purpose and were working under the supervision of the Fish & Wildlife Service to stop the damage which porcupines were doing to the trees.

We hunted the first day in the Whitetail and Cox Canyon country, where we found lion sign fresh enough to trail. We were soon convinced, however, that this was a female and not the calf-killer we had set out to kill. This belief was strengthened when we found evidence that this lion had killed and eaten two porcupines within a distance of less than two miles. Remembering the C. C. C. boys and their rifles, the Judge and I commented on the

SLASH RANCH HOUNDS

comparative expense and efficiency of that method as against letting Mother Nature handle the problem in her own way, by means of the lion, and agreed that this particular lion might better be left alive if only to shorten the work of the C. C. C. crew. This suggestion earned no comment other than silence from Ranger Tucker; but, as it turned out, later events swayed his sympathies, too, in the direction of the lion.

It might be just as well right here to explain the reasons behind these conclusions we had drawn about a lion which we, so far, had not seen. Any experienced hunter can usually tell a good deal about an animal from the tracks and from the things the animal does or does not do on a trail. We had at least two reasons for thinking that this was a female lion. First, the tracks of female lions are apt to be smaller in comparison with other indications (such as depth of track and length of stride) of the animal's size; and the toes of a female lion do not spread as much as do the toes of a male of similar size. Too, we had found on this trail no markers or scrapes such as would have been made by a male lion. We had two reasons also for thinking that this was not the calf-killing lion. First, these tracks looked smaller to us than the tracks seen around the killed calf; and, second, we didn't think the calf-killer would bother much with porcupines when he had, at least, one half-eaten calf kill to go back to.

We worked this trail most of that day, keeping to the top of the ridge on the south side of the canyon. The trail freshened finally, and toward mid-afternoon, the hounds jumped the lion on the south slope of that ridge and ran her down into the canyon. This was really rough country and the hounds were so close that the lion treed in the bottom of the canyon rather than attempt the bad bluffs that faced her if she tried to run farther. The hounds barked "treed" in great excitement, but we were faced with the problem of getting down to them.

It was finally decided that the Judge and I would go down

into the canyon on foot while Tom and Eddie and their wives rode several miles west to where a break in the rim would enable them to ride down and bring our horses up the canyon to us. Judge Botts wasn't too enthusiastic about that climb down into the canyon, but I insisted that the lion had gone that way and where she could go we could follow, and the Judge is too good a sport and too good a hunter not to agree. I'll have to confess that there were places in that climb that made me wish I hadn't insisted quite so much on it, but we finally made it and picked our way up the bottom of the canyon to where the lion was treed. We waited there, of course, until the others came up to us.

It was while we were waiting there that Judge Botts made a remark I have heard him make often, to the effect that no man ever really saw this country unless he had followed a hunting pack through it on the trail of a bear or lion. His argument is that such a trail will take a man into and through country he would never otherwise attempt; and that is true. This is apt to be the roughest and most beautiful country in a given area, and Judge Botts is a man with a keen eye for scenic beauty.

This time, perhaps because we had a considerable time to wait, the Judge's appreciation of the scenic beauty of the spot gradually narrowed down to increasingly flattering comments about the beauty of the lion itself as she posed or moved about in the tree in response to the excited barking of the hounds. We had been right in thinking that this was a female; and, although not large, the Judge became more and more convinced that this was a particularly handsome specimen. He was more and more enthusiastic, too, about the chase she had led us.

I guessed where this was leading and was not surprised, when the others finally joined us, to hear the Judge enter a veiled but well-worded plea for the lion. We were all agreed, were we not, said the Judge, that this was not the calf-killing lion? This was a porcupine-killing lion and, as such, a sort of guardian of the forests, if not actually a partner of the Fish & Wildlife Service. Besides, we'd had a fine day's sport trailing her . . . and so on.

Tom Jones fell right in with this. He said, "That's not the lion that killed my calf. And, since we all planned to be out longer than this anyway, why not run her again? There's a chance here to prove a point. Dub brags a lot about his hounds; and I've heard people say that hounds wouldn't pick up a trail away from a tree where they've once treed. Let's leave her and come back tomorrow and see if Dub's hounds will do it."

Ranger Tucker wasn't very enthusiastic about this, feeling that the time when a lion was treed was the time to shoot her; but we argued that there was no doubt at all but what my hounds, with a sure point of departure, would tree the lion again tomorrow, and Eddie finally agreed to let us try it.

Next morning, we laid out careful plans for the renewal of the hunt. It looked most likely that the lion would go out of the canyon on the same side from which we had trailed her the day before, so it was agreed that Tom and Eddie and their wives would ride back along the south rim while the Judge and I took the hounds up the canyon to the tree where we had left the lion. The idea was that when the trail took us out of the canyon, the others would be waiting to join us.

It is true that it is not always easy to get a trail started away from a tree, so when we reached a point about a hundred yards from the tree the Judge and I stopped and waited for the hounds to work it out. They went to the tree and checked all around it and soon a young black hound named Kirk opened on the hillside a short distance from the tree. This trail was promptly checked by an older hound who gave it his okay, and the pack took off up the hillside—in the direction exactly opposite that in which we had sent the rest of our party. The lion was crossing us by going out on the north rim instead of the south.

There was nothing for the Judge and me to do but to follow the pack, which we did as best we could over very steep, rough country. The trail led up into some bluffs that were bad even for good rock hounds and completely out of the question for horses; but this time there was no question of leaving the horses, because this trail was at least twelve hours old and might lead on for many miles after topping out of the canyon. We would never be able to overtake the hounds on foot, so the only question was to guess which way the lion would turn after reaching the rim. We took a chance on going up canyon, which we had to do for several miles before we could top out with the horses.

We finally got up on the rim and turned west to try to cut the trail. Soon we noticed fresh tracks of running deer all headed east and figured that the deer had been disturbed by the noise of the chase and were moving out ahead of it, so we knew we were headed in the right direction.

This proved to be good figuring, because in a little while we heard the hounds. They were not far ahead of us but, although they had been gone from us for more than two hours, they were not treed but were still trailing. In fact, when we came up with them it was evident that the trail was no fresher than it had been when they left us.

This was something of a mystery, but it was soon explained. We had followed the hounds only a short distance when they came to a halt beneath a big pine tree. They worked busily there for a time and then began working back along the old trail, going now in the opposite direction. They went back a ways, barking very hesitantly. Then one hound opened on a different note, indicating a fresh track, and the whole pack joined in, heading off over the mountain again. This incident convinced us that the lion had doubled back repeatedly, each time giving the hounds some trouble in straightening out the scent and thereby explaining the time they had taken.

The trail got fresher soon and the real race was on. We kept close enough to the hounds to see them check and work out still another switch-back; and this time, after back-tracking nearly a hundred yards, the lion (judging by what we were able to work out from the tracks later, and from the actions of the hounds at the time) must have jumped a considerable distance at right angles from her back trail, hit the tree high up, and so left no scent at the base of the tree at all. This puzzled the hounds at first but soon they caught the body scent and barked "treed."

It was right here that the incident occurred which gave this lion her name, "Old Shot-tail." The Judge and I were, you might say, in a sentimental mood about this lion by this time. Not only had she given us two good chases, but she had also showed us repeated examples of animal cunning that seemed to us to make her deserving of a longer life. So when it occurred to us that, if we could get her down out of the tree, the country here was ideal for a "sight chase" that we could follow and watch, we began discussing methods by which this could be accomplished.

We had a .22 rifle with us and it seemed likely that, by shooting close to her and possibly "barking" the limbs around her, we could force her down. So we started shooting. The whine of the bullets annoyed her, and the "spat" of a bullet into a limb near her, accompanied by the resulting shower of bark and splinters, would make her flinch and change her position. But the sight and sound of the hounds still kept her treed—until we hit upon the idea of trying to graze her tail with a bullet.

That took some shooting. The tail was a pretty small target and not by any means a stationary one; but one bullet finally found the target and out she came, leaving the tree twenty feet above the hounds in a tremendous leap that took her well beyond them. She landed running, with the hounds in full cry close behind her, and Judge Botts and I lost no time in scrambling into our saddles.

The chase was short but something to see. No doubt a sore tail

DOUBLING BACK

lent speed to the lion, and the sight of her ahead of them provided an equal incentive to the hounds. This time she had no time for tricks or strategy; it was sheer speed while it lasted, and then up a tree with the hounds shouting "treed" again below her.

This time, Judge Botts and I didn't even discuss the idea of shooting her. This lioness, in our opinion, had earned a name, a character, and a lease on life that we had no intention of foreclosing—that day, at least. In fact, she gave us and other hunters as well a number of other fine chases, always recognizable by the characteristic tricks of trail-laying that were hers, and by the sight, when she was treed, of that crooked tail that was the result of our bullet.

CHAPTER IV

DEER ANTELOPE AND BEAR

Most hunters over-estimate the weight of the game they kill. This is true whether the game be deer, antelope, bear, or lion. I have heard many hunters boast of having killed mule deer weighing "over three hundred pounds," but the heaviest one I have weighed in the Southwest weighed two hundred and seventeen pounds. One season the Game Department had a checking station for deer hunters at the Slash Ranch, which was on the road at the gateway to the Diamond Creek and Black Canyon country. Officers at this station checked the weight on about seven hundred mule deer and found that, in that number, the average mature ten-point buck weighed from one hundred thirty-five to one hundred seventy pounds. Mule deer do grow bigger than this in more northern areas; but, in this particular part of the country, it is rare indeed to find one weighing over two hundred pounds.

Some hunters (and others) think that the number of points on a deer's horns is an indication of his size and/or of his age; but such is not the case. A normal full head has five points to the side, and a mule deer may attain maximum size still having only ten points. Sometimes a very large, mature buck will have only one fork on horns that are big in diameter as well as long. Again, in rare cases, a buck will have more than ten points. But such heads are freakish and not necessarily an indication of either size or age.

Deer shed their horns in this area around April first if feed conditions are good. Usually both antlers fall at the same time, coming off smooth at the head, without any special jolt or exertion on the part of the deer needed to dislodge them. I have many times seen complete pairs of antlers on the ground as if they had fallen simultaneously at a time when, judging by the tracks, the buck was either walking quietly or standing still.

The new horns start growing very soon and grow rapidly. Usually by September they have attained full size but are still soft at the ends, which are blunt and covered with "velvet." These points harden quickly, and by early October the points become hard and sharp and the velvet begins to shed. The buck speeds up the shedding of this velvet by rubbing his head against small saplings. Many small trees are literally peeled by bucks "hardening their horns."

Exceptions do occur in this matter of shedding antlers. In April, 1927, I saw a mule deer carrying only one antler. He was running away from me and he jumped a gully while I was watching him. That jump caused the remaining antler to fall. Also, if range conditions are extremely bad, as they were in 1934, some bucks may retain both antlers all summer. In one specific case, I shot a buck during the hunting season and the one horn he was still carrying came off as he fell to the ground. I tied my license on the horn and tied the horn to the deer's neck, took the buck to a checking station and asked Bob Lewis, representing the Game Department, to record the incident. This was a "last year's" antler, carried throughout the summer and fall and so never replaced by new growth.

Deer give birth to their young during the last ten days in July and in early August. The earliest I have ever seen new-born deer in this area was on July eighteenth. We had a quite conclusive example of this timing one summer when the Game Department asked us to pick up some mule deer fawns to supply a little park at Roswell. We usually made our cattle round-up for calf branding in July on the Beaverhead ranch, and we asked all the cowboys to be on the lookout for young deer. We could tell from the looks of the does that they were still carrying their young, and it was not until July 26 that we found even a single fawn. On that day, the boys came in with six. All six were just a few hours old and were the first ones any of us had seen. Since this incident involved a considerable number of men engaged in careful search of a wide area in which deer were more plentiful than cattle, it would seem to fix pretty closely the time at which birthing begins in that area.

Antelope drop their fawns a month to two months earlier, mostly during the first days of June, and their birthing season seems to cover a somewhat longer period. I have seen very young antelope in August, when the area was full of fawns two months old or older. Antelope, like mule deer, sometimes drop twins; but it seems to me that the incidence of twins is much more frequent with deer than with antelope.

Antelope are, of course, much smaller than mule deer and are more uniform in size. Of the hundreds of antelope bucks checked out of the Magdalena area, the average weight, hog dressed, was around 90 pounds, rarely reaching 100 pounds. The heaviest buck checked from that area weighed 112 pounds.

Contrary to general belief, antelope also shed their horns, although not in the same manner as do deer. In the case of the antelope, only the shell is dropped, the pith being a permanent part of the head. Toward shedding time, which is usually around December first, a new growth, looking like skin covered with hair, begins to cover the pith under the old horn. The shell of the old horn begins to loosen and finally comes off, leaving the new

DEER, ANTELOPE, AND BEAR

horn only a soft, hairy mass. This finally hardens at the point and the characteristic single prong develops.

Another fact of which many hunters seem to be completely unaware is that doe antelope frequently have horns also. These are not as large as the horns on a buck, and are never pronged; but these differences frequently are overlooked and many hunters have been embarrassed by having to explain possession of a doe which they had shot in good faith for a buck, having seen the horns.

Hunters could avoid any possibility of such embarrassment if they would remember that bucks have a black patch at the base of the jaw, under and sometimes extending up to the base of the horn. Does, even with horns, do not have this marking. Actually, the head of a buck antelope is darker over all than the head of a doe, with black extending to and around the muzzle. But the black patch at the base of the jaw is usually even easier to see than horns, and is a much more infallible means of identification.

Naturalists say that antelope shed their horns every twelve months. I do not know this from personal observation but believe it is true, judging by the number of horns one sees on the ground where antelope are abundant. I do know that antelope, like deer, sometimes shed one horn at a time. One very foggy morning early in December, 1933, as I was crossing San Augustine Plains in a car, a bunch of antelope crossed the road just ahead of me. Two of these bucks carried one horn each.

The best news for a bear-hunting party in the early fall is the report of finding the trees "lapped." This means finding the sign of bear feeding where there is abundant feed, such as acorns, red haws, wild cherries, juniper berries, or any natural mast for bear, still in the trees. Bear have such an appetite they begin feeding on the food they like before it is matured. If a tree is loaded, a bear will climb it, find a comfortable seat in a fork or on a big limb and reach out, pulling the limbs in to him, and will not move as long as he can reach branches that have acorns or berries. In doing this some of the limbs are broken from the tree and fall to the ground, where the fruit is later eaten off by the bear. Most of the limbs are not broken from the tree, but may be broken or split so they do not straighten out again, and in cases where many limbs have been thus drawn in toward the top center of the tree, the lapping effect is accomplished. Before the leaves dry up, the tree looks something like an umbrella.

In the fall of 1950, while hunting bear near Raton, New Mexico, with Ed Jeffers, as guests of the T O Ranch, we heard one of his hounds, a Kansas hound named Lead, barking "treed" in the bottom of a canyon. We went to him and found he was barking up an oak tree with the limbs so matted toward the top that one could not see through them. This hound was expert at treeing coons but had not hunted many bear. There must have been lots of bear scent in the tree, not only on the trunk, but in the top, where the bear probably spent two or three hours feeding the night before. We didn't blame the hound for barking up a tree with no bear in it, but, rather, felt kindly toward him for finding this fresh sign. It was late in the day when this happened and some of our men and hounds were separated from us, but we returned next morning and picked up the trail of a bear which we caught.

Later in the season, when the mast is ripe and has fallen from the trees, bear either pick it up off the ground or rob the winter storehouses of birds, rats, squirrels, or anything that has the habit of storing feed for future use. Woodpeckers drill holes in the bark or trunks of dead standing trees, press a sound acorn into the hole, go back for another, and keep at this until there are thousands of nice cured acorns in one dead tree. When acorns and other nuts are scarce, bear really hunt these storehouses. They let the birds gather feed from miles of surrounding country, and conveniently feed at their expense.

Mr. Bruin has a wonderful nose and with little difficulty lo-

DEER, ANTELOPE, AND BEAR

cates these trees. He climbs up, and if the acorns are in the bark, he will tear off great slabs and drop them to the ground; if in the dead wood he will tear out long chunks that are filled with acorns and drop these to the ground, where, when he comes down, the acorns are removed and eaten. I have seen big dead trees, well filled with cured acorns by woodpeckers, that show by the claw marks on the trunks where bear have made many trips up and down to get this food. Woodpeckers will not store faulty nuts. I have also seen where bear had robbed rodent nests that had a storage of feed for winter use. When bear first begin to fatten they eat acorns, hull and all, but when fat, they peel the acorns. It is easy to examine the stores and tell whether they were made by a fat bear or one not yet fat.

In summer, before other feeds are available, bear eat many bugs or grubs. Much of this feed is found under rocks and it is not uncommon to find hundreds of rocks, running in size from ten to a hundred pounds and over, turned over on one mountainside. The big, white-backed, hog-nosed skunk also turns over many rocks, but never any large ones. There is always evidence of rooting in the leaves, ground, or around the disturbed rocks, where it is the work of skunk and they leave a lot of sign that is often confused with bear sign by the inexperienced. With bear, the ground is not disturbed, they simply reach over a rock, hook a paw under the edge and lift up or turn it over to expose whatever is beneath. By watching a hound closely on the cold trail of a bear, it is easy to tell just where the bear caught hold of the rock with his paw. Rotten logs that contain woodworms or grubs are clawed open by bear, and the dead bark is also torn off.

Bear are also carnivorous, eating any kind of fallen carcass; and occasionally there is a killer of hogs, sheep, or cattle. Once they develop a taste for fresh meat, nothing else seems to satisfy them, and they will continue to kill even when acorns, nuts, and berries are plentiful.

SLASH RANCH HOUNDS

I had proof of this in the late summer of 1946, when I saw Hal Bruner, owner of the Diamond Bar outfit, who told me that he was suffering very heavy losses from bear. He said his foreman, Bo Hobbs, had found as many as five freshly killed calves in one day's ride, and he wanted me to bring my hounds and try to catch the bear that was doing the killing. He would furnish horses and equipment if I would bring my hounds.

I told him I had agreed to take Jerry Vinson, of Wichita Falls, Texas, on a bear hunt in October, and I would make the hunt at his place. All I wanted was the use of a pasture or trap for our horses.

Bruner had this outfit stocked with cows and the range is from the top of the Black Range, on the east, to the East Fork of the Gila, on the west. In this range proper are all four branches of Diamond Creek—Bonner, Black Canyon, and Big and Little Rocky, and far too many side canyons to mention. Two of the shorter canyons that head in the Diamond Bar range in Winchester Ridge, between Black Canyon and the Rockies, are Squaw and Apache canyons.

We sent horses to Bonner Field, which is on Black Canyon, about two miles above the Diamond Bar headquarters and near the mouth of Bonner Creek, which comes into Black Canyon on the north side. As it was too far to move horses in one day, Benito, the wrangler, stopped over night at the D Bar and went on to Bonner Field next day. We loaded our camp outfit onto the G I Dodge truck which G. W., III, drove, accompanied by Parker Sorrel, the cook. I went by car and met Jerry and his brother Garland at Beaverhead, and Lee and Lou C. joined us at Bonner Field. Graves Evans came in from his ranch near Winston, bringing a good hunting horse in a trailer.

In Diamond Bar Canyon, the first day out, we jumped a bear which the hounds couldn't stop. We finally took them off on Sheep Creek Mountain. The next morning was better. We jumped

DEER, ANTELOPE, AND BEAR

a bear early, south of Black Canyon and treed in Black Canyon about one mile above camp. Beulah, Lou C., and the camp cook, heard the race from camp and also the shots that killed the treed bear.

Next day we went southeast from camp and jumped a lightweight, fast-running bear that led us into the Mimbres country but was too fast for us. Lee, mounted on a black Mexican pony, named Python, finally cut the hounds off while the pursued bear was still going south.

We went back into the same area the following day, as we had found lion sign between Mimbres and Black Canyon, and Jerry Vinson was eager to get a lion. Instead of a lion we got the trail of another small bear traveling west. We followed the hounds on this track most of the day and called them off near Squaw Creek without having jumped him. On our way to camp via Meecem place, we discovered an area abundantly covered with bear feed: good acorns, juniper berries, and lots of piñons. These little nuts are very delicious and we filled our pockets as well as eating a lot at the same time.

Graves and Lee said they would have to leave next morning, but because of the unusual amount of mast in the Squaw Creek area we planned to return next day. Where there is lots of mast there is always an accumulation of game. We saw many turkeys, deer, wild pigeon, and bear sign. Before we really got to the main hunting country next morning, the hounds picked up the running trail of a big bear that had run from us the evening before without our knowing it at the time. This trail led southeast and off into the head of Big and Little Rocky canyons.

G. W., III, and Benito followed the hounds and the two Vinsons and I stayed on higher ground where the riding was better. Even so, in the fast ride, Jerry's horse ran under a low-hanging limb and lifted Jerry out of the saddle but left him on the ground, standing up, with no injury. After picking up his hat which was knocked off, we were soon on our way again. We played in luck. The hounds circled left and passed near us but were still on the old trail where the bear had passed the evening before. They were now crossing the high country between Little Rocky and Black canyons. In fact they were approaching the area where we had jumped the fast-running bear two days before.

We knew the hounds were moving too fast for us possibly to stay up with them as they started over the high, rough peaks ahead, so we crossed the divide south of the highest peaks and got on a long ridge leading toward south Black Canyon. We followed this ridge about a mile and I hurriedly pulled to one side, dismounted, ran away from my fast breathing horse, and listened. I was rewarded with just one bark from Blue, but it told me they had jumped and were heading east.

We stayed on the same ridge and ran a mile or more without even checking. I pulled away from the men and horses hurriedly to listen again and heard what is the climax to all bear races—the hounds barking "treed." We had just happened to be in the right place every time that day. We rode to a point just above where the bear was treed in the bottom of a very steep header.

Since Garland had killed the first bear, it was Jerry's time now, so we left Garland with the horses and Jerry and I crept down to the tree. Jerry brought the bear out with one shot and, as we approached, I told Jerry that we were really in luck as I believed we had killed the Diamond Bar bear.

I recognized the bear from a description given me by a state hunter, who had come to our camp at Bonner Field to tell me about the killer bear. He said he had spent three months on the Diamond Bar range trying to kill this bear, which he had run several times, and had shot at, but the bear had fought off his hounds each time. He said, "You will readily recognize this bear, because he is shiny black, big, and extra wide between the fore

DEER, ANTELOPE, AND BEAR

legs. I know this because I saw where this bear went off a dirt bank, and could see by his marks that he was eighteen inches wide between his front legs." Because of its size, we had thought that this was a male bear. We now learned that we were wrong. It was a female, the largest female bear I ever saw. But she was the Diamond Bar bear all right, as was proved when I hurriedly cut her open, and, instead of a paunch full of mast, found about fifteen pounds of the prettiest meat—nice red chunks rimmed with tallow —and not a juniper berry, acorn, or piñon nut, although the ground was literally covered with that most desirable of bear feed. This bear had become so fond of beef that she went right on killing after other feed was available and plentiful.

We packed this bear to camp with the skin on and sent word to Bo Hobbs. He came to look her over as he had also seen and shot at the killer bear. As soon as he rode up, he said "That's the bear that has killed so many of our cattle."

I told him to come back next morning and I would show him the paunch contents that we left at the tree where the bear was killed, so he could see for himself just what she had been eating. He made this further check and felt completely satisfied that the depredations would cease.

Bear seem to be especially fond of the stuff that is in yellow jacket nests. I don't mean the wasp-like yellow jackets that build nests in trees or ceilings, but the little yellow kind that are about the size of a honey bee, and have nests under rocks, roots, or just in a hole in the ground. A bear will go out of his way to dig them out, either for the young bees or the honey-like stuff in the nest. Plenty of grief for hounds and riders is caused by suddenly coming up on a swarm of hornets that have just been robbed by a bear. They cover hounds and horses alike and cause a hound to let out yells while he rolls and paws at his head. I have seen the gentlest of ponies run and buck while also pawing at their heads trying to get rid of the angry hornets, while the innocent hunters were hanging on for dear life and wondering what they had done to cause such a commotion. I've had them sting me and it really hurts. Bear either are immune to their sting or stand the pain because they are so fond of the nests, for they dig out every one close to their route.

One often hears that bear tracks, especially tracks made with the hind feet, are very similar to human tracks. There is a resemblance, but nature provided an unmistakable difference. I have called this to the attention of many woodsmen who hadn't observed it for themselves. The big toe is on the outside of a bear's foot, just the opposite of the human foot. (See Illustration 18.)

One other distinct characteristic of bear that differs from the cat family, is that when a bear comes out of a tree he backs down, either all the way to the ground or very near the ground before he jumps. A lion will hop down from limb to limb head first, and jump from the bottom limb to the ground, even twenty to thirty feet.

Bear claws are not concealed, show in the track, and are used in climbing trees and rocks. The grizzly's claws are much longer, come more out of the top of the toes; and it is said that grizzlies will not tree. I have had experience in hunting only two with hounds. One, and the only grizzly ever recorded killed in Texas, was killed in the Davis Mountains, November 2, 1898, by my uncle, John Means, and Otie Fenley, both of Jeff Davis County. My father's Old Brownie made the strike, and his pack, together with other hounds of the neighboring ranches, bayed the bear. I was on the hunt but didn't get in on the shooting. The other grizzly was killed by me in the Black Range of New Mexico, and the story is related in detail in another chapter. Both of these bear were killed on the ground. Both skulls are now filed in the collection of the Smithsonian Institution, Washington, D. C., and are

DEER, ANTELOPE, AND BEAR

tagged as follows: "Texas, November 2, 1890.* Length of skull, 14½ inches. Width, 9¼ inches." The other, "New Mexico, April, 1930. Length of skull, 15½ inches. Width 9½ inches." We don't have the weights or skin measurements of either grizzly.

The biggest bear of the brown or black type, commonly called "little bear," that I have seen killed in Texas or New Mexico was killed by G. W., III, while with me the first of November, 1946, on Indian Creek, about two miles south of Horse Camp. We had no way of weighing him, but we cut him up three ways and brought him out, loaded on two pack horses, and I carried about 150 pounds in front of me on my pony. We rendered 150 pounds of lard or bear oil. The skin is on the wall in front of me now, and measures: head, 13 inches; between ears, 9 inches; from front paw to front paw, 7 feet 3 inches; from front paw across to back paw, 8 feet 4 inches; nose to tail, 6 feet 1 inch; and from flank to flank, 5 feet 5 inches. We guessed him at six hundred pounds. The average adult male, when fat, runs from three to four hundred pounds, and the females about one hundred pounds less.

A bear characteristic about which little is known is the habit of biting and scratching trees. The following extract from a letter from E. E. Lee throws more light on this interesting subject.

From our own observations and limited experience with bear, we are sure your father is perfectly right, or was, in his statement that bear do the biting on trees during the rutting season. Just why there seems to be more of this sign in some mountain ranges than others, we do not know, but this is true. There has been lots of this sign in the Chiricahua Mountains for many years, and that is not near as good bear country as other sections where we hunt. While in some seasons, from late spring to early fall, there are a great many bear in this range, but few bear ever stay there until late fall and very few of these winter in the Chiricahuas. Still there is, or used to be when we hunted lion from time to time the year around, a great deal of

---

* This hunt has been described elsewhere as having occurred in 1890. I know this date is wrong, because I was on the hunt and I was born in 1887. Not even Evanses start hunting bear that young!

the "biting sign" as well as the claw marks, and while we have heard old hunters claim this was all done by the common black bear, never by grizzlies, we know the latter do this, too, and some individuals do a great deal of it.

For many years there was one old, large grizzly that came into the Chiricahuas in late May or early June but never could find his fresh sign after the last of September. We are sure he wintered in Mexico because his sign would show up first in the south end of the Chiricahuas, then soon in the Fly's Peak and Chiricahua Peak country, the highest part of that mountain range. This grizzly did not come in there every summer; sometimes he would skip one but we did not know of his failing to show up the next year. For years we felt sure we could have killed him easy in the summer but would not try to do this as we thought he would be poor, with a skin that was no good. Sometimes, when we were hunting high on the mountain, our hounds would strike his trail early in the morning when we would call them off, but did let them trail far enough a few times until we learned where he was laying up during the day. We had quite a collection of his hair, where he had rubbed it off when shedding, on trees, stumps, and snags. With a handful of it all mixed up it was a light blue color. He was seen several times and before shedding off well he looked very light colored.

This grizzly did a great deal of biting trees and also clawing them. I often showed people a tree that was badly bitten and clawed by this old grizzly as the tree was right by the main Government trail along the main divide; and where he would rear up and bite the tree it was just even with my head when riding a fifteen hand horse. We have hunted in other ranges of mountains which was good bear country, but saw very little of the biting sign.

A strange thing about the Chiricahua grizzly is that he never killed any cattle, to our knowledge, and we are sure in the years he ranged in there if he had killed cattle we would have known it. We have caught quite a number of the common black and brown bears in those mountains, who were killing cattle, but never found one killed by the grizzly.

There is one habit bears have that we have never heard other hunters talk about and have never read of it, and this is the bawling they do in the summer time, say late in July and all through August. This sounds so nearly like a yearling that it passes in cattle country for that when heard by anyone, including cattlemen and hunters. We learned about this "bawling" from a captive bear we kept for a number of years, and while we do not think it is a mating call, they do seem to bawl much more during the mating season and we have heard them in the mountains ever so many times. However, maybe you know all about this and have heard them bawl many times when you knew what it was.

CHAPTER V

CHARACTERISTICS OF LIONS

Mountain lions are meat eaters and prefer to kill their own. In southwestern New Mexico, they usually are satisfied with deer, but I have found cattle and horses killed by them in areas where deer were much more abundant than the domestic animals. In January, 1931, Lee and Lou C. were with me at Horse Camp. Scotty also was with us, but spent most of his time scattering stock salt, riding fences, etc., while we prowled around with the hounds. On one of these "prowls" the hounds picked up the trail of a very large male lion along the north rim of the Middle Fork near where Canyon Creek empties in. This track soon led us across the Middle Fork, at the mouth of Clear Creek, which comes into the Gila from the Mogollon side to the west. Clear Creek heads in the Lilley and Jerky mountains which are separated from the main Mogollon by Turkeyfeather Creek.

In following this track all day we saw the tracks of hundreds of deer and many wild horses, including colts, in the snow on the north slopes. No cattle are permitted in this area because it is the summer range for Otero sheep, although a few cattle belonging to the Heart Bar Ranch were there. The Heart Bar is much lower down on the Gila.

Late in the evening, when we had followed halfway up Lilley Mountain, the hounds had lost the trail and were working all around us. We were sitting on our horses watching them when Lou C. said, "What is that piled up there?" Not ten feet away there was a kill; a yearling heifer so completely covered with sticks and bark and small limbs that it looked exactly like a huge rat nest. On close examination we found the flank had been opened and most of the guts pulled out; the left shoulder had been eaten into, the shoulder blade disjointed, and completely cleaned of all meat and laid on top of the heifer.

It was easy to see why the hounds were acting differently. Instead of the single track always leading on they had found many tracks where the lion had been around this kill. It must have taken many short trips to gather up enough stuff to cover the yearling with a heap the size of a wagon bed. The hounds soon found the right track, leading to where the big lion was lying nearby on the hillside and when he got up they were close enough to put him up a tree in short order. Fortunately, we had been seeing lots of lion sign on previous trips and had borrowed Scotty's .30-30, otherwise we would have been unarmed. We tried to get Lou C. to shoot the lion but she refused. We were about three or four hours' ride from camp and the sun was going down, so with no further argument the lion was shot, skinned, and a start made for camp. It was well into the night when we got in and plenty cold. When we rode across snow, Lou C. said it squeaked like little pigs.

In December, 1946, with deer season over and hunters gone, some of the family came to Horse Camp for a hunt and visit. They were Lee and Lou C., G. W., III, my nephew, Jodie, and our daughter-in-law, Lee Evans, whose husband, Bob, we lost in World War II.

The young folks were busy most of the time scattering enough

CHARACTERISTICS OF LIONS

stock salt to last through the winter, but the two Lees and I were trying to catch a bear or two. Late one afternoon, along the rim of the Middle Fork and in the area where the Horse Camp cattle live the year around, instead of a bear trail the hounds found a lion trail. Nearby there was one of our very nice Hereford heifers, which had been killed by the lion, dragged under a big log, and covered up with any loose stuff the lion could find handy. We didn't stay around there long as it was real hot, and we thought it best to call the hounds off and return to camp, picking up the trail early next morning. The lion had returned in the night and after a short trail and race, was soon put up a tree. The dead heifer belonged to G. W., III, and there was no argument about whether the lion should be killed, so he shot it as soon as we reached the tree.

The young folks had work to do next day, so Big Lee and I went back where we found the trail of a big female lion. She crossed the Middle Fork and didn't tree until she reached the mouth of Hell Canyon, in the West Fork. The limited grazing permit at Horse Camp permits 134 head but only produces fifty or sixty calves yearly and, with no one living there during the winter, we thought if these two big lions were not killed they would eat up the calf crop before spring.

The calf which we had found was killed in an area where there were easily twenty deer to one calf, indicating that one or both of these lions were stock killers.

Stock-killing lions will also kill sheep and hogs, and, occasionally, horses and colts.

I have not seen a skin removed from a lion in this whole general area that did not have porcupine quills in and under the skin, mostly around the paws and forearms, evidence that all lions around here kill and eat porcupines. I have found quills in the mouth and face of a few young lions, but this is rare. The lion reaches under and turns the porcupine on his back to avoid the quills. The many porcupine kills I have found consist of just the well-cleaned skin, flesh side up, quills to the ground, with all edible portions gone as if the lion had made only one meal. Other than a few rodents—I have found a whole rat in a lion's stomach—this about covers a lion's diet. Lions sometimes eat a lot of hair with their meat.

I have observed that, contrary to common belief, varmints generally lay up on the cold side of a hill or mountain on winter days instead of in the sun. I think this is nature's way of protecting them from the subzero night temperatures. About all varmints do their prowling and feeding at night, and at high altitudes, where the cold is extreme in winter and there is ice nine months out of the year. They are provided with only one coat, and cannot go inside, build a fire, cover up, or put on more clothes, but by staying on the shady side during the day, where the snow and ice do not melt in winter, their blood and natural coat of hair develop to where the extreme cold at night can be endured.

By lion hunters, lion "markers" or "scrapes" are the most commonly looked for of lion signs, and this sign can be seen much easier than tracks, lion kills, or any other sign. Also, the direction the lion is traveling is always indicated by the "marker."

If you want to know just what a lion "marker" or "scrape" looks like, double your fists, put your thumbs together, then press down on the soft ground or under a tree where there are pine needles or duff. Draw your doubled-up hands back about six or eight inches, pressing down all the time, and you will create a small mound, the size will vary according to the depth and softness of the debris. These two parallel marks made by your knuckles, and the resulting mound is enough like a "marker" or "scrape" to fool anyone.

This is a mating sign of the male lion, made frequently along his "runs." These "markers" are not made indiscriminately over

CHARACTERISTICS OF LIONS

the country, but follow a common pattern, so true to form that one with experience can go into any mountains anywhere on the North American continent, and soon tell if there are lions in the area simply by checking for lion "markers." The place to look for "markers" is on top of rimrocks or ledges, close to the edge. Mostly under trees, under rimrocks, especially if there are hangovers, in the bottoms of the canyons, and more often at forks under big trees, on top of hogbacks or narrow rocky ridges, in saddles, or on top of peaks.

This same sign is made by the male bobcat in similar places but is easily distinguished from lion "markers" by the difference in the width of the "scrape." By the same token it is easy to tell if the "marker" is made by a big lion or a smaller one. Usually there is a small amount of urine left either before or after the "marker" is made.

A female lion will follow these same runs, and often leave urine on the "markers." Naturally with the added scent, many a lion trail, both male and female, has been picked up by hounds at "markers" that would have been passed up otherwise.

I was hunting horses, without any hounds, along the rim of the Middle Fork once in the late afternoon. I was facing the wind when I saw a whitetail deer come running out of a small header from near the rim. Knowing there was no one else anywhere in this area, and that the deer had been disturbed by something, I investigated. Under a pine, I found a "marker" made by a big male lion and so fresh there was a drop of urine still hanging from a pine needle on top of the "marker." The deer had run away from the lion.

There have been many arguments about whether these "markers" are made by the fore or hind feet. It seems reasonable that a lion could hunker down with most of his weight on his haunches, draw his front paws toward him in a parallel position with claws concealed to make the "marker," and I, for one, thought this was the way it was done; but never having seen a lion make this sign, I wrote to some of my friends whom I regard as completely reliable, and men who have had the best chances to make observations pertaining to "lion markers." After these reports, it seems one must conclude they are made with the hind feet.

Following are quotations from replies to my inquiries, which shed considerable light on this interesting practice:

Mr. J. Stokley Ligon, of Carlsbad, N. M., Field Biologist, U. S. Fish and Wildlife Service, writes:

My knowledge from actual observation on this controversial subject is not such that you can safely tie to it. In my earlier experiences with mountain lions and their habits of raking leaves or soil, I assumed such rakes or marks were made with the front paws. In my association with Mr. Lilly in later years, I learned from him that the rakes are definitely made by the hind feet. As I recall, he said by both hind feet. Had I been so informed by another with less experience, I might have doubted the source of information, but knowing Mr. Lilly as I did and his insistence that facts be supported, I could not but accept his word. He has had many mountain lions in confinement with opportunity to observe their habits.

It was also Mr. Lilly's opinion that the males were usually responsible for the marks, although there might be exceptions, just as is true of dogs and wolves; when in an aggressive mood, the female will also make the backward movement scratches or "dare marks" common with males at registering places.

Bobcats, likewise, have the rake-making habit and both they and the common tom house-cat will back up to a bush, tree or other object and spray their scent. It is my understanding the lion does likewise, after which the rakes are made.

Like the much mooted question of lions screaming like a woman, the habit of raking leaves or soil will continue to be a campfire subject of interest. If solved to the satisfaction of all, many interesting camp arguments will never again be revived to heighten the enjoyment of campfire tales.

Homer C. Pickens, of Santa Fe, N. M., Assistant State Game Warden, gives the following information on the subject:

It is a controversial subject, and very few of us have had the opportunity actually to see a lion making a scrape. I think that I was very fortunate

CHARACTERISTICS OF LIONS

one time while living in Albuquerque to see a lion in the zoo make a scrape on the cement floor.

Our three boys were small at that time and Mrs. Pickens and I took them down to visit the zoo late one afternoon in the summer. We noticed this mountain lion walking back and forth in his cage making a "meowing" noise that could have been heard about 150 yards away. In the still forest it could have been heard farther away. As the lion was pacing along inside his cage he would jump the water drain or "trough" and twice after jumping the trough he would urinate on the pavement and scrape with each of his hind feet, seemingly trying to cover up the wet spot. This is the only time that I have ever witnessed a scene like this and it may not be natural, since the lion was caged.

Many times have I trailed and treed lions that did not make any kind of a scrape, but my observations have proven to me that most male lions usually make scrapes at certain places along the route they travel.

I remember one time while trailing a lion north of Cimarron the dogs were traveling fast, mainly following the many scrapes. When it was treed and killed I found it to be a female lion. I knew at once that there had to be a male lion near although the country was such that tracks could not be seen. Immediately the dogs picked up the male lion's tracks and treed him within five minutes. They were adult lions traveling together and were mating, and it was the month of May.

Another time I caught a large male lion northwest of Las Vegas during the winter months. The snow was about eight inches deep and he was making a lot of scrapes. At every scrape his tracks indicated in the snow that his hind feet were used in making the markers. In all the experiences while lion hunting, my observations have proven to me that the scrapes or markers were made by male mountain lions, using their hind feet.

In a few cases around a deer kill I have seen cone-shaped scrapes piled up high, which, in my opinion, were made by a female lion that had kittens. In most of these instances I killed the lioness and her kittens near the deer kill. [See Illustration 14 for typical deer kill.]

E. E. Lee, of Tucson, Ariz., one of the famous Lee Brothers, big-game hunting guides in Arizona and New Mexico, says:

We will have to string along with the hunters who think an adult male lion does his scratching, or scraping, with his hind feet.

Of course, we do not know that all of them do this, but from our own observations, we think they do. We have seen them scrape with their hind feet and never saw a full grown one do this with his fore feet, although we have seen the young ones of both sexes use their fore feet. However, this sign of the young ones is not a true "scrape" but looks more like the sign of a house cat.

We have also seen both the Bengal tiger and African lion males scrape with their hind feet, and to do this they get into much the same position a mountain lion does, kind of half squatted down on their hind legs with the fore ones almost straight, kicking first with one foot then the other.

While watching tigers in a zoo in Jacksonville, Mississippi, when we were on our way to southern Florida for a panther hunt, I saw a male make the scrape. In Douglas, Arizona, while watching the circus African lions of Clyde Beatty, I saw one big male make the scrape twice in a period of less than ten minutes.

We have captured many lions and have raised a number of them in captivity, having spent many hours watching them when they did not know we were near them. We meet quite a few hunters, and read of others, who claim a mountain lion is practically silent. I am now (at 4 P.M.) listening to a yearling female who is calling, crying, or squawking, and she does this often either day or night. A little over two years ago we captured four grown lions in five days on a mountain a short distance from Tucson. Might have caught all of them in one or two days, only in taking them alive we would pack one into camp as soon as it was tied up and do no more hunting that day. Anyway, these lions were probably all very well acquainted, two old males, an old female, and a young female, probably not more than two years old. We had them in separate cages, but all in the same building so the lions could not see each other. The second night, after bringing the fourth one in, we heard an awful commotion and it seemed all of the lions were jumping against the cages and making a number of calls, yowling and squawking, and after we were in among the cages they kept this up, would yowl with a powerful flashlight held within two feet of their faces, and this bunch of lions continued to be very noisy as long as we kept them here.

The average weight of adult female lions is around 100 pounds, and of males 125 to 150 pounds. It is a rare exception when a male weighs over 200* pounds. Hunters often exaggerate weights and

---

* Young and Goldman, *The Puma, Mysterious American Cat,* Plate 6, "largest male puma . . . taken to date [Feb. 14, 1901] in the Americas. Killed by Theodore Roosevelt, near Meeker, Rio Blanco County, Colorado. Length . . . (tip to tip), 96"; weight, 227 pounds."

Page 53, "Musgrave (1926:285) states, 'The heaviest lion taken in this state [Arizona] weighed 276 pounds.' . . . This Arizona puma was killed near Hillside, Arizona, in March, 1917, . . . the weight of this creature was ascertained 'after the intestines had been removed . . . He measured 8 ft. 7¾ in., from the tip of his nose to the tip of his tail. . . .' "

CHARACTERISTICS OF LIONS

lengths of mountain lions as they do fish, deer, bear, or any other game. I have always felt that there is only one way to obtain weights and lengths, and that is by actually measuring or weighing and not by estimate. Game or fish never actually measure up to what they are estimated. Young and Goldman* show some very conclusive records of weights and lengths of mountain lions which compare favorably with my observations for half a century of some two hundred mountain lions taken in the Davis Mountains of west Texas and over the southern half of New Mexico. In New Mexico, the count of over a hundred is by actual tally recorded by me, and gives the date taken, sex, area taken, and who was along at the time. There was a similar record of the Texas hunts left by Will Evans.

Bear in mind that none of our family has been a professional hunter, but the hunting has been casual and only in connection with ranch operations. Another thing to remember is that less than 1 per cent of the lions and bear were taken with the tracking advantage of snow on the ground, but depended entirely on the trailing ability of good hounds.

Mountain lions that live in small mountain ranges and feed on stock, such as cattle and horses, get much heavier, as a rule, than those of bigger ranges where they travel greater distances. Kills of domestic animals are easier to make and the amount of edible meat on a horse or yearling carcass is greater than on a deer or smaller animal, hence less time is spent in hunting. I have followed the feeding trail of lions after deer for many miles without finding kills, and have seen, from signs left on such trails, where there had been passes made at deer that were not successful.

Lion tracks, when plainly seen, show all four toes, but never the claws, which are located one above each toe, unless on a running turn or where the lion has slipped. On the back bottom part

* Ibid.

of the heel, there are three little lobes that make an imprint in dust or soft ground almost like toes, and, if plainly seen, will identify a lion track beyond doubt from that of a dog or wolf of the same size, which also shows four toes; the claws of the latter two are never concealed and show in the track. A bobcat or a house cat have these same lobes on the heel. The lion has a fifth claw, called the killing claw. This claw is located on the inside of the leg, probably two inches from the ground and is always sharp and well protected, not being used in climbing trees and bluffs where the regular claws are sometimes broken and often dulled. But even if a claw is dulled or broken, a new one is soon grown and sharpened by natural methods known to all cats. Just as a house cat will sharpen its claws on your furniture, so will a lion sharpen his on trees or rocks. Among the soft-footed animals that make tracks in this area, all show four toes, except bear, coons, and badgers, all of which have five toes.

There have been many statements about panthers "screaming" and some of them must be true, so when I state that in all of my experience I have never heard one I wouldn't want it understood as a contradiction. I have lived in a mountain lion country nearly all of my life, and have camped in remote areas where opportunities for hearing nighttime noises were perfect. I have caught part of a family of lions late in the evening, laying out at night to finish the job next day, thus proving there were others in the vicinity; still I have never heard a lion in the woods. My opinion is that it must be unusual for them to scream. I have heard owls make awful noises at night, some of them rather frightening, but not what I would think sounded like a lion.

Another thing about mountain lions is their ability to stay out of sight. I have never seen one in the woods that hadn't first been put up by the hounds, while, on the other hand, I have frequently seen all of the other varmints that prowl the woods—bear, lobos,

CHARACTERISTICS OF LIONS

coyotes, cats, coons, and foxes. So it must be admitted that mountain lions are seen less often than any other varmints. During deer season, when the entire area is thick with hunters, an occasional lion is seen and killed by deer hunters. I think this is because there is so much noise and the woods are so thoroughly combed as to cause abnormal movement of lions that otherwise would remain in well-concealed beds all day.

CHAPTER VI

MT. TAYLOR LION HUNT

My first lion hunts in New Mexico occurred in March and April, 1920. The first of these hunts was in the Mt. Taylor country on my brother Lee's ranch.

In March, 1920, we loaded up the Buick car which I had at that time. With our two children, Pansy and G. W., III, Beulah and myself and all of our luggage, together with the two hounds, Alice and Redbone, we were loaded right up to the top of the side-curtains—it was in the days before the modern sedan. In the Mt. Taylor vicinity in those days the roads were merely ruts made by wagons passing between the little settlements—Marquez, where Lee gets his mail, and some of the other little places north of Old Laguna, such as the Indian villages of Seboyeta, Paquate, Mokina, and others.

It began to snow soon after we left Laguna and with visibility very near zero, it wasn't long until we were completely lost. As we approached the first settlement, I saw a man chopping wood, and, thinking we would surely get directions from him, I got out of the car, walked up to him and asked him if he knew where Lee Evans lived. He just kept chopping wood; didn't even answer.

MT. TAYLOR LION HUNT

I asked him the same thing in Spanish, and still he did not answer. This was my first experience with a New Mexico Indian. Lost in a snowstorm in a strange country, with my family at the mercy of the elements—I never felt worse in my life as I got back in the car and kept driving.

Not far from this place we came to a narrow wooden bridge, with no side rails, across a gully at least thirty feet deep. I drove across the bridge very slowly and started up a slippery hill beyond, but just before reaching the top the car stalled. I applied the brakes, but the car kept sliding back downhill toward the bridge, fortunately sliding off to one side just short of the bridge and the chasm below. I got out, and after scotching with rocks, finally got the chains on. We could then handle the car a little better across the ditches and up the hills. When this sticky clay and shale gets wet it is very difficult to negotiate.

The many wood-roads all looked alike, led mostly to deadends, and none of them were more than barely passable for an automobile. Lee had an automobile, the only one in that part of the country at the time. By close observation one could see little traces of oil and grease on the road leading to the ranch—and this was the only difference between the right road and the many wrong ones. Every time the road forked we looked closely for oil stains on the grass. Sometimes it was necessary to follow a short distance on foot to be sure; but by this method we finally trailed Lee's old yellow Cadillac right up to the ranch house. Never did smoke coming out of a chimney look so good.

Having gone in over a winding, crooked road in a snowstorm and not being able to get my bearings at any time, I was completely turned around in my sense of direction when we got to Lee's ranch; and until this day, I have never been able to get my directions straight there, although I know of no other place where I am turned around.

Lee's headquarters is out some distance from the rimrocks that mark the boundary of the Mt. Taylor mesa, with an altitude of over 8,000 feet, and the lower country around Lee's, with an altitude around 6,500 feet.

Lee had not seen any late lion sign, nor had he heard of any. We went out with the hounds the next day after my arrival, but found no sign at all. Returning to the ranch about noon, Lee said it would be necessary for him to ride up to Marquez, four miles from the ranch, and up around the rimrock country and rough canyons that looked more promising for lions. Upon his return that evening he made a remark that proved him to be a real prophet in his own country. He said, "I know where there is a lion."

Of course we wanted to know how he knew it. He said, pointing west, "See that little rocky peak up there? Anyone can tell by looking at that peak there has to be a lion there." Whether his opinion was based on a hunch, or on his knowledge of the kind of place a lion would be likely to be, I don't know. Next morning before daylight, after a fine ranch breakfast, Lee, Jack Garner, his ranchman, and myself were mounted and headed straight toward the little peak.

Just as we approached the base of this peak the hounds winded something and broke into a run. We later learned that lions had killed a wild horse and the hounds had winded them on the kill. We followed, but came to a very good wire fence soon after starting, and by the time we got our horses through to the other side we could no longer hear the hounds. We knew where we had heard them last, and they were heading up toward Garter Mountain (so named because of a white rimrock about halfway up that circled the mountain and looked much like a garter. We were riding as fast as possible and as we approached a pile of rocks, some of them thirty or forty feet high, on a small, benchlike mesa, we came upon Redbone baying a big male lion that was standing on a rock looking down at him. (See Illustration 15.)

MT. TAYLOR LION HUNT

I think Jack Garner was carrying the only gun, and one of us, I don't recall which, shot the lion. We were much concerned about Alice, so we soon made a little circle to pick up her sign. Redbone hit another trail almost at once and headed up the side of Garter Mountain, where a huge rockslide, some fifty feet across and three hundred feet long with rocks the size of an automobile, extended down the mountain near the top. Redbone reached the slide ahead of us, and when we got there Alice and Redbone were both baying another lion as large as the one we had just killed. This lion was down in the rocks instead of being on top like the first one. After shooting this one, and learning that it also was a male, we figured there must be a family of lions, and therefore one or more females around. We were soon on the fresh trail of another lion which led to the top and over Garter Mountain. In the rim on the other side we jumped another lion. Lee was the only one that sighted this one. Females not only make less scent, and are harder for hounds to follow, but usually are more alert and make faster time on the ground. Redbone and Alice were pretty old dogs and not very fast, so we were unable to crowd this lion close enough to make it stop.

It turned out that there were two females—one probably was the mother of the bunch, and the other must have been the same age as the two males we killed. If a female does not have another litter, it is not uncommon for a family of lions to stay together till maturity. At another time in my life, we found and killed just such a family—the old mother lion, two males, and a female, all full grown. On numerous occasions we have found two or three half-grown lions still with the mother.

Jack Garner left us to pack the two lions in to the ranch, but Lee and I stayed on the chase until nearly night, when we had to call the hounds off and go back to the ranch. Jack had both the lions skinned when we got in.

Lee and I went back early the next morning and picked up

the trail again, but could not get close enough to shoot or bay a lion. They always managed to take advantage of the many huge rock piles common to the Mt. Taylor country, and while the hounds were slowly following the trail through these bad places, the lion would slip out. By the time the hounds picked up the trail again it would be almost cold.

By nightfall of the second day, we were about fifteen miles from the ranch and were just as tired as Redbone and Alice, as we both had to do a lot of walking because the course we were following was too rough for a horse. The one advantage we had over the hounds was that we could alternate, while one followed through the roughs on foot the other would take the horses and make contact on the other side.

Again we quit the trail about dark, reaching home well into the night. As the hounds were worn out, we did not take them out again, and so wound up the first of many hunts. As we look back on it now, with the knowledge of later experience, we know how foolish we were to wear ourselves out on these hard trails when we might so easily have gone back to that first kill and there picked up a fresher trail made by the lions returning for another meal. But knowledge of this sort comes only from experience.

In November, 1922, Albert Pickens came to Horse Camp with his two well-trained lion hounds, Nig and Sam, to hunt lions for the Government. Slash headquarters was then the voting place for Indian Peak District, Precinct 14, Catron County, and when Albert came there to cast his ballot he told me that he had trailed a lion into Indian Creek the day before and asked if I would go back to Horse Camp with him for a lion hunt. My first New Mexico Brownie was about a year old at that time and I was eager for a chance to work him with such experienced hounds as Nig and Sam, so I took him and went to Horse Camp with Albert.

MT. TAYLOR LION HUNT

We went directly to Indian Creek next morning and picked up the lion's trail where Albert had left off two days before. We found where the lion had laid up not far from where Albert had quit the trail, so, from there on, the trail was about as fresh as it had been when Albert left it.

Sam and Nig were smart, fast-working hounds on a trail in narrow canyons, rimrocks, or brushy country. In such terrain, they took the scent high from rocks or canyon walls or brush and, going south along under the top rim of Indian, they made such good time that Albert and I could hardly stay up with them, and Brownie hardly knew what it was all about. But when the trail left the roughs and turned east across the big mesa between Indian and Brother West canyons, the picture changed.

Here, Nig and Sam were at a loss and Brownie began to work. Brownie had been trailing a lot of cats and was trained for close trailing, even to the point of taking a difficult trail a track at a time over barren, open, mesa country. He did so here, and this was very impressive to Albert; so much so that plans were made then and there for him to have hounds of Brownie's blood. He later owned and enjoyed to the limit hunting with a full brother of my famous Little Brownie. This hound also was named Sam and made a great record for himself as a lion hound.

We kept on after this lion until dark overtook us, crossing all the rough canyons along the north rim of the Middle Fork without water for ourselves, our hounds, or our horses, and without finding either a kill or where the lion had laid up. So at dark we were still on a cold trail; but we decided to lay out and follow the trail again next morning.

We were rewarded by finding where the lion had laid up in Cassidy Canyon, not half a mile from where we had camped; and from there on the trail was fresh and easy to follow. Crossing Cassidy, the going was too rough for horses and Albert followed the hounds on foot while I took the horses to a crossing farther up

SLASH RANCH HOUNDS

the canyon. I finally made the very difficult crossing and, when I reached Green Fly Canyon, just east of Cassidy, I found the hounds with a female lion bayed on a big rock. She was where the hounds could get close to her, and she was in a vicious mood. I could not see one of Albert's hounds and thought sure the lion had killed him. As I arrived, the lion jumped straight out from the rock right onto Albert's other hound and started to maul it. I reached for my carbine, only to find that the scabbard had torn loose somewhere earlier and spilled the rifle, leaving me without a weapon.

I went back as quickly as I could and found Albert and took him back with me. The battle was still going on when we got there, and I used Albert's rifle to kill the lion. We then found that she had four healthy cubs denned right under the rock she was bayed on. There was a freshly killed and half-eaten deer right near the den.

The lion had not succeeded in killing any of the hounds, although Sam was mauled so badly that we thought at first he would have to be packed to camp; but, by riding slowly, he was able to keep up with us and, in a few days, was none the worse for the experience.

This was the only four-kitten litter I have ever seen. The usual litter numbers from one to three. Elliott Barker, in his book, *When the Dogs Bark "Treed,"** tells of finding one four-kitten litter; and I believe that Ben Lilly is quoted, in the book, *The Ben Lilly Legend,* by J. Frank Dobie, as having found one litter of four and one litter of five kittens in all his years of lion-hunting experience. Such litters are extremely rare.

---

*University of New Mexico Press, Albuquerque, 1946.

CHAPTER VII

WOLF CUNNING

Speaking of Albert Pickens reminds me of the way he killed the last lobo wolf in the Black Mountain-Cooney Prairie area; and that reminds me that I have never explained the statement made much earlier in this book that the lobo was one predator I would like to see exterminated.

My hatred for wolves goes clear back to my early boyhood in Texas, and has been strengthened by countless experiences with them throughout my lifetime. Never once have I known a wolf to do anything to change my bad opinion of him; and, although I would very much regret the passing of bear and lions from these Southwestern mountains, I would shed no tears whatever over the death of the last lobo.

In my opinion, the lobo is the cruelest, most wanton killer of all of our Southwestern predators. Bear and lions do sometimes become stock killers, and both do sometimes kill wantonly, beyond the need for food. But such animals are the exceptions to the rule; whereas the opposite is true, in my opinion, of the lobo.

Years ago, when I was a boy in Texas, a lobo adopted as his home range the area immediately around our ranch headquarters.

SLASH RANCH HOUNDS

I think he chose this location at least partly because of my father's pack of hounds. I have seen many instances since then of wolves choosing a locality around a ranch headquarters where dogs are kept, partly no doubt because of the opportunities for food to be found around such a headquarters, but partly too, I think, because the wolf delights in annoying and trying to kill the dogs. This particular lobo became an immediate threat to our stock, and he made our nights miserable by the way he stirred up and harassed our hounds. He would come in close to the house at night, arouse the hounds, get them to chase him a mile or so, then turn on them and chase them back—time after time and night after night, all to the tune of much barking and general uproar.

This is a favorite trick of wolves, one I have since seen repeated many times. Dogs in their own back yards are bold enough to chase a wolf; but they fear the wolf and, once they get out into the darkness and away from familiar surroundings, that fear grows and, when the wolf turns, they will run from him. Often too, dogs will string out in such a chase and the wolf will turn and kill them one by one, as he catches them. Our Texas hounds in this particular instance had been wise enough to stick together and this wolf had not, so far, succeeded in killing one of them; but we knew that sooner or later this would happen or that the wolf would kill some of our stock, and we grew to hate him bitterly.

One night we heard the hounds take off after the wolf, and my brother, Joe, and I decided to slip out into a nearby arroyo and hide there in the hope of shooting the wolf when he chased the hounds back. We waited until the hounds came pounding back past us and, sure enough, there was the wolf close behind them, visible enough in the moonlight to make a target. Joe, being the older, had the rifle and he stood up to fire. The wolf turned swiftly at sight of us, but Joe's quick shot knocked him rolling. I have learned since that few wolf stories end so suddenly or so simply.

WOLF CUNNING

Cole Means tells of another very similar but less easily solved instance that occurred on the Means Y6 ranch. Here, too, a wolf took up headquarters near the ranch and proceeded practically to disrupt the work of the ranch. Every night he would come in and play this game of "you chase me and I'll chase you" with the hounds, and nearly every night he would kill stock. This went on for a considerable time, with sometimes as many as fifty men working on the problem of exterminating this one wolf. This wolf finally was killed, but at great expense both in stock killed and in man-hours.

Just a few stories out of my own experiences will show why I, and all cattlemen, hate wolves. A favorite wolf method of killing large animals is to hamstring the animal, breaking him down and making him completely helpless. Raw cowhide is extremely tough, and the heavy tendons in a full-grown steer's legs are even tougher, yet a lobo's sharp teeth and powerful neck and jaw muscles enable him to leap past a steer and cut through those tendons with no seeming effort. Once the animal is down and helpless, the wolf will gorge himself off the steer's body, sometimes not even taking the trouble to kill the animal first. I have seen these hamstrung, helpless animals still living after wolves had eaten great chunks out of them. I remember one night hearing an animal moaning as if in great distress. We could not get to her in the darkness but, next morning, found a fine heifer, hamstrung, still alive and suffering in spite of the fact that a wolf had eaten at least twenty pounds of flesh off her living body. A few incidents like this will teach anyone to hate wolves.

I have a painful memory, too, of finding, in one corner of a small pasture where the wolf had trapped them, eleven ready-for-market steers, some hamstrung and waiting to be shot, some already dead. This was the work of a single lobo, and the wolf had eaten from only one carcass. The rest of the slaughter had been merely to satisfy the beast's lust for killing.

SLASH RANCH HOUNDS

Incidents like these, repeated many times in my own personal experience, may give the reader some idea why I hate wolves and why cattlemen have repeatedly offered large rewards, sometimes up to $5,000, for the destruction of a single lobo.

Hound men have still other reasons for hating wolves, as I mentioned earlier. I well remember one fine pack of trained hounds that was ruined on one chase after one lobo. This pack belonged to my brother, Joe Evans, and represented generations of breeding and years of careful training. The pack strung out on a hot but long trail—long because the lobo is fast and will keep ahead of hounds for a long distance. The wolf turned finally and, one by one, killed the lead hounds. Naturally, the best hounds in the pack were in the lead. When Joe rode up and found his best hounds dead or dying, he swore never to run wolves again. Joe and his family loved those hounds, and losing them was almost as painful as would have been the loss of human friends.

A person not familiar with wolves might wonder why dogs, even strong trained hounds, unafraid of either bear or lion, should be so easily killed by a wolf. After all, the wolf is only another kind of dog, and not the biggest of the dog family either. Yet he is death to dogs. I have never seen a dog that would stand a chance in a fight with a lobo. Neighbors of ours once owned one of the biggest, one of the most vicious dogs I have ever seen; so big and so vicious that he had to be kept chained constantly to keep him from killing other dogs and injuring people. He was truly a gigantic animal and about as dangerous a fighter as one could imagine. We took this dog to a ranch where a lobo was making regular visits and one night, hearing the lobo outside, turned the big dog loose. He charged out eagerly enough, and met the wolf. We heard the sounds of that meeting, but not for long. I don't know what the lobo did, but whatever it was cured the dog of any desire to fight him. The big dog turned tail and ran, not stopping at the ranch at all but fleeing miles across country to his own

WOLF CUNNING

home and the safety of his own pen and chain. The lobo was unhurt and continued his depredations.

I recently read an article in which the writer defended wolves, claiming that they were brave, gallant animals, that their killing of other animals was no worse than that of any other predator, no worse than that of the human hunter "who kills for sport," and that the wolf was a necessary part of Nature's plan for the control of wildlife populations, since the wolf "kills only the weak, sick, or crippled" and so tends to strengthen and improve existing supplies of game animals such as deer, antelope, sheep, etc.

I have no patience whatever with such sentimentality; can only believe that the writer knows nothing whatever about the actual habits of wolves. It is absolutely untrue that the wolf kills "only the weak, sick, or crippled," whether of game animals or of domestic stock. He will kill such animals, yes; but he will also kill any other animal he happens to feel like killing, regardless of size, health, or value. The writer's contention that the wolf is necessary to maintain a natural balance in deer and antelope herds, that without him deer and antelope would either die out or become tame as sheep, is simply childish. In the area with which I am most familiar, there have been no wolves at all for many years; yet the area is well populated with deer and antelope, and I could prove by the testimony of countless hunters who have walked or ridden these mountains in search of game that neither the deer nor the antelope are "tame."

It is true that the other predators kill game animals, and a few individual lions and bear do become stock killers; but these animals rarely kill beyond the need of their own hunger. Sometimes they do, but not often. On the other hand, the lobo is a butcher, killing at every opportunity whether he is hungry or not.

The comparison of the lobo with the human hunter also is childish, in my opinion. Even if we grant that the human hunter also "kills for sport," game laws today control and guide his

SLASH RANCH HOUNDS

killing toward the beneficial control of game populations and limit it to the degree needed for that purpose. You can't limit a lobo to one deer a season; nor can you tell him, "This year you can kill only a doe, because does are too numerous!"

Too, the hunter actually provides, through his license fees, the money without the benefits of which game of all kinds would have long since ceased to exist in this country. The wolf kills aimlessly, needlessly, and heartlessly without contributing anything at all. He has been praised for his stubborn survival against the centuries-long and world-wide war man has waged against him; but, to me, this survival is only an evidence of his cunning and ruthless courage. The very fact that man has, throughout the world and from earliest times, hated him and waged relentless war against him, seems to me to be far more telling evidence on the opposite side of the picture. Such general hatred must be, and is, deserved. Granted that the wolf is brave, and granted that courage is an admirable quality, even courage becomes less than admirable when it is used, as in the case of the lobo, only for self preservation and wanton murder.

I have kept my hounds off wolf trails whenever possible, but there was one time when, using every possible precaution, I did encourage them to help toward the extermination of wolves in this area. During the work of clearing the wild cattle off Black Mountain, the hounds one day jumped and ran down a lobo pup. Figuring that other pups of the same litter would be in the vicinity, we let the hounds work and soon found the trail of a full-grown wolf, probably the mother. We called the hounds in immediately, following the wolf's trail to where she had topped out of a canyon. Knowing that the hounds would never cross that canyon except on the trail of the wolf, we put a man at that point to stop them if such an attempt were made. I knew that, if the hounds got away from us on the trail of a full-grown lobo, the wolf would

1 My father's original Brownie, an American Foxhound. In 1903, when this picture was taken, Brownie was fifteen years old and had helped kill 100 bear.

2 Unusual shot of climbing lion.

3 CATTLEMEN ALL—Twenty-four members of the Evans family, spanning two generations, attended the 35th annual convention of the New Mexico Cattle Growers' Association in Albuquerque. Male members of the Evans delegation were (top row, left to right) Joe, Jr., Marquez; Graves, Hot Springs; G. W., "Dub," Magdalena, president of the association; Joe, El Paso; Lee S., Marquez; and John P., Marquez. (Lower row) Rube, Hot Springs; Jim, Magdalena; G. W., III, Magdalena; E. B., Jr., Silver City; and Truet Evans, El Paso. Also attending, but not shown, was George Evans, of Lovington, N. M.

4 Judge C. M. Botts, of Albuquerque (standing), Dub Evans, with lion taken on Mt. Taylor.

5 J. W. Kirkpatrick (left) and Hoxie Thompson, with lion taken by Hoxie Thompson.

6 Prize-winning steer raised by Dub Evans. Steers from Montosa ranch were entered in many of the big 1951 stock shows, including the International at Chicago.

7 Beaverhead Headquarters.

8 Little Brownie.

9 Old Brownie.

10 Biggest single drive ever made from Beaverhead (1,632 head, 1937).

11 From left to right: Harvey Blair, of Wichita, Kansas, holding Brownie; Lee Evans, of Marquez, N. M., holding Dan; Dub Evans, holding John, a son of a hound sent to Dub by the Lee brothers, of Arizona. Spotted hound between Lee and Dub is Katie.

12 Will D. Parker, Bartlesville, Okla.; Mark Taylor, Amarillo, Texas; Dr. McBride, Oklahoma City; Arthur M. Hughes, Bartlesville, Okla.; Carl Shappiro, Virginia, Minn.; Moss Patterson, Oklahoma City; George C. Oberfell, Bartlesville, Okla.; Jack Comer, Santa Fe, N. M.; Phil Phillips, Bartlesville, Okla.

13 Forrest Parrott and his lion.

14 Harvey Blair holding remains of deer killed and partly eaten by a mountain lion. Note twigs and debris with which lion covers his kill.

15 Lion bayed on a high rock, looking down at hounds below.

eventually turn and kill some of them, and I took every precaution to keep this from happening.

We then went back and used the hounds to trail and run down five more lobo pups. These pups, dead, were turned over to the Government hunter then working in the district.

A Government hunter-trapper named Ritchie did fine work toward the final extermination of lobos in this area. One by one he weeded them out until, finally, only one wolf was left. This was a female, and she was smart with the cunning of long experience. Mr. Ritchie worked long and hard to kill her and once did catch her in a trap; but a small stone caught in the trap and prevented its jaws from closing tightly, so that the wolf was able to, and did, shake the trap off.

After this experience this wolf would not approach even the most carefully laid traps, and of course no man could come within gun range of her. Her sex made her particularly dangerous, since she would certainly attract males into the country to mate with her, and her pups might well repopulate the area. As a matter of fact, well after it had been established that she was the sole survivor in the area, Mr. Ritchie did catch and kill a male wolf apparently drawn in from some other section of the country by this female. But as for the female herself, Mr. Ritchie used every lure and every trick of trap-setting he knew but finally admitted defeat and suggested that another hunter be sent against her. He felt that this wolf knew his scent and that of his mounts, as well as all his lures and tricks, too well for him ever to catch her, and that another hunter might have better success.

Albert Pickens was the man chosen for the job, and Albert spent two or three months in the area without setting a trap, studying this wolf's tracks, habits, and the reports of her doings brought to him by the ranchers and cowboys who were also on the alert for any sign of her. Albert patiently tried every scent lure he knew or which was suggested to him, leaving the various scents on bushes and rocks and then going back to search for tracks to see whether or not the wolf had been drawn to the spot, but never once did he find that she had been lured to where a trap would have caught her had a trap been set. Apparently she was just too wary of all scents to be drawn to any that might have been laid by man. During this period, Albert did kill another male wolf attracted to the area by the female; but this merely renewed the possibility that she might soon birth a new litter.

One day Albert, on horseback, followed the wolf's tracks to where she had stooled. Albert got a long stick off a nearby tree and, without dismounting and without leaving his body scent on any spot of ground or any object that would be left there, managed to move the dung a few feet to one side of its original position. He then rode away.

The next day he went back to the spot and saw where the wolf had returned, examined the place, and finally circled to find and examine the dung in its new position.

Days later, Albert succeeded in finding another similar deposit. This time, he moved off to one side a little distance, dropped a piece of canvas and dismounted onto the canvas so as not to leave scent or sign, and, using every possible precaution, set two traps a few feet to one side of the stool. He did not move the dung at this time but let several days pass so that time and wind and weather might wipe out any trace of scent he might have left in the immediate vicinity of the traps.

Next, he rode back to this place some days later and, as he had done the first time, without dismounting at all, using a long stick, he moved the dung over between the two traps.

If all this seems like undue precaution, bear in mind that all other tricks known to trappers had failed, whereas this one worked. The next day, Albert went back to his set and found tracks showing where the wolf had returned, noticed the moving of the dung, went (as she had done safely before) to examine it

WOLF CUNNING

in its new position, and had been caught in both traps. The traps were attached to drags, of course, because a wolf caught in a fixed trap will gnaw off its feet to get free. Albert followed the tracks of the wolf and the furrows left by the traps and drags and soon came upon the wolf in a thicket where the drags had caught and stopped her.

That was the end of lobos in this area. This happened in the early '20's, and no lobo has taken up residence in this locality since.

Since writing the above, I have received a letter from my brother, Joe, who has read the same article defending wolves which I referred to earlier in this chapter. Joe was so indignant about that article that he wrote several pages on the subject, some of which I quote:

> This article merely proves to me that the writer never raised sheep or cattle for lobos to kill! There were only a limited number of bear that killed stock, as they lived mostly on acorns, piñons, and berries. The mountain lions fed principally on deer or antelope, and were easy to control because they could be caught with hounds. They would usually kill one deer or antelope and go back to the carcass day after day until it was eaten up. But the lobo wolf lived on cattle whenever possible because they were easier to catch than deer or antelope, and would kill a fresh yearling about every three days. Think how much this would amount to, at the present price of beef!

Joe reiterates my own remarks about the wolf killing for sport, and reminds me of the incident already mentioned of the lone lobo killing eleven ready-for-market yearlings in one night. He adds:

> The slaughter of lobos was not limited to yearlings, either. And it is not true that he killed only the weak, sick, or crippled animals, whether beef or wild game. I remember seeing a grown bull, about as far from being a weak, sick, or crippled animal as you could imagine, which was cut down by lobos and eaten off of while he was still alive. . . . This writer's idea of preserving the lobo is no more sensible than it would be to pet a rattlesnake or coddle a bandit or rapist who was endangering the lives of your loved ones or the sanctity of your home. If this writer had ever shed tears, as I did, over the torn and bleeding body of a well-loved hound as I carried him in my arms back to the ranch to die after an encounter with a

lobo, he would sing a different tune! To kill the lobo wherever you find him is to render a service to mankind and to all wildlife.

I agree with Joe, and want to add here that the Fish and Wildlife Service (formerly The Biological Survey) has rendered an invaluable service to the livestock and game interests of the Southwest by the determined warfare they have carried on against the lobo. I and all the stockmen of my acquaintance, as well as the hunters, commend them for it.

CHAPTER VIII

WHEN BELL CAME AFTER SCOTTY

In November, 1924, Lee and his wife came to Beaverhead for a visit and a hunt. They brought with them a friend, Howard Walker, telegraph operator for the Santa Fe Railroad, stationed at the time at Suwanee, about fifty miles west of Albuquerque.

As the most desirable hunting camp in the Beaverhead area was Horse Camp, we loaded up chuck and beds on some good pack mules and sent Scotty, one of our best ranch hands, around north of Black Mountain with the pack outfit. Lee, Howard, and I went through the mountains with the hounds to look for sign. We learned that the bear that had been using Black Mountain earlier, had moved into the Middle Fork of the Gila.

The Middle Fork is from six to ten miles south of Black Mountain, and is extremely rough country, with a mass of high, broken bluffs, some as high as a thousand feet straight up and down without a break. At intervals of a mile or more this bluff is cut with side canyons that cannot be crossed near the rim of the Middle Fork, nor can man or dog go down any of these side canyons into the Middle Fork between Jordan Canyon on the east and Indian Creek on the west. Such extremely rough and inaccessible terrain is ideal for bear in the late fall after they are fat, because they are pretty helpless against a good pack of hounds in a less rough country. Nature has provided the bear with the natural instinct to seek the roughest country for self preservation at a time when he is too fat to run.

In my observations over a period of half a century in the Davis Mountains of Texas and the many ranges of New Mexico, whether there is hunting in the area or not, the habits of bear are the same. As the nights get colder and the bear get fatter, they begin to retire to the dark canyons and the rougher country, and their nightly feeding tours become more limited. It usually is in such a place that they den up for winter, which is one reason why few bear are found in hibernation.

I have seen many of these dens, but seldom one that can be reached on horseback. I have found most of them while following the hounds on foot while trailing bear. About the only time bear will vary from this procedure is when there is no mast at all in the rougher areas, and at the same time plenty for them to eat elsewhere. Because of a bear's hog-like appetite and the necessity for taking on more fat before hibernation, an abundance of food in more accessible places will sometimes lure him out into the open country, even in the late fall; but in my experience such cases are rare.

It was only in this very rough country that we could find a bear trail fresh enough for the hounds to follow on this hunt.

Some duty in connection with the ranch operation made it necessary for me to return to headquarters for a day. During this time, Lee, Howard, and Scotty hunted with the hounds in the very roughest part of the Middle Fork country, along the north rim where Cassidy, House Log, and Brother West canyons empty in. I was late getting back to Horse Camp, and so were they. They had been on a fresh bear trail and the bear had piled off into the Middle Fork, with the hounds following as far as they could. In their enthusiam they had even gone off some falls and could neither get down or climb back. The boys had to go to their rescue on foot and use saddle ropes to get them out.

We knew that we could get on this same trail by going into the Middle Fork west of Indian Creek, on what is known as the Meadows Trail, and we figured that we might get another bear trail by going down through this rough country. We were curious to know also just where this bear had gone after "bluffing" the hounds. We found no other trail, but as soon as we reached the mouth of House Log Canyon the hounds readily picked up the trail of the bear they had lost the day before. This was a place about an hour's ride down the river below the Meadows Trail.

Our enjoyment in watching the hounds work on the trail was short lived, as they soon left the bottom of the canyon and began to climb out on the north side, where they had had trouble the day before. This trail led up to a place out of which the hounds could not climb. Smart hounds usually find a way around and then come back and pick up the trail, but in the Middle Fork country the continuing bluffs and rimrocks prevented them from doing this.

I didn't mind walking in those days, and being able to follow hounds on foot through rough places allowed me to see lots of things and learn a lot about the habits of both bear and lions that I could not have learned otherwise. This knowledge has been useful on other hunts which otherwise might have failed.

When I volunteered to follow the hounds on foot I did not hear any arguments from the other boys. Howard did offer to go with me, but after looking over his bulky frame I decided I might have to assist him, as well as the hounds, through some of the rough places. The hounds on this hunt were Bell and Brownie, litter mates, about three years old, and two younger hounds, Ranger and Blue. I knew when I left my horse that the going would be rough, but if I had known just how rough, I probably would not have tried it. This kind of going is extremely slow; and lifting four hounds up over ledge after ledge became very tiresome.

After passing through the first little saddle out of the river over into Brother West Canyon, I neither saw nor heard anything of the men with the horses until late in the day. They had taken the horses back up the river to the Meadows Trail and topped out on the west side of Indian Creek. Lee is unequaled when it comes to being in the right spot with the horses at all times.

Just before sundown when the hounds and I topped out of Indian Creek on the west and reached the first place on the whole trail where a horse could be used, there were Lee and the other boys all mounted and leading my horse. Never did it feel so good to be on a horse. It was late and we were still on the trail of the bear that had gotten away from the boys while I was gone.

We decided to go back to the river and lay out for the night so if we hit the trail again we might run the bear out of the rough country instead of back into it. All the while we had nothing to eat, but one of the boys had killed some squirrels and we cooked them over an open fire, salted with a little stock salt we found on the river. I think that was the best squirrel meat I ever ate.

Next morning, we figured that it might save time not to go back to the trail where we had left it, but to go up the river for a few miles and try to cut the trail farther ahead. Lee, Howard, and I were to take the hounds and hunt for the trail, and Scotty was to go back to camp, get fresh horses and cook something to eat. We traveled up the river to the Homestead Trail, about five miles above the Meadows Trail, and had barely topped out when the hounds hit the bear trail. Luck was with us, because the trail at this point was real fresh, and led away from the rim and rough canyons. Even out where it was good riding, we could not stay up with the hounds. They were moving fast and traveling almost north.

Howard and I stayed together and Lee took off alone. The hounds were soon out of hearing, but I thought the bear would circle back towards the bluffs, as Lee was working more to the west when I last saw him. Howard and I hunted more to the east. There was some good rough country on upper Indian Creek a little east of where we last heard the hounds and I felt sure they would tree in that country. We kept going; stopping often to listen, for if the hounds tree in a header, and are pretty hot and not barking much, it is easy to miss them in such a big country. We failed entirely to find them.

This bear was doing just what a bear shouldn't do—going away from rough country instead of toward it. About noon, Howard and I decided we would go to camp and see if Scotty had heard anything. About the time we got to camp, Lee rode up. He was peeved because we had not found the hounds and we felt the same about him. There was a corral full of fresh horses, but we didn't see Scotty. We went in, and there was a pot of fresh coffee, a nice pan of biscuits, a big platter of fried steak, and "dough" gravy in the frying pan. Scotty had cooked this meal, but had not eaten. We couldn't figure out just what had happened, but thought it possible he had heard the hounds and had gone to them. We turned our tired horses loose, ate dinner, and had saddled up mounts to make another search for the hounds when we saw Scotty riding into camp at a fast trot, with all four hounds following him. He rode right up to the front gate, reached into his shirt front and pulled out a bear's foot, reached in and pulled out another, and another. He threw all three on the ground and said, "If you will notice, you will see that they are each off the right hind leg of a bear."

We could hardly wait until he told us what had happened. He said that just when he had cooked the meal, but before he began to eat, Bell had come to the door and began to bark as though she were trying to tell him something. He went to the corral and got on his horse, and no sooner had he mounted than she took off up the old road leading out to the north. After a while he met another hound or two, but Bell was traveling ahead of him at a pretty good gait, and seemed to know where she was going. She led him over to Canyon Creek Mountain, about five miles from camp, to where the hounds had three bear up one tree, an old she-bear and two big husky cubs, brown in color and very pretty.

When the old bear had gone back out onto the same side of the Middle Fork where the boys had run her three days before, it was to get her cubs. We took a couple of pack mules and went with Scotty to bring the bear in. Just as we were leaving camp, Lt. Paul C. Febiger, who was visiting Forest Ranger Bloom, rode over to tell us someone had seen a big bear on Eagle Peak, and he wanted us to bring our hounds over there. We told him we were so busy packing bear in at the time that we couldn't go. He joined us to help pack the bear in, and get some pictures. He was stationed in Wyoming, but went from our ranch to visit his mother in Palo Alto, California. He took some of the cub meat with him and later reported that his mother had fourteen for dinner, with a big turkey at one end of the table and the bear ham and loin at the other. He said: "Believe it or not, we cleaned the platter of bear meat before we touched the turkey."

I can believe that, for a fat cub, properly cooked, can be mighty good eating.

Another sportsman's treat, not generally known, is fish cooked on hot rocks.

We usually rest the hounds for a day after four or five days of really hard hunting, and in fishing season, when we are within reach of a trout stream, we can spend the time very well along the banks of a mountain stream catching trout. One of my favorite tricks is to cook the trout with hot rocks on the bank of the creek in which they are caught. In order to do this right, a big fire is made about an hour before time to cook the fish. A number of smooth, flat rocks, the kind always plentiful along creek bottoms, are put in the fire. The rocks need not necessarily be flat if there is a smooth side wide enough to hold a brook trout ten or twelve inches long. Extra rocks should be heated as some will crack. By the time the fire has burned down, the rocks will be hot.

With a brush out of a tree the ashes can be brushed off the surface where the fish are to be cooked. After the fish are cleaned and salted, they are laid on the hot rocks, and they will begin to cook at once. Plenty of time should be given for one side to cook thoroughly, so the fish will have to be turned but once. A spatula can be made out of a dry stick an inch or more wide; when the fish are ready to turn, the spatula is worked carefully between the fish and the rock as the skin will stick to the rock, or come loose from the fish, if this is not done properly. After the fish are turned, they will cook on the other side in about the same length of time. The rocks should be at least twelve inches in diameter so that the heat will be held long enough to cook the fish properly. This is the best-tasting fish of all. Mountain trout are good anywhere, but this is mountain trout at their best. Salt is all that is necessary, but coffee and cold bread add a lot for a complete meal.

Build the fire close to the water and far enough from any kind of growth to avoid any chance of spreading; and see that it is completely out before leaving.

One doesn't necessarily have to be resting hounds on a bear or a lion hunt to enjoy this rare treat, so I suggest that you try it sometime.

CHAPTER IX

UNUSUAL HUNTS

TWO COMBINATION HUNTS

In November, 1926, J. W. Kirkpatrick, known as "Kirk," or "Mr. Kirk," made arrangements to bring a big party to New Mexico for a deer hunt. We decided to use our D Bar camp, on the East Fork, for our central camp, as at this place there were a good two-room log cabin, barn, corrals, and a horse trap. The cabin had a cookstove and a fireplace, with ordinary ranch conveniences.

Because of the large amount of supplies and camp equipment this party required, they wanted a campsite that could be reached by car or truck. The previous year, we had packed the same outfit into South Diamond Creek, and the actual weight of the equipment was 4,600 pounds, not including small duffle, guns, and cameras, which the hunters carried on their own mounts, so we were glad to use a more accessible camp such as the D Bar.

There was open season for bear at that time, and I had agreed to hunt bear with some of the party, while the others hunted deer. The whole party consisted of thirteen hunters, a porter, cook, and two horse wranglers. I provided the horse wranglers. Our plan was to hunt from the general camp with parties of from two to six, taking bedrolls and light camp outfits into the high country for a day or two at a time.

The first time we started out for bear, the hounds and the pack outfit looked so tempting that six of the deer hunters decided to go along. After a couple of nights and no bear, they were glad to get back to the main camp.

When we started on our next bear hunt, only four volunteered to go back into the high country with me. We camped on East Diamond Creek and, although we found old bear sign, we caught no bear.

On the third hunt, camping at the head of Diamond Bar Canyon, I was accompanied by Lee Wilson, of Rose-Wilson Motor Co., Dallas; and Barry Hagedon, of Peak-Hagedon Undertakers, El Paso. Zane Smith was our horse wrangler for this hunt and it was our last chance to get a bear.

Lee and Barry were both good deer hunters, and already had their bucks, as had most of the others, and they were anxious to get out. Our camp was about four miles above Diamond Bar headquarters, in reach of some mighty good bear-hunting country, especially at this time of the year.

I saw Bob Steele, one of the Diamond Bar cowboys, while we were packing in, and invited him to hunt with us the next morning, which he agreed to do. I got breakfast while Zane rustled horses, and we were ready for an early start on a frosty morning.

We had been gone from camp only about an hour when the hounds broke away at full speed, making music. I yelled at the hunters, "This is the moment we have been waiting for." We followed as fast as possible and soon heard the hounds overtake the bear when their barking changed from that of giving chase to the short, coarser barks of baying. We slowed down at once, for a party of five men on horseback makes so much noise riding through thick brush that the bear will come down. This bear did come down and another race was on. The hounds were coming in our direction, and we could hear the brush popping. They came out of the thick brush right on the heels of a huge black bear, and we saw him take a tree in the bottom of a little header. This was high up on the divide between Bonner and South Diamond canyons, and close to Sheep Creek Mountain.

Just as we rode up to the tree the bear started backing down. He was just ready to leave the tree as Wilson let him have it with three fast blasts from a .35 automatic. It was still only a quarter after seven, and it was cold on this November morning in that dark header.

I suggested that we remove the bear's entrails, hang him in the shade, and then hunt some more. Very close to this place the hounds picked up the trail of a bear that had been feeding, and the track was just the size of the bear we had recently killed. The only way to find out if it were a different bear was to let the hounds follow the trail.

Winding around through oak thickets, where there were plenty of good acorns on the ground, the hounds were working farther south all the time. When the trail straightened out leading toward a densely covered mountainside high up on the head of Bonner Canyon, I knew that it was another bear going to a place to lay up. This was really wild country, and the riding was bad.

We decided to separate. Bob and Barry were to top out and work the high saddles, while Lee, Zane, and I followed the hounds. From the looks of the country, this was not going to be easy. The hounds jumped the bear on the big, rough mountainside and were soon out of hearing. We hoped that Bob and Barry had gotten out in time, but learned later that the bear had already passed through the saddle between Bonner and Hell canyons, with the hounds in hot pursuit, just as the boys reached the saddle.

UNUSUAL HUNTS

The hounds piled off into Hell Canyon at about the roughest spot in the Black Range.

Bob and Barry had the advantage of being close enough to hear the hounds, so they followed them, but by the time we topped out all was quiet, and there was nothing for us to do but follow their horse tracks. These tracks led off into Hell Canyon between two spiral rock pillars, and it was almost straight down. I knew we could go any place they could, so off we went. Lee said, "Dub, I have starred on a football team with thousands cheering, but for real excitement, it is mild compared with this."

Bob Steele was a real bear hunter and could follow the hounds in the roughest country on this mountain. It was really a bear heaven, but the bear could not get away from these four hounds, the two main ones being Brownie and Little Brownie. Little Brownie was only a year old at the time, but Bob said he was the lead hound all the way. He dealt this big brown bear so much misery, even in Hell Canyon, that he backed up against a big tree for protection and stayed there till Barry shot and killed him on the ground. We trailed their horses right to the spot.

Our problem now was how to get these two big bear into camp whole so that the other hunters could take pictures of them. We selected the best horse in the bunch, loaded the brown bear on him, and took turn-about walking to lead him back to camp. We loaded the other bear on another horse, then two of us had to walk. We reached camp after dark, tired but happy. By morning the bear had thoroughly cooled out, and we loaded them and the beds and camp equipment on some good pack animals and headed for D Bar.

Lee and Barry felt so good about this hunt that they presented me with a brand-new saddle that Lee had had made just before coming out, and it really was the "apple of his eye." I appreciated this very much, and still have the saddle.

Soon after this combination hunt, the Game Commission

passed a regulation prohibiting dogs in the woods during the big-game season.

Elliott Cowden, of Midland, Texas, arranged to bring two of his oil-men friends out for a bear, deer, and turkey hunt in November of 1932. His guests were E. J. (Jim) McCurdy, Jr., and B. F. (Bert) Weekley, both of Fort Worth. Elliott and his party arrived November 11, with four days open season remaining for deer and turkey.

We sent our horses and hounds on to the Diamond Bar headquarters, on Black Canyon, where we were to leave our cars, and from there we were to make a long day's pack to the head of the Mimbres in the Black Range. To avoid packing them out of the Black Range, we wanted to kill deer near Beaverhead and leave them at the ranch to freeze while we were bear hunting.

We loaded some bedrolls and light camp outfits for Chet McCauley, one of our hands, to take across Black Mountain to Cassidy Spring, where we would spend only one night, hoping to get bucks. We reached Cassidy Spring about 3:00 P. M. on the twelfth, and had a hurried lunch so we could spend the hours before dark hunting for deer. The Fort Worth boys were tired after their long ride across Black Mountain, and wanted to hunt near camp on foot, while Elliott and I rode west of camp.

Although this was the tail end of the deer season, all four of us had a buck before sundown. Bert and Jim killed their bucks real close to camp, while Elliott and I got ours a mile away. We had brought extra pack animals for the purpose of packing the buck in to the ranch, and we did this the next day.

Lee Evans joined us at the ranch to go with us on the bear hunt. We spent the night of the thirteenth at the ranch and left early the next day for Diamond Bar, which was thirty miles to the south, to help move a heavy pack outfit over to the Mimbres.

UNUSUAL HUNTS

We wanted to spend the last day of the season, the fifteenth, hunting turkey.

Bert Weekley was feeling ill when we returned from Cassidy Spring, and instead of going with us, he went to Silver City with Chet, where he spent a few days in the hospital. Chet returned and joined us on the Mimbres. We had good luck with turkeys, taking seven, and, after eating one gobbler in camp, took the other six out with us.

The main objective, however, was to hunt for bear. I had made a scouting trip into this area earlier, and had found plenty of acorns and lots of bear sign there. We rode far the first five days until our hounds, horses, and men were worn out, and not a hound ever barked. The bear had all left there. Our time was running short, and Elliott said they could hunt only two more days, so we decided to pack back to Diamond Bar and hunt in upper Black Canyon and Bonner Canyon.

We helped Scotty, Chet, and the cook do the heavy packing, and they were to take the pack outfits and the extra mounts across to Diamond Bar while we hunted bear on the way. Our luck changed, for soon after leaving camp the hounds jumped a bear from a little header. The bear soon treed, but Jim's shot in the shoulder didn't kill him. He came down and a terrible fight followed. The underbrush was very thick and, with the hounds attacking from every side, there was little chance to shoot the bear without killing a hound. Elliott is cool headed, and an expert shot. He went in the thicket on foot, getting closer and closer, and finally delivered a fatal shot to the bear.

Lee hurried down the canyon to intercept the pack outfits, while we removed the bear's entrails and let it drain out, ready to pack. He reached the main canyon and had been there only a few minutes when the pack outfit arrived. Lee and Scotty soon reached us with a good pack horse and we loaded the bear. Scotty took him in and joined the boys who were waiting on the main trail.

SLASH RANCH HOUNDS

We went on with our hunt, and about two miles farther on, in a rough side canyon, the hounds picked up the trail of a lion. Brownie had hit the trail of the bear which we had just killed, but Boots, a black-and-tan bitch belonging to Lee, gave us the start after the lion. The trail got better all the time, but the hounds really had to get down and work on it.

About the middle of the afternoon they jumped, and after a most exciting race through quaking asp thickets, on steep hillsides, and over rock slides, they put a male lion up a tree. Lee, the two hunters, and I were able to stay together on this race, and were all present at the tree. After this lion was killed and loaded on a horse, we started to Diamond Bar, reaching there just after dark.

The hounds were pretty well worn out, and we decided to stop hunting. Bert joined us that night at headquarters. We were a little disappointed about bear, but otherwise, this combination hunt turned out pretty well. Bud McGahey's motto: "Never stop hunting," worked out fine for us on this hunt. It was rather unusual to move camp, and to kill a bear and a lion all in the same day.

LION KILLED WITH BARE HANDS

Mr. Kirk participated in another unusual event in August, 1931, when he came to Horse Camp and brought two of his friends: Judge Morrow, of El Paso, and Walter Browning, head of an automotive finance company in Dallas, Texas.

We hunted around a day or two without striking a lion trail. Then one morning we woke up to a pouring rain. We sat around camp playing dominoes and talking about past hunts until noon, when the clouds broke, and soon it cleared off. We were tired of camp and eager to get off with the hounds, even if we could find nothing but bobcats, which commonly come out and prowl after it has rained, even in the daytime. Judge Morrow was not a strong man, and he decided that chances for a lion after an all-night and morning rain were so slim that he would stay in camp.

UNUSUAL HUNTS

Mr. Kirk, Mr. Browning, and I rode along the rim of the Middle Fork, between Indian Creek and Canyon Creek. Suddenly Brownie threw up his head and piled off into a header, having winded a big lion in his bed. The hounds were right on the lion before he knew what had happened to him, and they had him up a tree in a couple of minutes. They crowded him so close that he climbed an old dead tree or stump with very few limbs. When we approached the tree after a mad dash through the brush, during which Mr. Kirk not only tore all the sleeve off a shirt but also scratched his arm until it bled, the lion was standing straight up with both hind feet on a limb, holding to the tree trunk with both forepaws, with his back to us. Mr. Kirk shot him with a .22 high-power, the bullet entering the center of the back, between the shoulders. The backbone split the bullet, so none of it came out, and the hole where it entered was so small that it was almost impossible to find it. (See Illustration 2.)

While we were gutting the lion, the difficulty we had in finding the bullet hole was inspiration for a practical joke on Judge Morrow, who had a most congenial personality and was quite a practical joker himself. We agreed to tell the Judge that the lion was bayed on a rimrock, and Mr. Kirk, following the hounds, came around a ledge and met unexpectedly with both the lion and the hounds. The lion made for Mr. Kirk, and the hounds covered him. When the big commotion was over, Mr. Kirk had the lion by the throat, his shirt was torn and his arm bleeding, but he and the hounds had killed the lion. The story was substantiated by Mr. Kirk's torn shirt and scratched arm. We rehearsed this tale all the way, and by the time we got back to camp, we almost believed it ourselves. With a straight face, Mr. Kirk told the story to Judge Morrow, who at first was not at all impressed. But we backed him so convincingly that the Judge began to wonder, though he said very little. Along in the late afternoon, some of the boys were resting, and Mr. Kirk went to the spring for a bucket of water, when I noticed Judge Morrow going over the lion for some evidence of a bullet. He was very thorough in his examination, but he could not find the very small bullet hole between the lion's shoulders.

After a while, in a voice of complete surrender, he said to me, "Dub, how in the hell can a man with only the help of dogs kill a beast of that size with his bare hands?" Mr. Kirk had really put one over on a man that was plenty keen and hard to fool. After Judge Morrow learned the truth, he wanted to try the same thing on the folks at the Slash Ranch, but Mrs. Evans knocked the props out from under him before he got well started.

CHAPTER X

LION MARKERS*

BY J. FRANK DOBIE

One of our most outstanding hunts was made in the winter of 1928, with Mr. J. Frank Dobie, who wrote the story of the hunt for the Country Gentleman. *This story follows in Mr. Dobie's own words.*—G.W.E.

> Way up high in the Mogollons,
> Among the mountain tops,
> A lion cleaned a yearling's bones
> And licked his thankful chops.

That is where Paul Branson and I went to hunt the mountain lion—the American lion, the Mexican lion, the panther, the painter, the puma, or whatever other name one wishes to bestow upon the cougar species of the cat family. Westerners generally refer to him as mountain lion, or simply as lion. Texas nearly always called him panther, and panther is the word, with its corruption "painter," that connotes the great hunters of old days, like Daniel Boone and Davy Crockett. Some people call him catamount, but the catamount proper is the wildcat, or lynx. I propose to use whatever name sounds best in the place and at the time it is used.

---

* From *The Country Gentleman*, May, 1928.

SLASH RANCH HOUNDS

Eighty-five miles by automobile from Magdalena, New Mexico, across the winter-browned Plains of San Augustine, then to the road's end in the Black Range, and we were at the Evans Brothers Slash Ranch, at Beaverhead. Twenty miles with pack mules over a trail of the Datil National Forest, and we were at the Horse Camp on the middle prong of the Gila River, perhaps the best mountain lion country left in the United States.

Formerly the panther ranged over entire North America, but a lion country nowadays must be inaccessible. Inaccessibility means brush and rocks and a country that is rough. The forks of the Gila, with their intersecting canyons, are as rough as a million years of ice and snow and rain and wind and sun and volcanoes—ages ago extinct—can make and unmake, scar and weather the rocks.

It is the malpais country. Here are mountains covered with pine, spruce, and fir and fringed with manzanita and stubborn shinnery. Here are slopes and plains dotted with alligator junipers and sweet-nut-bearing piñons. Here are wide mesas of grama grass, and moating the mesas are canyons that cut down a sheer thousand feet—Jordan, Cassidy, House Log, Brother West, Indian, Panther, Butcher Knife, and many a lesser.

Finally, a lion country must be prolific of lion food. The lion's staff of life is deer meat. He likes turkeys, and there are plenty of turkeys in the Mogollons. He licks his chops over antelope and beaver, both of which survive in numbers along the Gila.

Frequently, other food being scarce, he kills calves and yearlings, but seldom does he bother cattle in the Datil National Forest. He grows fatter on colts and mules than on anything else, but horse raising is pretty much an obsolete business now.

All he asks is venison, and anywhere on the upper forks of the Gila, venison may be had for the taking. Every day we rode I saw forty or fifty deer. But even in the best of lion country rigid requirements are necessary for catching a lion. The requirements

LION MARKERS

are trained hunters, trained dogs, and, generally, persistence and endurance. Lions are shy and wily creatures. Men who have hunted them a lifetime and have killed scores of them have told me they never saw one until after he had been jumped by the dogs.

The Evans brothers, Dub and Joe, are certainly experienced hunters. Seventy-five years ago their grandfather was ranching and hunting in southwest Texas. Nearly fifty years ago their father pioneered into the Davis Mountains on the western edge of Texas, where the lion and the Apache had for ages held possession. By the time Joe and Dub were ten years old they were running Ladino longhorns and following the hounds. In a single year they helped catch fifteen lions out of the canyon on which the Evans home ranch was established—Panther Canyon, it is called. Altogether they have caught hundreds of lions. In the few years they have ranched in New Mexico they have caught thirty-three. They are what the Mexicans call *hombres del campo*—men of the camp.

As for their dogs, there is not a better pack in Texas and New Mexico. The family of hounds of which they are the latest generation have been with the Evans men for thirty-nine years. When a year old the original pair of pups, Bell and Brownie, began hunting lion and bear and soon developed into remarkable dogs. By line breeding, with an occasional cross with bloodhound and Redbone hound, the characteristics of old Brownie and Bell have been strictly preserved. The original names pass down from generation to generation. Today the leader of the pack is Brownie, mighty of foot and mouth and muscle, as confident of himself in the field as Nelson at the Battle of Trafalgar. As good, and more energetic is Bell, beautifully spotted and amiable of disposition. Then there are Short Brownie, Little Brownie, Francis, Trumm and Lee Wilson.

The older dogs never notice the tracks of deer, coons, coyotes, foxes, and the like. They will take a wildcat's track, but are easily called off it. The only animals they really hunt and, once they have struck the trail of, follow despite hell and high water, are lions and bears. Our hunt was at a time when most bears have gone to sleep for the winter.

The moon was yet shining, the thermometer was at zero, and the dogs were comfortably filled with the flesh of a slaughtered mare when we struck out across Black Mountain the first day of our hunt. About noon, as we were riding down in the very bottom of a deep canyon, the dogs opened up, but the trail soon proved old. After much searching, Dub Evans made out two lion tracks, one of a full-grown lion going down the canyon, and the other of a young lion going up; neither track fresh enough to follow.

We went on, the dogs smelling at the foot of trees and nosing along the base of boulders and palisades. The lion likes to walk on a narrow bench under a bluff. He likes to cross rough saddles, or dips, between highlands. He likes to prowl the length of narrow hogbacks that look down into chasms on either side. He likes to meander along projections and indentations of a naked rimrock, following the ragged edge sometimes for miles.

Brownie and Bell and their followers knew all this. They never failed to examine any log so fallen that there was space between it and the ground. The lion likes to walk under such logs, bow up his back and rub it, like a cat. If a twig is bent over the trail the dogs sniff it, for the lion often leaves the scent of his body or tail on weeds and bushes. We were topping out of Brother West Canyon when the dogs opened cry with immense energy.

"Sounds good but not very fresh," remarked Dub. The trail followed over a malpais ridge. Once in a while the dogs would lose it for several minutes at a time. Then Brownie or Bell would pick it up. There was no soil for the track to show in. It was the kind of country that a lion feels safe in traversing, for the lion depends on sight more than on any other sense. He sees everything, and he thinks that if he leaves no visible impressions he is safe from pursuers. Sometimes while prowling over the country he winds about in all sorts of ways, apparently for no other reason than to keep rocks under his feet. How dogs can smell where a padded foot stepped on a rock perhaps forty-eight hours before is truly marvelous.

"Over yonder is the canyon of Indian Creek," Dub said. Beyond a blue vacancy I saw a line of cliffs. Suddenly the dogs stiffened their tails, stretched out their heads, worked their noses, let out a long and peculiar bay, and were gone. "They have smelled a kill!" said Evans.

We followed at hot speed. Presently we came upon the dogs tearing at barren deer bones over which no lion would ever again lick his "thankful chops." The ribs were still red with dried blood, but they had been picked several days before. The kill was under a gnarled juniper tree on a shelf of rocks overlooking the junction of Indian Creek with the Middle Prong of the Gila. The bark of the juniper was scratched with lion claws.

Spread out below us, like the ruins of some incomprehensible and fantastic mammoth, was a skeleton world over which the hounds of the elements had gnawed and snarled for dizzy aeons. The dried and scattered ribs of the skeleton were cones of rock, red and yellow and gray. The twisted and broken legs were ridges of wrecked boulders. The grave of the skeleton was walled in with cliffs that only an eagle could surmount. It was not *the* Grand Canyon, it was *a* grand canyon. On the point of an escarpment I saw a blotch of red. It was possible to work one's way out to it. The blotch proved to be a bone of the lion-killed deer.

"That raven we just saw put it there, I guess," said Dub. "Always watch for ravens. They locate the kill every time."

We had trailed a lion either to or from the kill, we did not know which. It was entirely possible that we had back-trailed. Certainly it was an old track to an old kill. The dogs seemed unable to work away. "Lead my horse around to yonder point," said

Dub, "and I will take the dogs and skirt over some of those ridges below us." He pointed to a saddle half a mile around the head of a side canyon.

When, an hour later, he came up without having discovered a sign, the sun was far down. Camp was six or eight miles away. Before we headed for it I looked back. It was a magnificent, an ideal, lion country, and we had little doubt that a lion was in it within finding distance. During the night he might, out of curiosity, pass the abandoned kill. We would come back in the morning. Dawn found us, Indian file, rimming out of the deep canyon in which we were camped.

As we topped out onto a mesa the dogs took an east by north course instead of our intended east by south direction. But the Evans boys refused to change them. Luck, destiny, providence, something might be directing them. We were outward bound, bound to get a lion. The fact had as well be told. We did not even strike an old trail that day. We cut for sign over some of the ground we had traversed the day before, but the dogs were too intelligent to take up again a trail they had worked on and abandoned.

The next day bore the same lack of luck and the next and the next. We scouted east and west, north and south. It snowed, rained a little, and the southern slopes melted. It snowed again, and the northern slopes were as slick and hard as glass. We slid down those slopes into warm, deep canyons and somehow wound and climbed out of them.

Often we were afoot, leading our horses. I discovered that by grasping the tail of the horse in front of me as we plodded upward I could get my wind and my footing with much less heaviness. Those mountain horses climb like Rocky Mountain sheep and are as fearless as rock squirrels. They went up desolate steeps that would literally pen in to death and starvation a trainload of plains

LION MARKERS

horses. I would not have traded my mount, Insect, for the finest stabled steed in Newport.

One day we saw an eagle maneuvering to catch a fawn. Another day we let the dogs tree a wildcat. On the iciest, shadiest, roughest slope in Catron County we found where a huge black bear had spent a week not long before. Flocks of piñon jays jeered at us. Tassel-eared squirrels played bopeep from the branches of great pines. We saw more deer than cattle, mule deer and whitetails both. Often we looked eagerly at ravens, but the fact that ravens locate a panther kill does not mean that every raven denotes one.

Up at four o'clock in the morning. Before dawn a hot and meaty breakfast, saddles, and the clear bugling of a hunting horn. Some raisins and nuts in the pocket to munch on for lunch. Hours and hours of riding and hoping and looking. Such was the order of the day for three, four, five, six days. On one of those days, Sunday, it was snowing, and we rested ourselves and the dogs. The Evans boys don't hunt on Sunday anyhow.

And the shadows of evening always found us back at the Horse Camp, ravenous, tired, every fiber in the body yearning for hot food and a roaring fire. How much hot beefsteak one man can eat I do not know, but had a weigher been present at the Horse Camp any night we were there he might have found out. Plenty of meat, plenty of tobacco, gallons of coffee, forests of pitch pine to burn, a snug cabin, company immensely congenial, grain for the horses, and mare meat for the dogs—what better camp could a man ask for?

The two log rooms and open hall of the cabin, unfurnished though they might appear to some eyes, contain a hundred details that cry out stories and character.

Where the puncheons about the stove in the kitchen have decayed from water, heat, and salty grease, they are carpeted with cowhides. The chuck box—ponderous, iron-braced, the lid lined with copper—used to be the combination box and seat of the Silver City-Magdalena stage. The hooks on the walls are old horseshoes and eagle talons. On one log a bear's foot is tacked. At another place a pair of eagle wings are stretched. Ancient elk horns are hung and thrown here and there. Out in the hall, brass cartridge shells stud the ends of logs. The door into the bunk room shows a storied bullet hole. The logs about the same door and next to the great fireplace are burned and carved with cattle brands.

Never was there a better camp for the spinning of yarns than the Horse Camp. The winter nights in New Mexico are long, long nights, and Joe Evans is one of the best story tellers west of the Pecos. In the lore of American animals the bear has no doubt figured as the subject for more tall tales than any other beast, but the panther, particularly in the Southwest, has provoked more strange stories. So when the talk turned to panthers, as it did hour after hour, night after night, we could all help Joe along. How lions kill, how they cover their kill, their strength, their size, their disposition to travel, their scream, their fear of man, their ferocity, their playfulness, their patience, their markers—every phase of lion nature we discussed and yarned over.

We must have talked more about panther kills than about any other feature of the great cat. We were hunting all the time for kills. If we could find a fresh kill we were reasonably certain of jumping the killer. He might stay away from it for a night, but the chances were ninety to ten that he would return the next night, eat, leave a fresh trail, and be lying up somewhere near when the dogs were turned loose in the vicinity at dawn. The lion is more prodigal of meat than any other predatory animal. Sometimes he merely slays for exercise or nothing more than a drink of blood from the jugular vein of his victim.

At the same time in the care of his meat he is probably the most intelligent and meticulous animal in the world. He likes his meat fresh and clean. As soon as he makes a kill he removes the entrails

LION MARKERS

from his prey; unlike the wolf, he begins eating on the fore parts of an animal. If the place at which he has slain a buck or other game does not suit him, he carries it to a proper place. Then he carefully covers it with leaves and twigs.

And so the nights passed, with talking on many things really, but never long off the subject of lions and lion dogs and lion hunts. One night we settled the mooted business of panther screams. They do scream, although seldom, and sometimes in a blood-curdling note, the testimony of certain hunters to the contrary.

And the days passed with hunting. It was the morning of the seventh day and we called it good. We were down in House Log Canyon. About ten o'clock Brownie let out a bellow, Bell sent up a cry, and the other dogs turned loose a varied and stirring noise that sent the blood tingling to the roots of the hair. "Lion sign and no fooling," said Dub as I rode up to where he had already dismounted at the root of a pine. The dogs were slowly working away up the canyon.

"I've been telling you about lion markers," Dub went on. "I never saw one in Texas, but New Mexico and Arizona lions make them all the time. Here they are. Some hunters call 'em scratches."

What we were looking at were two parallel scrapes on the ground about eight inches long, at the base of them a little mound of pine needles. They had evidently been made by the lion with his claws hooded. Double up your fists, dig them down into leaf mold or pine needles, draw them back to you at one stroke about eight inches long, and the result will be something very much like a lion marker. The little ridge between where the lion's hooded paws have scraped in parallel lines always shows. As the lion rakes back toward his body, a marker always indicates in what direction he is going, whether any tracks are visible or not. Of course the markers remain for weeks after tracks have vanished. Only males make them.

For an hour or more we worked up the canyon, so slowly that

most of the time we were on foot, trying to help the dogs with the trail. It was oldish, but still it was a trail.

"Look here," called Dub, who had followed the dogs to a bench fifty feet above our heads. He had found another marker made in gravel against the bluff.

The trail finally climbed out of the canyon and struck across a lava mesa. It came to a kind of barren place with not a twig or a blade of grass to hold the lion smell. It took us an hour to go less than half a mile. "Just as well pull for the top of that mountain," said Dub. "Once a lion starts up a mountain, he is going to the top."

When we struck the southern slope, where the snow had all melted and run over the tracks, we were absolutely stalled. We were a day too late, and the day's work was about over. People don't hunt mountain lions at night as they do coons. According to the course he was taking, the lion was making for the very broken country along the Middle Fork between Indian and Butcher Knife canyons. We had not yet been in that territory. We headed for camp, determined on the morrow to hunt out the promise.

On the trail in, Dub told me a remarkable story about the lion markers. A year or more ago a Government hunter in the Middle Gila country got on the trail of two lions, a male and a female. He followed them for two days, camping out both nights without food. On the third day he caught the female lion; then, seeing nothing of the male, he went on into camp.

Two weeks later while riding after cattle Dub struck a fresh kill made by a male lion. He knew the lion was a male from markers right at the kill. It was in the country the Government man had hunted over.

Dub went to the ranch, got his dogs and was at the kill early next morning. He had no trouble in striking a good trail, but the lion was not lying up to digest the food. He was roving, day as well as night. Over Black Mountain and down into the canyon country, Dub followed the trail at a good gait all day long. And every little distance he found a lion marker. He is sure that he found a hundred markers, all made in one day's time. The lion was putting out signs for his mate. He was searching the country for her.

Late in the evening the dogs jumped him, and even after he was jumped he made a marker—a very, very unusual act. After Dub killed him he cut him open. There was not a bit of food inside him. He had been too desolate to eat.

When the morning of the eighth day dawned the world was white with fresh snow. Hardly a quarter of a mile from the camp the dogs opened up on a hot trail. Joe and Dub called them off without even looking at the trail. What the dogs said to them was "wildcat."

Well, when the day closed, the magazines of our guns were as full of cartridges and our hands were as empty as they had been for a week. We were thoroughly disgusted with the Middle Fork and all its eastern tributaries. The lions might be on the other side of the Gila. They were not on our side, for certain. They might be ten miles away, and ten miles of canyons that include the Gila River in the Mogollon Mountains is as far as two hundred on pavement.

Our plan was to leave very early the next morning without packs, but carrying on our saddles a ration of grain for the horses, some mare meat for the dogs, and coffee, bread, and meat for ourselves. We would cross the Gila and let luck direct us. We wound headlong down Meadow Trail, worked around cold bluffs for an hour, and then headed up Fiddler Trail for the land of luck.

It must have been about two o'clock when we struck a fresh kill. It was a ten-point buck. One fore quarter was gone and the tongue eaten out. There were two, three markers under the trees about it. "We've got the check and all we have to do is to cash it," I yelled.

"Wait," said Dub.

"Just wait," said Joe.

It happened that the kill was on the mountainside where very little snow had fallen, but there were plenty of rocks and timber. Before we had time to do anything the dogs were coursing off at a lively rate. If a lion has smeared blood, the contents of a deer's entrails or other fresh animal matter on his paws, he leaves a trail that can for many hours be scented at a long run. The way our dogs were making tracks indicated that they were on an outgoing trail made by a lion with well-smeared feet.

Still there is only one sure way for a man to know whether his dogs are going with the tracks or back-trailing. That is to see the tracks. The blindness of dogs to tracks is as remarkable as their acuteness in smelling them. Some hunters say that if a dog goes faster uphill than downhill over a trail, the chances are that they are back-trailing; the explanation being that lions in going downhill put more weight on their feet and therefore leave a stronger impression than when climbing. However that may be, the only sure way of telling an out-trail from an in-trail is to look at the tracks. Our dogs were going fast enough downhill.

We followed them, now galloping, now pausing, looking all the while for tracks. Joe discovered a track, but the impression was so light that it was impossible to tell which way it was pointed. Unless the ground is soft the knobs on a lion's heel sometimes look almost like toes.

When we came to where the dogs had crossed a gulch in the bottom of which was sand, the tracks were plain. We were back-trailing. There was nothing to do but call the dogs off and return to the kill for a fresh start. Quickly the eager dogs found another track that we made sure was outgoing. It went down into rough country, and it was as tortuous as a corkscrew. The dogs came to bluffs over which they had to be lifted. Even if a lion were jumped there, he stood a good chance of getting away. With night about to close down it was folly to trail further.

LION MARKERS

"It's only a mile from here to a spring in Little Bear Canyon," said Dub. "I packed some deer hunters into that place a month ago. A quarter mile above the spring I saw a cave. We'll spend the night there."

Dogs, horses, and men were all glad when we struck the soft bottom of Little Bear. At the camp we found a side of deer ribs that the hunters had left and that a month of cold weather had not injured.

When I fed the dogs I noticed for the first time that their noses were bloody raw. No wonder! Those noses had been without letup grazing over malpais rocks by the tens of thousands and poking under acres of snow, snuffing, snuffing for lion sign. Galley slaves never worked harder than those dogs worked for us. They were used to sleeping out, but when we found a place for them in one corner of the long cave before which we built two fires, they were very grateful. The pleasure of seeing them warm was about the only pleasure I realized that night.

We discussed an Indian proverb, then each man made himself a wallow. The Indian, according to tradition, said, "White man heap fool. Build big fire and have to stay long way off. Burn and freeze. Indian wise man. Build little fire. Stay close to it. Warm." We had a saddle blanket apiece, we kept on our overcoats, and we replenished the big fires at least every forty minutes. I am inclined to think that the Indian was right.

With the first light we saddled. A short hour's ride and we were at the kill. The lion had been there during the night, though it was apparent that he had not eaten more meat than he could well carry. He might be lying down within a hundred yards, or he might be off at some distance. We took his trail at a gallop. It made for the rough canyon we had quitted the evening before. As the dogs struck the canyon rim they all at once hushed, apparently nonplussed. Dub and Joe were down on their knees, working like dogs themselves.

It took ten minutes to discover that the lion had leaped from the rim into a juniper tree which grew out of the canyon wall, had climbed out on a limb of the tree and then dropped off under the rimrock. A lion does not often play fox tricks.

As the dogs, with a joyful bound, again took off, we remained on top, where we could hear and see and come as near being with the dogs as we could be anywhere. They followed down the canyon under the rimrock on our side, crossed, and began working back up the canyon on the other side. Above them towered an uneven wall of rock that could be scaled only at intervals.

"Look at old Brownie in that grass over yonder," said Joe. "Acts as if he were hunting rabbits."

A tolerant grunt at the joke was all the response that Dub gave.

All of us could see Brownie, though none of us had seen him climb out. The other dogs were still under the bluffs. Brownie was at least two hundred yards out from the canyon rim on a smooth mesa. Between him and the canyon was a growth of scattering cedar.

"Look! Look!"

It was the first time I had seen Dub excited.

"I caught a glimpse of a panther in that cedar, I'll swear I did."

Nobody else saw a panther in the cedar, but what we all saw a minute later was a long, tawny form gliding through the grass away from the canyon of barking dogs and toward silent Brownie. With the corner of my eye I saw Bell about to climb out. The tawny form was gliding, drifting, moving like an effortless ghost straight toward Brownie. And Brownie had turned and was coming in a long run back toward the canyon and the lion.

In midprairie they met.

It is a mystery of nature why such a powerful and lethal fighter as the mountain lion will run from a dog. But run he will invariably.

The lion we saw wheeled like a released bowstring. I would

LION MARKERS

not attempt to say how high or how far he jumped. As he whirled and leaped the slant morning sun showed his breast dazzling white. When he reached the canyon rim he was at the climax of his speed and he never checked a second but spread himself flat like a flying squirrel for the awful leap. It was a hundred and twenty-five or a hundred and fifty feet to the first bench below, but the space was not altogether clear. Some rocky spires jagged up part of the way. With outstretched paws the lion caught one spire, swinging himself a quarter round and slightly breaking his fall. A second rock he barely scraped.

While he was making that leap I do not think that one of us drew breath. By the time he hit, Brownie and Bell on the rim above were simply having fits. It was a lucky thing that the younger dogs had not topped out. One of them must have seen the lion leap. In a minute's time they were in full blast behind him. The race could not last much longer now. With long tail straight over his back, the lion was doing his best but was plainly flagging.

Directly he came to a series of rocks that ran out at right angles to the main canyon wall and sloped sharply up. He ran out on them, leaping over a little gap that the dogs could not negotiate. On a pillarlike abutment he halted. Far above him Brownie and Bell, who had kept up with the race, hung their heads over and cried. Below him the other dogs gave the cry of conquerors. He was bayed.

When we got down to him he was still panting hard. He lashed his tail and opened his mouth and spit. He seemed to consider trying another desperate leap. He was game and noble game, the noblest and most beautiful predatory animal on the American continent. As a bullet found its mark I felt, momentarily, mean and ignoble. I shall never forget him. That last bit of chase, that leap, the fervor of the dogs, the tawny bundle of cornered killer bayed up there on the pillar of rock were worth all the ten days of grueling work we had put in.

SLASH RANCH HOUNDS

When the lion's body fell to the ground and we examined it we found that all the claws of his right paw had been pulled out by the clasp he gave the rock that checked his fall. One claw of the left paw was out. But he did not have a bone broken. He measured eight feet and six inches from tip to tip.

CHAPTER XI

*HUNTING LIONS WITH A LASSO**

BY DR. HENRY M. CALVIN

Roping of live mountain lions, I believe, furnishes about as much excitement as can be had on any hunt. The following story of how we roped two of these animals and brought them in alive was told by Dr. Henry M. Calvin, of New York City, in Forest and Stream.—G.W.E.

It was cold—bitter cold. The train from Socorro coughed and wheezed to a stop at the Magdalena station like an old man who had just plowed his way through a blizzard. A lone passenger descended to the platform and gazed about him. The deep snow, smoothed and banked by the icy fingers of a bitter north wind, stretched for endless white miles over New Mexico. The handful of buildings that made up Magdalena seemed to shiver under the icy blasts and huddled together like a brood of motherless chicks left out in a storm. For it gets bitter cold in New Mexico in the winter as it does scorching hot in the summer. And, in the words of the sun-scorched, frost-bitten men of the range country—"that's sayin' a heap."

---

* In *Forest & Stream*, July, 1929.

SLASH RANCH HOUNDS

The station master, bubbling over with curiosity and questions, scurried out to assist the visitor with the mountain of luggage which had been thrown down beside him. A battered service car which stood in the road nearby suddenly came to life and a head was poked out from beneath the curtains. "You the N'Yawk doctor what's bound for Beaverhead to rope lions?"

"Yes," replied the new arrival. "I expect you are the man scheduled to meet me. If you will help me with this paraphernalia, we'll get started."

The driver climbed from his car and silently went to work. An elderly cowpuncher, who had been standing in the station doorway, stumped across the platform. He leaned casually against a convenient post and dived into a hip pocket for a scarred plug of tobacco. He bit off a chew that warped one side of his face, and smiled cynically as he watched the men stow away collapsible tents, dehydrated food, and other modern camping equipment.

Silently he watched the last piece of baggage disappear in the back of the car. He was still leaning against the post as the car started its hundred-mile trip to Beaverhead with the tire chains clanking a medley all their own against the rear fenders. Then he marred a nearby snowdrift with a brown streak and snorted: "That city doctor a-goin' to rope lions," he muttered to the station agent, "he's goin' to rope hell." "That city doctor" was myself and the puncher probably was thinking of "High Chin Bob," that famous cowboy song character who "roped a lion and couldn't turn him loose."

Like "High Chin Bob" I have roped a mountain lion—two of them in fact. But unlike "High Chin Bob" I managed to "turn 'em loose," and in the Prospect Park zoo in New York at that.

Early last winter I became aware of the fact that I was getting "fed up" on the city. I was nervous and irritable. The roar of the subway and the clang and clatter of the elevated jarred against my eardrums. It was another attack of "sportsmen's fever," and I

HUNTING LIONS WITH A LASSO

knew but one cure for it. So, I laid my plans to penetrate the Tonto Basin country in Arizona, made famous by Zane Grey. And just as I had keyed myself to the nth degree and was preparing to start west, my guides wired that they would be unable to make the trip.

Determined not to be done out of a taste of the wide open spaces, I headed for El Paso, Texas, with Old Mexico as my goal. I had hunted there for five winters and decided to try it again.

On the border I met the owner of a famous health resort on whose vast holdings of thousands of acres I had hunted before. My friend from Old Mexico persuaded me to pass up his hunting ground and stay in the United States. "If you want to rope 'em instead of shootin' 'em," he declared, "there's not one bit o' use goin' clear into Mexico. The bears are all denned up for the winter and the lions have lit out for the high country. You might as well stay in the United States and then if you get a lion you won't have any difficulty in transportin' him."

I took his advice and through him met Joe Evans, one of the Evans brothers who own a large ranch at Beaverhead, New Mexico, a hundred miles across the snow-mantled range from Magdalena.

It took us two days to make that hundred miles, counting engine trouble, broken axles, poor roads, and deep snow, and by the time I rolled into Beaverhead ranch I was so blue-cold that I had lost all desire for hunting anything except a crackling fireplace. Dub Evans and his wife and three children welcomed me to Beaverhead.

The Evans Brothers ranch is one of the few spots left in this civilized country that still smacks of the Old West. The ranch headquarters consists of many buildings which nestle in a valley high above sea-level. The main building is a many-roomed bungalow with modern improvements, where Dub Evans and his family make their home. Beaverhead is the post office for that section of the country, as well as headquarters for the Government rangers, and is part of the Datil Government Animal Refuge, which embraces hundreds of thousands of acres. It is also part and parcel of the Mogollon Mountains.

Joe Evans had been rather dubious in El Paso when I revealed that I was out to rope and not to kill, but Dub was thrilled over the prospect and my first night at Beaverhead was spent in front of the open fireplace laying plans with the enthusiastic Dub.

The following morning, lashed by a severe snowstorm, the lion-roping expedition got under way. Our outfit consisted of myself, Dub Evans, a cofpuncher named Dick Etheridge, five pack-mules, five horses, and six hounds. Dub and I mounted our horses and struck out over the snow-blanketed mountains for the camp twenty-five miles away, the hounds at our heels. Dick took the pack mules, and the extra horses the long way around the mountains where the snow was not so deep.

The hounds knew full well that the hunt was on, and the valley and mountains resounded with their excited barking. They leaped excitedly about the horses as we got under way and broadcast to the world the news that they were out after big game. One of these hounds was Old Brownie, an eight-year-old hound, who had sustained a fractured thigh bone only two months before. Old Brownie really wasn't in any condition to make the trip, but he wouldn't take no for an answer and he hobbled along anyway. Several times I was tempted to pick him up and carry him, but each time the wise old hound seemed to read my thoughts and with a mighty effort he would get to his feet and stagger on.

As we urged our horses over the mountains the elements seemed to conspire to discourage us. The biting wind increased and the snow beat down more furiously than ever. The temperature dropped lower and lower, and I was more than thankful for a pair of heavy angora chaps and an old, heavy mackinaw which pulled me through the day. As our horses plodded upward through the drifts, we kept a weather eye out for sign of deer or small animals on which lions would and could exist. Seeing none after hours on the trail I began to feel blue and discouraged. Then suddenly Dub shouted. Far ahead up the mountain two brown spots came to life and leaped away.

"Deer," I shouted joyously.

Dub nodded and grinned.

A few minutes later we saw where a great herd had gone through just ahead of us. Their fresh tracks were easily discernible in the snow. The farther we traveled and the more tracks we encountered the better I felt. For where there were deer we would find a lion or two and I was bound to rope a mountain lion even if I did go the way of "High Chin Bob" doing it.

Late in the afternoon we arrived in Green Fly Canyon, where we were to camp. A blinding snowstorm beat about us wildly. And to add to my discomfort, my aching body convinced me that the Western saddle was a product of the Spanish Inquisition. Riding a horse through a blinding snowstorm and belly-deep snowdrifts up the side of a mountain is hard work.

The hounds found shelter under rock ledges while we fed and hobbled the horses and mules and made camp. Did you every try to cook a meal at an altitude of nine thousand feet in a blinding snowstorm? No? Well, try. However, we accomplished this feat under the most trying conditions. As the streams were frozen solid, it was necessary to melt snow both for drinking and cooking purposes. And I was surprised to learn that it takes at least three-quarters of an hour to melt a pail of snow at that altitude. But you'd be surprised how appetizing beans and coffee, diluted with rapidly falling snow can be after a hard day's ride.

Dub and I slept in the tent that night with everything on except our wet boots and socks. Yes, we even wore our hats. But even with our clothes on and a rubber poncho and mattress beneath and quilts and blankets over us, topped by a heavy tarpaulin, we slept cold and little. My lion roping expedition was beginning to look like a "frost" to me in more ways than one and my aching bones from the day in the saddle prevented me from giving much consideration to lions or anything else. The fact that my toothpaste was frozen and had to be thawed out didn't help much either. My automatic motion picture camera was frozen stiff too, and refused to budge. I thought a bit of oil might help it, but the biting temperature had turned the oil into a thick jelly. I gave up in despair and was content to rest my aching bones in camp for the day.

Dub went scouting, however, and though he covered a great amount of territory he found no lion tracks. It snowed and snowed, and then snowed some more, and that night the temperature dropped to eighteen degrees below zero and I spent a sleepless night trying to keep warm. The following morning the snow ceased, the sun came out and my bones quit aching. The lion-roping fever returned. So, shortly after nine o'clock we took the pack of hounds and started out.

Halfway down Green Fly Canyon one of the hounds sent a mournful note heavenward. The others, all except Old Brownie, scrambled to his side and sniffed the trail doubtfully. Then Old Brownie, veteran of many battles, shouldered his way through the pack and took charge. He sniffed the imprint in the snow—once, twice, three times. Then his head and nose went up towards the sky, sniffing the air two or three times. Having thoroughly satisfied himself, he raised his deep bass voice to corroborate the finding of the younger hound. His decision, given, after his careful examination, in such a majestic manner, was such as to direct and encourage the younger hounds who chorused their approval and followed his rapid and unfaltering gait in the path of the animal's trail.

The lion-roping hunt was on. When we reached the spot where the hounds had commenced baying, we discovered they

HUNTING LIONS WITH A LASSO

had picked up a wildcat trail. But wildcat or mountain lion, it made little difference to us. Down the canyon went the hounds for a half mile; then they rimmed out on the east side and over the ridge into Jordan Canyon. They followed this canyon to the point where it boxed up, or became impassable. At this point they lost the scent, for the wildcat had taken to a hole at the top of the cliff where the hounds could not follow.

We went west up a hill on the opposite side of the canyon and for a distance of three-quarters of a mile rode so perilously close to the edge of the cliff that one misstep would have plunged us to the rocks three hundred feet below. I had a rather empty feeling as I gazed down the sheer wall of that canyon at the jagged rocks below. One look was enough. From then on I gazed straight ahead and trusted to the sure-footedness of my pony to bring me through without mishap.

In a short while we arrived at a point opposite where the hounds were. Old Brownie discovered the wildcat's hiding place and chased him out. Another hound joined him, and off they went up the trail after the streak of fur. The other four hounds took the trail in the other direction, and we knew they were after the mate. Dub followed Old Brownie, and Dick and I took out after the other hounds.

A half mile north we found them baying around a small hole on top of the rim of Jordan Canyon. We dismounted and gazed into the hole. After our eyes had become accustomed to the darkness, we could see, about five feet back, the blazing eyes of a cornered wildcat. We decided to wait for Dub. In a few minutes he joined us with a dead bobcat. Old Brownie and the younger hound had treed it and Dub had brought it down with one shot.

We held a council of war and then decided the best thing to do was try to move some of the rocks away from the opening so we could reach the cat with a forked stick with a rope looped over the end of it, which we could slip over the bobcat's head.

SLASH RANCH HOUNDS

It took five hours of back-breaking labor to clear that hole so we could get at the cat, but we finally made it and the forked stick and looped rope worked like a charm. One thrust and we had a snarling, fighting wildcat on the end of a rope. We'd roped our first wild game even if we did have literally to move mountains to do it. It was an easy matter to throw another loop over his head as we pulled him out into the light, and then with Dick on the end of one rope and Dub on the end of the other, and a snarling, raging wildcat between them, I started my motion picture camera and "shot" the cat we had roped. Then came the ticklish business of trussing up this snarling cat so we could carry him back to camp. This was managed by roping one hind leg, then throwing him, and then, while Dick and Dub held him down with a stick across his neck, I lashed his legs together and gagged him with a piece of wood. We then turned back toward camp, Dub with a live cat in front of him and a dead one at his back.

About half a mile to the left, however, we heard one of the hounds baying frantically. "Must've treed something," Dub declared; "I'll take a look and you all go ahead." With that he turned his horse and rode off and Dick and I proceeded to camp.

Just as we arrived Dub's voice floated down to us faintly from the top of the mountain. Again and again he called and Dick finally mounted and rode off to find out the trouble. After what seemed like hours he came back to me.

"Get your ropes and camera," he shouted enthusiastically, "we've treed a mountain lion." Up the mountain to Buck Point we rode, urging our horses to the limit. We found Dub and the pack of hounds surrounding and barking up, not one tree, but two. Little Brownie, one of the youngest hounds in the pack, had crowned himself with fame. He had treed two lions in trees a hundred yards apart and kept them there more than three hours. He had kept his vigil until his tongue was hanging out, but there

HUNTING LIONS WITH A LASSO

wasn't a prouder hound in the pack than Little Brownie, over his achievement.

The sun was already casting long shadows on the snow, and realizing that it was a long, rough way back to camp, we decided to shoot one lion and rope the other. I was delegated to do the killing and rather reluctantly I brought him down with a bullet through the heart. Then started the sport which had brought me all the way from New York over snow-covered desert and wind-swept mountain passes—roping a mountain lion.

I climbed up almost to the top of the tree in which the lion had taken refuge, carrying with me a six-foot forked stick with a rope looped over the end. I tried again and again to slip the noose over the head of the lion. Each time he would snarl and spit like a huge, cornered house cat of the Brooklyn apartment variety. And with each snarl he would slap the stick and rope away with a huge paw. Finally he grabbed the rope between his teeth, but finding it not to his liking, spit it out.

All this time I had been clinging precariously to the tree with my right hand and trying to manipulate the rope and stick with my left. After fifteen minutes, without doing any more than driving the lion from the dense foliage out on a bare limb, I returned to the ground.

"Let me try it," Dub declared. "I'm left-handed and maybe I'll have better luck." Up he went, hand over hand, and ten minutes later he succeeded in roping the lion and shoving him off the limb. Halfway down, the snarling beast checked his fall on a convenient limb. Then pulling himself up like a trained athlete, he shook off the noose. But he lost his footing in doing it and crashed to the ground between Dick and myself and the hounds. It was one grand mix-up, and what really happened probably never will be known. All I can remember is hounds, lion, and men, and a lot of shouting, and then Dick and I picking ourselves up off the ground; and the lion was up another tree, a hundred yards away.

Dub followed him, and a few minutes later the big beast again struck the ground and a second scrimmage started. The hounds were all over him, but he shook them off and streaked out for a third tree about fifty yards away. As he leaped for this tree the hounds caught up with him and down they went in a snarling, yapping heap. Fearing the hounds would be killed, we rushed to the scene of battle and began pulling them off the lion, who was using his teeth and sharp claws to good advantage. But it was a useless task, for as fast as we would tear one hound loose and fling him aside he would get to his feet and attack the lion from another angle.

Finally the big cat shook off his attackers and the hounds paused to rest at a safe distance. The lion rested on his haunches and glared at us. We had him completely surrounded. He was facing me, and his teeth were bared and his claws curled ready to strike. He seemed undecided which way to strike first, and as he hesitated Dick roped him, and a few minutes later we had him trussed up tight and ready for travel.

Our first day of hunting lions with a lasso was over and we had a live lion and a live bobcat and a dead lion and a dead bobcat to show for it. We lashed these beasts to our saddles and started to return to camp when we discovered a dead doe under a nearby tree. "Mountain lion's work," declared Dub as he noted that the doe's abdomen had been ripped open by a slashing paw. The lions evidently had killed it the night before and had eaten the liver and other organs, but had not touched the meat. Dub explained that they always did this and would return the next day and finish the kill. It was pitch dark when we rode into camp, and with the aid of a flashlight we chained the lion and wildcat to trees and then untied them.

The crackling warmth of the campfire and our success of the day put us in excellent humor, and after supper we joked over the day's events and laid our plans for the next day's hunt.

HUNTING LIONS WITH A LASSO

The next morning found us up with the sun, and after a hasty breakfast we took the hounds and back-tracked to the spot in the snow where we had found the doe. We found that it had vanished during the night, but the hounds soon picked up the trail of two more lions and we were off again with the baying pack ahead of us. The tracks told a mute tale of the passing of an aged monarch of the mountains and a younger lion, probably a year old. The hounds led us to a tree a quarter of a mile away, where we found the head and shoulders of the deer. Here the hounds paused and yapped excitedly as they tried to pick up the trail again. Soon they found it and their baying echoed and re-echoed through the mountains and canyons as they circled west over the Main Divide between Green Fly and Jordan canyons. Suddenly they changed their course and loped across the divide between Green Fly and Cassidy canyons and down to Cassidy Spring. There they treed their quarry.

When we rode up to this spot we found one young lion crouched on the highest limb. The hounds circled and picked up the trail of the other lion, an old female. They jumped her out of some bushes and she streaked out into the east and then circled south along the line of Cassidy Canyon. The greatest race I ever hope to witness was on. Dub left Old Brownie with me to guard the treed lion, and he and Dick set out after the hounds. The excited baying of the hounds carried me to the top of a large rock, where I could see the race and keep an eye on the lion still crouching menacingly at the top of the tree. What a race it was. The white blanket of snow provided a perfect stage and the baying of the five hounds was the music for that drama of the mountains.

The lion was a scant twenty jumps ahead of the hounds, leaping terrific distances and picking out spots where there was little snow in order to get better footing and travel faster. The hounds, with their quarry in plain sight, were straining every muscle to overtake her. What an effort that beast made to outdistance her pursuers. The hounds streaked over the snow carpet like lightning, running breast to breast, head to head, shoulder to shoulder, their tails moving in circles, and baying madly as they tore through the icy air. Dick and Dub, pressing their horses hard, brought up the rear.

The lion vanished under a tree about a mile from where the hounds jumped her, and then I noticed they began circling this tree, and their wild baying changed to excited barking. The beast was treed and the great "Mountain Handicap" was over.

After treeing this big female lion, Dub left Dick and the hounds to guard her and returned to where I waited.

"Haven't got enough collars and chains to handle all these lions," he said as he rode up. "Reckon you will have to kill that other one down yonder and we'll rope this youngster here in the tree."

I agreed with him and joined Dick. I found that three of the hounds, in their excitement, had managed to leap to the lower branches of the tree where they were having difficulty in finding a foothold and were barking furiously. The lioness, the largest of the four we found, was crouched on a limb about halfway up, and her flashing eyes were fixed on the barking hounds beneath. Other than a slight switch of her heavy tail, she showed no signs of excitement. I fired from about seventy yards and she tumbled from the tree, with a bullet behind her shoulder, stone dead.

"One down and one to go," smiled Dick as we loaded the dead beast on my saddle and started back for the other lion. Dick went up after this one, and profiting by our experience of the previous day, he deftly slipped two loops over the lion's head and tossed the loose ends to us. Dub and I grabbed hold and heaved. The snarling beast came down with a crash. In two minutes we had him bound and lashed to the saddle ready to start for camp.

Lack of chains at the mountain camp made it necessary to kill

HUNTING LIONS WITH A LASSO

the bobcat and use the chains which were holding him to fasten the second lion. We packed the live lions by mule the twenty-five miles over the mountains to Beaverhead. Binding them in kyaks, or boxes made out of heavy wooden frames covered with rawhide, made this possible, and sundown found us seated again in front of Dub Evans' crackling fireplace with the lions safely locked in improvised cages outside.

My first experience of hunting lions with a lasso was over and two live lions, two dead ones, and two dead wildcats were the result.

Those two New Mexico mountain lions pace cages in the zoo at Prospect Park in New York today, and I never see them that I don't think of old "High Chin Bob," the man "who roped a mountain lion and couldn't turn him loose."

CHAPTER XII

"GET AWAY FROM THAT BEAR"

Forrest Parrott, of Oklahoma City, came to our Slash Ranch for a hunt in March, 1929. As usual, we moved over to Horse Camp to hunt along the Middle Fork, and the first morning out we rode along the west rim of Indian Creek all the way to the Middle Fork. About halfway down on the Meadows Trail the hounds opened up on lion sign, which was barely fresh enough to follow.

The country was all rough, and in some places very hard to navigate on horseback. The trail led through a small run-around with big pine trees, not far from the river bottom, where the hounds found a kill, covered with pine needles, under one of the trees. Here the remains of a whitetail buck and the legs of a turkey gobbler, with spurs, had been buried together under the same tree. But the kills were old, and we did not expect the lion to return. A little farther up the river the trail began to lead out on the north side, the same side where we had struck it.

Bill Benton, one of our good ranch hands, was along to act as guide, and to be of general help on the hunt. I told Bill that I would follow the hounds on foot, as they were then climbing up through some rims where I might have to help them up over the

"GET AWAY FROM THAT BEAR"

high places. Bill was to take Forrest and the horses and climb out as best he could.

They had come to a place which was too steep to ride up, so they dismounted, and Bill started out, leading his horse, with the other two horses following single file, each horse tied to the tail of the one ahead, while Forrest grabbed the tail of the last horse. All was going fine until they came to a gully washed out on the side of the hill. When Forrest's horse jumped this gully the sudden jerk tumbled Forrest into the bottom of the gully, but he was bundled up in so many clothes the fall did not hurt him. Nevertheless, he must have been pretty miserable; and, when Bill went back to help him up he made a remark typical of his own good sportsmanship and of sportsmen everywhere. He said, "Just think, Bill—I'm *paying* to do this!"

When they topped out they could hear the hounds coming right toward them, and they passed just in front of the horses. Though still a cold trail, we followed it in the general direction of Canyon Creek, until late dark, then called the hounds off and went to camp.

After a good meal and night's sleep, we were up early and back along the rim of Middle Fork looking for the trail. The lion had completed a circle toward Canyon Creek, and was headed east, back the way we had been the day before. But the hounds got the wrong end of the trail, and it was some time before we discovered the mistake and got them turned in the right direction. Since the trail was leading in the same direction that we had followed all the day before, we were really surprised to find later that we were back-tracking. It was about noon when we got back to where we had picked up the trail in the first place.

About one or two o'clock, when the sun was coming down hot, the hounds led off some bluffs, going under the main top rim of the Middle Fork, and I followed on foot. They went downhill a short distance, then turned back up into the big bluff. The lion was lying just under the main bluff, and when the hounds got close he climbed out on top, jumping onto some high rocks right in front of where Forrest had stopped to rest. Forrest saw the lion, but his gun was in a scabbard on his horse. He ran for the gun and got it just in time for a very hurried shot that barely burned the hair across the lion's belly. The hounds couldn't get up where the lion did, but they soon found a way out, picked up the fresh trail, and were away on a run. They put the lion up a tree within a mile, and Forrest killed his first of many lions.

While here, Forrest reserved a date to hunt bear the following October. He came back with William P. Holly and S. F. Peavey, Jr., of the Chase National Bank in New York City, and they each got a bear. The hunt was made in the Black Range, and our camp was on South Diamond Creek just below the box.

The first morning out we hit an easy trail and the bear was soon treed. Forrest suggested that Mr. Holly have the honor of shooting the first bear, which he did.

We had no luck the next day, but on the third day we jumped a bad-running bear that scattered men all the way to the top of the Black Range. Forrest and I were together and finally got ahead of the bear and turned him back. When he headed back down country he was running fast, but we came down the ridge between Bonner and Black canyons where it was good riding and we could make good time also.

The hounds were off to our right, where aspen thickets formed a real bear country. The hounds must have crowded the bear too much, for they put him up a tree just where the canyon begins to get rough.

I was a little ahead, and ran out to the edge to listen. The bear was treed just under us in a wild-looking place, with dense aspen and spruce thickets and high, spiral rocks scattered about. When Forrest rode up, I said, "They have him treed right under us about

"GET AWAY FROM THAT BEAR"

halfway down. Jump off with your gun and get down there quickly, and try to kill that bear." He said, "*Do you mean—me—by myself?*"

My only thought was to stay on high ground, so if the bear moved again I would know which way he went. Forrest started to the tree, but the going was rough, and just before he was close enough for a shot, the bear came down. But the hounds crowded him closely and he took another tree in a minute or two, where he stayed until Forrest shot. After the shot I heard limbs popping as they broke when the bear fell through. Without further delay I started with the horses, knowing that I would have to go back up the rim some distance before I could get off into the canyon.

About the time I reached the canyon I saw Lee, for the first time since morning, and it was then two o'clock or later. We both had been close enough to hear the shot and hear the bear fall out, and we couldn't understand why the hounds were still fighting and baying.

We rode into the thicket where the noise was, and there was Forrest sitting astride the bear, trying to stick a hunting knife into the back of his head with one hand while holding him by one ear with the other. We yelled at him to get away from that bear and shoot him again.

Mr. Holly had shot twice to kill his bear, and Forrest wanted to do better and kill his bear with only one shot. It was lucky for him that the shot had in some way paralyzed the bear's jaw, although he had good use of his head. We told him never to go to a bear as long as it was still moving, as they have been known to hurt men and hounds in their death struggle.

While on this hunt Forrest told me to keep him posted if fresh signs of lions showed up the coming winter, as he had some friends in Oklahoma City who had heard him tell of his hunts with me so many times that they, too, would like to hunt for lion with me.

SLASH RANCH HOUNDS

I saw some lion sign in the Horse Camp country in March, 1930, so I called Forrest in Oklahoma City to tell what I had seen. I phoned him from Albuquerque advising him of the exact day I would go back to the ranch.

In answer, he said, "I will call you back." He called soon to say that if I could meet the train at Belen the next day at noon a lion hunter or two would get off, ready to go to Beaverhead with me. I was very much surprised next day when only Forrest left the train at Belen. He said that after thinking it over he decided he wanted the two-man hunt for himself.

We made a pack trip into Horse Camp the next day, and in seven days we caught two very large male lions. It turned out good for both of us—Forrest got just the kind of a hunt he wanted, and I had to take care of only one guest at the price I had agreed to charge for the two.

While on this hunt Forrest made reservations for another bear hunt the following October. He arrived with Pat Dunham, also of Oklahoma City.

We camped on North Palomas Creek, on the east slope of the Black Range. Lee, Scotty, and myself, completed the party.

Pat got the first bear, which we treed early the first morning out. During the next two days we got after some bad-running bear that the hounds couldn't stop. About the third day out we hit a bad-running bear again, but he went up a tree to rest, right on top of the Black Range. I happened to be pretty close and got a shot at him before he came down.

On the last day out the hounds hit a good trail and treed a huge black bear, which Forrest killed. We reserved a date at this time for the following October to hunt bear again with his New York friends, Mr. Holly and Mr. Peavey. We camped at the head of Diamond Bar Canyon, and hunted about a week, getting two bear and three lions.

"GET AWAY FROM THAT BEAR"

This wound up the hunts with Forrest in this area. He was a fine fellow in every way, and an enthusiastic hunter for all kinds of game. He enjoyed still hunting when he was not hunting with the hounds.

The following Christmas I received a very fine pair of Ziess binoculars as a present from Mr. Holly and Mr. Peavey.

CHAPTER XIII

TWO TAYLOR CREEK MALES

In January, 1930, N. F. Frazier, of Kansas, brought his two sons, Nat, Jr., aged 18, and Bill, 14, out for a lion hunt—taking them out of school so that they could camp out in the mountains for ten days where they could be close to nature and watch good hounds work, and would have plenty of horseback riding in the rough mountains.

The Fraziers were coming by automobile and as the roads were pretty bad to Magdalena, I drove out to meet them on the road somewhere.

It is very cold in January at an elevation of 7,500 feet, but Mr. Frazier and his boys were well equipped with warm clothes, and each had an arctic sleeping-bag for the frigid temperatures of the camp.

We met about midway, and after introducing ourselves, Mr. Frazier rode in the car with me, and the boys followed us in their car. On the way in, Mr. Frazier told me that the boys were very eager to get a lion and a bobcat each.

We spent the night at the ranch, leaving the next morning early to hunt along the way to Hoyt Creek, about ten miles south-

TWO TAYLOR CREEK MALES

east of Beaverhead in the Black Range, where Scotty and Chet were to establish camp. From this camp some very good lion country could be reached, which included Taylor, Whitetail, Cox, Hoyt, and two or three prongs of the Diamond creeks. We didn't find much sign on the way over, but as we neared camp, the hounds hit a bobcat trail. Mr. Frazier wanted to ride on in to camp, so I told him how to go. Nat, Jr., went with him, and Bill went with me after the hounds. They didn't trail far until they jumped the cat, which soon went up a tree. Bill was really excited, and said a cat and a lion were just what he wanted, and this was the cat, with a lion to go.

When we reached camp with the cat, Nat, Jr., was sorry he hadn't gone with us. Next morning we hunted the south rim of Taylor Creek, and picked up the cold trail of two male lions. We knew they were males because of the markers and scrapes they made.

The lion trail soon left the Taylor Creek rim and headed southeast toward the upper Diamonds. The trailing was slow, but extremely interesting and gave us a wonderful opportunity to watch the hounds at work. This trail led us across many headers and side canyons of Whitetail and Cox canyons, and by late evening we had reached the drainage of Hoyt Creek. The trail seemed no fresher than when we hit it that morning, so we took the hounds off and rode into camp, where Scotty and Chet soon had us good biscuits, cooked in a Dutch oven and served with syrup and butter, fried beefsteak with gravy, hot coffee, and a choice of canned fruits; all of which tastes just a little better out in camp than anywhere else. The hounds had plenty of fresh horse meat and there was grain for our horses. Everything was comfortable for our camp.

Next morning we returned to the place where the hounds had last barked on the lion trail, and they picked it up right away, as the scent seemed to be about as it was the evening before.

The general course was the same, toward Diamond Peak, which is the summit of the Black Range, elevation 9,700 feet, and around which South Diamond, Middle Diamond, and Main Diamond creeks head. These canyons are all deep, with big side canyons, and the going was very slow all day. We hoped to find where the lions had made a kill and laid up awhile, leaving a fresher trail, but we were disappointed. Like all lion trails, in some spots it was almost impossible for the hounds to follow it; then it would get better for a ways.

Sometimes the tracks of the two lions would be a hundred yards or so apart, and then come together again to follow, one behind the other. There was no snow except on the north sides of the hills, and it was only in the snow that we could see any tracks. As evening was coming on, we called the hounds off and returned to camp, as we were all tired out.

The third day we went back to the trail and followed it high up on Main Diamond Creek, still headed in the same general direction, but it got no fresher. Because we were getting so far away, we would either have to move camp or quit this trail and try to find another one.

We called the hounds off again and returned to camp. As Mr. Frazier was tired out he stayed around camp with Chet to rest up and, in the meantime, we hunted in the upper Hoyt Creek country. We found sign of a female lion, but the trail was not fresh. We hunted the next day in the same general area and treed a bobcat, which Nat, Jr., killed. Each boy now had a cat to his credit.

About this time, we were joined by A. L. Inman, who lived on the East Fork of the Gila about five miles below the D Bar. He was a good lion hunter and had good hounds and he advised us to move camp and follow the trail of the two males. We were not equipped to do this, as we had brought our camp outfit to Hoyt Creek in a wagon drawn by mules, and there was no wagon road into the upper Diamond creeks at the time.

TWO TAYLOR CREEK MALES

There was much discussion as to where would be the best place to pick up a fresh lion trail. I remembered that Jack Francis, who had caught many lions, told me that a male lion usually made the same round in about a week's time, so I decided to go back to the south rim of Taylor Creek and check the area where we had picked up the trail of the two males the first morning.

We were joined by Les Ake, a ranchman who lived on Taylor Creek just above the mouth of Hoyt. Mr. Frazier was rested up, and rode with us. We headed for Taylor Creek, but had to cross Cox and Whitetail canyons, both good lion country, to get there. As we climbed out of Whitetail Canyon at a rough spot, the hounds got ahead of us.

Before we topped out, I heard Brownie open up fast and long drawn-out, saying, "We have what we want." I hurried on to the top and was delighted to find a fresh lion marker under a tree on the north rim of Whitetail, but headed toward Taylor. We followed in hot pursuit, not looking for tracks, but picking out the best course possible, trying to stay within hearing distance of the hounds. As always, when hurrying through rough country on horseback, it was difficult for the riders to stay together. I finally pulled up a minute to let my horse get his wind, and there was young Bill, his face beaming as he remarked, "Two men after a lion." When the hounds hit the rim of Taylor Creek only about half of the pack went off, the rest staying on top looking for a place to get down. Before they got off, the other hounds had jumped two lions. They were together when they were jumped, but one came back on top and the hounds that were still on the bluff hit the trail of this lion. This really was a break for us, as the pack was pretty evenly divided, with some experienced hounds in each bunch.

I stayed on top while all the other men were listening to the pack under the rim. When the hounds began to crowd the lion on top too much he circled back to Taylor Creek and went off the rim probably a half mile east of where the other hounds had gone off.

The side hills of Taylor Creek are really rough, with high bluffs and pinnacles, and heavily timbered, so when the hounds followed this lion off the bluff I prepared to leave my horse and follow on foot. About this time some of the other boys rode up and said the other hounds were treed about halfway down the hillside, and to the west. I told Scotty to let the Frazier boys decide which one would shoot the first lion, and to go with him to the tree.

I went on after my hounds on foot. They had gotten way ahead, but it wasn't long until I heard them coming toward me, as the lion had circled, or doubled back on his own trail, a trick common to them. It was some time before they had this second lion up a big pine tree near the bottom of the canyon. After I had located the lion, I climbed up on some high rocks in sight and hearing of the other boys and they told me that Nat, Jr., had gone with Scotty and that he had already killed a lion. I told Bill to bring his gun and join me.

There was ice and snow all along this slope and it was extremely steep. Bill must have been really eager to get to me, as I heard a noise and looked up, and here came Bill, sitting down with his feet out in front, sliding at breakneck speed and using the butt of a new rifle for a brake. It answered the purpose, but when he was able to stop, about even with me on the side of the hill, there was a chunk broken out of the stock. He was only thinking of a shot at the lion in the quickest possible time. I advised him to get his breath, take a rest on a tree, and let him have it, and this he did.

Inman, Chet, and Les Ake knew the country well, and, with Mr. Frazier, traveled along the rim of Taylor Creek Canyon to where they could get down with all the horses. They then came up Taylor Creek to where Scotty, Nat, Bill, and I were waiting for

TWO TAYLOR CREEK MALES

them, having dragged and rolled the lions to the bottom of the canyon. We loaded the lions on horses as soon as the men reached us, and headed for camp.

By going down Taylor to the mouth of Whitetail we could cut across through some low saddles and have good riding all the way into camp. We reached there before dark, and we were a happy bunch. We reached the ranch feeling fine, and the Fraziers left for home the next morning.

The next Christmas, which was nearly a year from the time they were with me on the hunt, I received from Mr. Frazier, Nat, Jr., and Bill, a very fine 6.5 mm. rifle with a hundred rounds of ammunition. I never had a gift that I treasured more highly, or that did me more good.

Thanks to Jack Francis for the remark he had made about a male lion making a round about once a week, we were able to bag two fine specimens. I don't know how often it holds true, but I firmly believe that the lions we caught on Taylor were the same two we were trailing so far away, high on Diamond Creek. It would be interesting to know just how much farther they went before they circled back.

CHAPTER XIV

MORE UNUSUAL HUNTS

HUNTING LIONS AT SEVENTY-FIVE

In the Spring of 1924, I had contracted to deliver fifteen hundred two- and three-year-old steers off the Slash Ranch at Beaverhead. Although my father had no financial interest in the steers, he realized that if I could make a good gather and delivery on these steers, it would be the turning point in my business life. After the droughts, snow storms, and low prices that left Evans Brothers insolvent, here was a chance to change the trend from continuously increasing debt to gradually increasing movement up the long hill to financial recovery.

My father came from his ranch in Texas and brought with him my youngest brother, Graves, and Alexandria Valdez, one of his best ranch hands. We moved the pack outfit to Horse Camp about the first of April, to start gathering the steers which we were to deliver in Magdalena the fifteenth of May, a trail drive of one hundred miles. The steers were scattered with about three thousand head of stock cattle over a mountain ranch of 250 sections. The heavy snows of the previous winter left all of the mountain creeks and even the small canyons with plenty of water. Conse-

MORE UNUSUAL HUNTS

quently, the cattle were well scattered, and much riding was necessary to find even 90 per cent of them.

While gathering steers out of the Horse Camp area, which covered about fifty thousand acres, from the top of Black Mountain on the east to Canyon Creek on the west, and from the rim of the Middle Fork on the south to the head of Houghton Canyon on the north, we often noticed the sign of a male lion, but we were too busy with cattle to do any hunting.

A day came when we needed to move camp to the D Bar on the East Fork. The cowboys took the pack outfit and the remuda along the old D Bar-Horse Camp pack trail that crosses Jordan Canyon about midway between the top of Black Mountain and the Middle Fork of the Gila. As usual, we kept the hounds in camp to eat the scraps, for there is usually much waste meat around a cow outfit. My father, who was then in his seventy-fifth year, had been riding with us every day all day and was keenly interested in the number of steers we found. Dad, my brother Lee, and I took the hounds, leaving ahead of the pack outfit.

As we crossed Sam Martin Canyon, about two miles east of Horse Camp, the hounds picked up the trail of a male lion. It was fresh enough to be good trailing, and we could tell by the markers that we were on the right end of the trail, which led generally east and in the direction of Black Mountain, the summit of which was about six or seven miles distant. Instead of going straight, the lion meandered around and made a scrape at frequent intervals. I began to count the scrapes soon after we picked up this trail and kept count until I reached one hundred and I announced to my father and Lee that I had seen this many.

We started this trail at 7:00 A. M. and killed the lion at six that evening in Bell Canyon, several miles east of Black Mountain. This was one of the most interesting lion trails I ever followed. Of course, it had the dull spots in it that characterize lion trails, when the hounds could hardly move it; then they would pick up again so that we would have to ride in a fast trot or "lope" to stay up. The nice feature was that instead of rock bluffs and rimrocks that lions usually pass through, the terrain crossed was good enough to ride over, and we were in sight of the hounds all day. My dad, being the great hound man that he was, and not having seen my pack in action, especially enjoyed the good work they were doing. With us we had Brownie, Bell, Ranger, and Blue (not the present-day Blue).

About one o'clock the trail led us very near Black Mountain lookout, where we could find coffee, water, and a can for making coffee. As we passed, I told Father that I could make him some coffee very quickly if he wanted to wait, and let Lee go on with the hounds. His reaction was a look of disgust to such a suggestion, and saying, as he spurred his mount forward, "I *like* to stop to make coffee while the hounds are on a lion trail."

On we went. We still had not jumped the lion. Just before sundown I told Dad that it was only about eight miles to the ranch and we could make it there before bedtime, if he wanted to call the hounds off.

He pointed down to a sheep-lined jacket which he was carrying behind his saddle, and said, "I will use this if we have to lay out."

So we stayed on the trail, and were rewarded by the hounds jumping and treeing a big male lion, after a very long trail, but a very short race. It was six o'clock and almost dark when my seventy-five-year-old father shot his last lion. Although he kept a fine pack of hounds, and had seen them bring many bear and lions to bay, he hadn't shot either in the past twenty-five years. He thoroughly enjoyed watching and listening to hounds, but he was always willing for someone else to do the shooting.

I opened the stomach of this lion and found about two tablespoons of a greenish fluid, showing that he had been a long time without eating. Since I had counted over one-hundred markers on

16 Blue, leader of Dub Evans' present pack.

17 While the hounds bark "Treed!"

18 A. T. "Cap" McDonald (left) and other hunters examine a bear kill. Picture shows conformation of bear's paw.

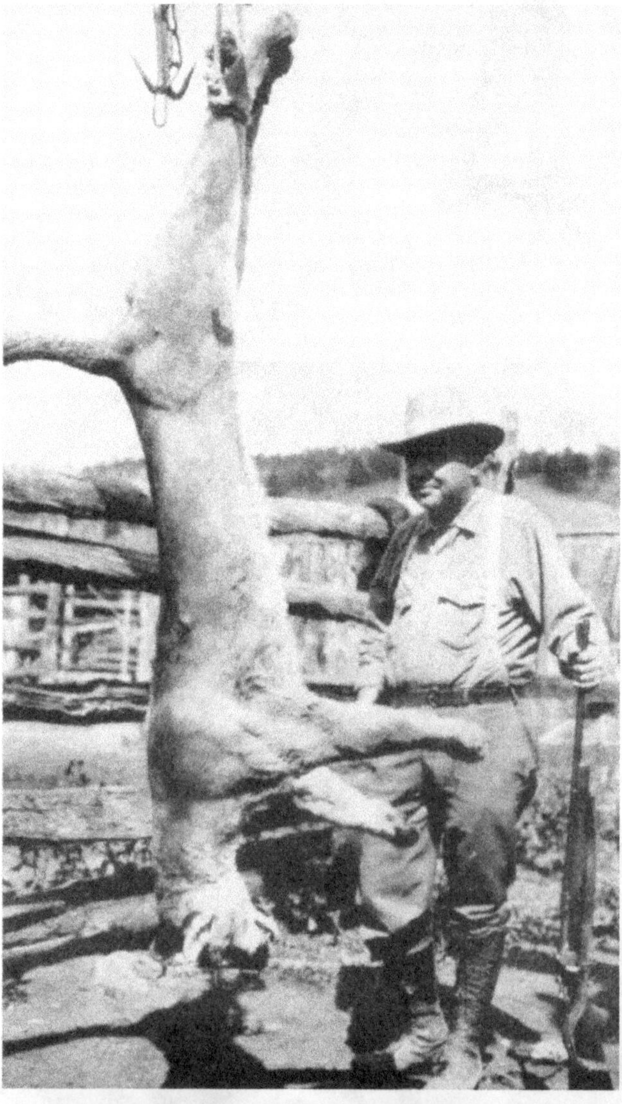

19 Tom Hunter, of Wichita Falls, Texas, hunted for eleven days without seeing a lion treed; gamely came back for five more days and his trophy.

10 This lion treed high.

11 J. W. Kirkpatrick (left), Roy Pratt, President, California Packing Corporation, San Francisco (seated), and Fred Austin, Sales Manager of the Southern District of California Packing Corporation, Houston, Texas (right), with trophies taken on the same day on Evans Ranch.

22 (Left to right) Dub Evans, holding Old Brownie; Lee Wilson, of Dallas, Texas, holding Little Brownie; and Barry Hagedon, after a successful bear hunt.

23 My father's original Brownie with one of the bears he loved to hunt.

24 K. S. Adams, Chairman of the Board of Phillips Petroleum Company, with his fine buck antelope.

25 (Left) Elliott Barker, New Mexico State Game Warden, and A. T. "Cap" McDonnald, with two antelope.

26 Lee Wilson, of Dallas Texas, and J. W. Kirkpatrick, with lion taken by Wilson at Horse Camp. Three lions were killed during this one week of hunting.

27 Trail Riders party in Little Bear Canyon.

Photo by Erle Kauffman

MORE UNUSUAL HUNTS

his trail, it would seem to disprove the theory that some hunters hold, that the markers are made only around kills and at distances of a mile or two apart.

Albert Pickens, a Government hunter, had killed a female in Jordan Canyon about two weeks before this, so we figured that this was her mate, on the prowl and looking for her.

We went in to the Slash Ranch headquarters that night, taking the lion with us. Lee and I left at four the next morning to join the cowboys at the D Bar, where we started in again gathering steers. We slipped out without disturbing Father, but he also was up early, skinned the lion himself (he later had the skin mounted), and rode to the D Bar and joined the outfit later that day.

We did make a satisfactory gather and delivery on the steers, and the records show that it was the turning point in our financial careers. Although Father died in January, 1925, he had lived long enough to see us headed in the right direction.

He always said that a hound, to reach the point where he was rated a "lead dog," had to have character and stamina enough to resist the temptation to chase deer, rabbits, and the many other things that tempt hounds off the trail. The same can be said of people—they must have the will-power to resist the ever-present temptations if they are to remain morally fit to take their place as leaders.

HOUNDS THAT HUNT ALONE

In October, 1925, Forest Ranger Harold Peckenpaugh, stationed at the Beaverhead ranger station, located a quarter of a mile north of the Slash Ranch headquarters, was at the Black Mountain lookout station, a distance of twelve miles via Forest Service trails, and connected with both the Slash Ranch headquarters and the ranger station by telephone. "Peck," as the ranger was commonly called, called the ranch from the cabin on Black Mountain and asked Mrs. Evans if I were with the hounds. She told him that I was working stock in the D Bar country and didn't have the hounds along. Peck stated that he could hear the hounds and would ride over into the head of Trap Corral Canyon to see what they were after.

He was surprised and wildly excited to find them with a lion treed! He had a pistol, and although we never learned just how many shots it took, he finally killed the lion, after it had moved to at least a couple of other trees. He left the lion where he made the kill, as he was too excited to load it on his horse and bring it in. He came back to the station, and, when I got home that night, there was a message for me to call him, but the word was out that he had killed a lion.

He was still excited when I called, and related his experience with much enthusiasm. He said he had killed a big male lion, too big for one man to handle, and wanted me to go with him the next day to help bring it in. I went, but instead of a big male the lion he had killed and dressed was a female and weighed eighty pounds. Nevertheless, it looked big to him and provided just as much excitement as if it had been the "big old male" that he thought it was.

The significant thing about this story is that the hounds had gone out on their own to get this lion, crossing several miles of mesa grassland or open country before reaching an area where there would be any possibility of striking a lion trail. Those Slash Ranch hounds must have had lion on their minds when they left the ranch, as they would naturally cross the scents of many other animals over such a distance. Brownie and Bell were in their prime along about this time, and probably had Ranger and another young hound with them, as Peck said there were four with the lion. It would be interesting to know what passed between the hounds and just how they understood to stay together and pass up the other trails until they reached lion country. I have had a lifelong experience with hounds, but I still don't know how they

MORE UNUSUAL HUNTS

communicate with each other, or what they say, but they undoubtedly do and have an understanding.

When I was a child living on the old E V Ranch in the Davis Mountains, where I was born, I was sent to look for the hounds many times when they would go off early in the morning for a hunt of their own and not return by mid-morning. The hounds would go out early and hunt while it was cool, and if they didn't bay anything they would quit and come in when it began to get hot. But if they bayed, and especially if the animal, usually a cat or a fox, was where they could see it, they would stay out a long time.

When I was eight years old, my Dad sent me one morning about ten o'clock, to look for the hounds. The old E V Ranch was located in Panther Canyon and was pretty well surrounded by rough hills. When one of us went to look for the hounds, he usually would make a circle out two or three miles from the ranch, ride to the highest spots, and stop often to listen. On this particular day, I went south toward what we called Wildcat Hills. When I stopped to listen on top of a high hill a couple of miles out, I could hear an occasional bark farther south. Upon reaching the spot I found several hounds scattered on top of a broken bluff thirty or forty feet high, indicating that there was something in the bluff, but not in sight.

I tied my pony and began to climb around in the rocks. I soon heard a little black hound we called "Coley" deep down in the bluff, which had some cracks in the rocks twenty feet or more in depth. Coley was baying, and he sounded as though he were barking at an animal. I kept climbing down, and finally got to a spot where I could see Coley a few feet below me, but a bend in the crack kept me from seeing what he was barking at. I was leaning way over, trying to see what it was, and I suppose my presence made Coley feel a little bolder, because, just at that moment, there was an awful noise that only a mountain lion makes when a hound gets too close to him. The lion sprang at the hound about six feet below me, and I really came out of there in a hurry. It was three or four miles to the ranch, and I probably made it in record time.

There were no horses even close to the ranch at the moment, except the one I was riding, so Mr. McAnally, our ranch foreman, armed himself with a .30-30 and rode my pony with me up behind the saddle. I directed him toward the spot where the lion was bayed, and we had almost reached the place when we heard a lot of noise behind us. Looking back, we saw Lee and Joe, two of my older brothers, mounted on a crippled old dun mare that we had left belled, and used only to keep a bunch of young mules together. She and the mules came in to water just as Mr. Mac and I left. Lee and Joe caught her, and, without even putting on a saddle or taking off the bell, both climbed on, and, with all the young mules following, came as fast as they could get the old crippled mare to travel, to join us after the lion. (In Texas we always called them panthers, and I had never heard of mountain lions until I came to New Mexico.)

We had some difficulty finding the panther, but we kept climbing around in the rocks looking into cracks, until we heard Mr. Mac say, from way down in the rocks, "I see two balls of fire, so look out, I'm going to shoot." He shot and killed the panther.

Only those who have seen a cat's or lion's eyes shining out of the dark can know just how much like "two balls of fire" they really look. This is another case of good hounds going out on their own and bringing a lion to bay.

LION HUNT IN THE NIGHT

In April, 1930, I had a guest from Los Angeles, Mr. Ross N. Boggs, a retired hotel man, who wanted a pair of lion skins, male and female, for a game room in a new house he was building.

We sent out beds and chuck to Horse Camp on pack mules

MORE UNUSUAL HUNTS

with Scotty and Fred Spaulding, while Mr. Boggs and I brought the hounds to check for sign. We got the trail of a cat in Houghton Canyon and decided to follow it to give the hounds a workout, but it turned out differently than we expected. The trail led in a northwesterly direction and the cat kept moving. When evening came we were on Elk Mountain and much closer to O Bar O ranger station than Horse Camp. We expected the hounds to jump the cat and tree him any minute, but he just kept traveling ahead of them all day. I never witnessed more interesting hound work, as this cat used all the known tricks to throw them off. Although he was unable to stump the hounds entirely, he did manage to delay them enough to avoid being treed. Just before night we called them off and went to O Bar O for the night instead of to Horse Camp.

Next morning, still being as far from camp as when we had left the ranch the day before, we decided to ride on into camp without doing much hunting, as we wanted to reach there before Scotty might start out looking for us. The area to be crossed between O Bar O ranger station and Horse Camp, a distance of about twenty miles via Middle Elk, Little Turkey, and Canyon Creek Mountain, is mostly a yellow pine country and not especially good for lions.

As we came off Canyon Creek Mountain, Brownie opened on lion sign not fresh enough to follow, but good enough for us to plan to return next day for further checking and to look over an area we normally would pass up.

Scotty and Fred had made camp with our supplies without incident and were not uneasy, as there were two of us together. Next morning, accompanied by Scotty, we returned to the Canyon Creek Mountain area after a most interesting day during which the hounds showed us one porcupine and one deer kill, and finally a female lion up a tree. This gave Mr. Boggs one-half of his order.

The next three or four days were spent in covering all the best haunts I knew of but didn't yield a bark. We had taken three male lions out of the Middle Fork, between Canyon Creek and Jordan, earlier in the winter and nothing had come into the area since.

We decided to cross the Middle Fork to check Lilley and Jerky mountains. This area brought us only a bobcat, which the hounds treed on the extreme north end of Jerky late in the evening. By the time we had killed and skinned the cat, we had hardly enough daylight left to get out of the rough country. By hurrying we managed to cross the Middle Fork and get on to a very dim trail out of Canyon Creek, just at dark. We felt that from that point on the horses would get us into camp.

On our climb out of Canyon Creek, the hounds opened with great enthusiasm. I scolded and called but to no avail. As it is never hard to call them off a cat, I knew it was a lion but we had no desire to try to follow a lion in the night. We wanted to call the hounds off, come to camp for the rest of the night and return next morning to check this sign in daylight. Fred Spaulding was with us that day and I borrowed his pistol, which I fired several times, calling the hounds as though I had found something. We rode as fast as possible for nighttime in the rocks and brush and, since the hounds had quit barking, we thought they would be coming to us.

We didn't slow up until we got completely out of Canyon Creek and came to an open, grassy mesa, where we stopped to see how many hounds had returned. The dry, white mesa grass, and no brush made it possible to see pretty well and we were happy to count all seven hounds.

We started for camp, riding pretty fast as going was much better now. About a mile farther on we came to another open, grass-covered spot where we stopped again to check on the hounds. Imagine our disappointment at finding none of them with us.

I told Mr. Boggs that we were well on the trail to camp and

MORE UNUSUAL HUNTS

that Fred could go to camp with him, cook something to eat, and care for the horses, but that I intended to go back to see what the hounds were doing. Mr. Boggs surprised me by saying he wanted to go back with me. We all went back, but instead of following the trail, which led around a high point back to the little mesa where we had last seen the hounds, we decided to ride up over the point so as to be on higher ground and in better position for listening. It was brushy and rough but when we reached the top and stopped to listen, we could hear the hounds barking "treed," back toward Canyon Creek. We started to them but were cut off by a rimrock on the last little canyon and the hounds were directly across, barking furiously, indicating they were in plain sight of the quarry.

We left our horses and made the rest of the way on foot. We felt around until we found a break in the bluff where we could slide down, and from there to the tree we made it pretty well, but stumbled over lots of rocks. Fortunately the lion was up an old dead pine and the bulk of his body could be seen silhouetted against the sky. I borrowed Fred's .30-30 and told Mr. Boggs, who also had a .30-30, that if he would sit right beside me I would count to three and we would both shoot and maybe one or both of us would hit the lion. We could not even see the end of the gun barrel, much less the sight, but we fired simultaneously and the lion fell out wounded. He ran a few yards and bayed up in some bushes. The hounds would crowd in on him and he would knock them off, but only for a moment when they would crowd in on him again. I kept getting closer, watching for a chance to get a shot without shooting a hound. The lion would knock the hounds all loose, then sit back on his haunches against a bush. I couldn't see him when still, but could see a flash as he would back up after knocking the hounds off. I watched this movement carefully and there would be just an instant before the hounds closed

SLASH RANCH HOUNDS

in again. Just as he knocked them off and backed up, I took a flash shot which luckily hit the lion in a vital spot.

We built a small fire, for light, by which we gutted the lion, which was a big male, and fed the hounds, but left the unskinned lion there. We climbed back up to our horses and arrived in camp about midnight. After a good rest and breakfast, we packed the lion in and got some pictures, winding up another very successful hunt, and the only lion hunt I ever made at night in New Mexico. I did kill one under similar circumstances in Texas, a long time ago.

CHAPTER XV

OLD MAN GRIZZLY

The following story of an unusual bear hunt that ended with the killing of a monster grizzly appeared in the El Paso Times, *Sunday, May 4, 1930. The weight stated in the newspaper story is, of course, an estimated weight; but it was an estimate agreed upon by Lee Evans and Bud McGahey, both experienced hunters who saw the carcass. I myself know that this was the biggest bear I have ever seen. He was fat, built like a prize bull, and his pelt actually completely covered a double bed.*

On this hunt with me were Lee Evans, Bud McGahey, A. L. Inman, his son, Deming Inman, and Chet McCauley. The big grizzly we killed was the killer of many cattle and sheep, and had been the object of numerous hunts.—G.W.E.

From out of the Black Range of the Rocky Mountains, in south central New Mexico, about 175 miles northwest of El Paso and 50 miles northeast of Silver City, comes an unusual story of an unusual bear hunt which ended with the killing of a monster grizzly bear—a genuine grizzly weighing more than 1,000 pounds—

SLASH RANCH HOUNDS

which had been foraging on stock of that region for more than fifteen years.

The story, as written by G. W. Evans, of Albuquerque, N. M., who was accompanied on the eight-day hunt by his brother Lee, Bud McGahey, of Borger, Texas, and A. L. Inman, of the Healy ranch in the Black Range country, will be broadcast over WDAH at 7:45 o'clock tomorrow evening by Joe Evans, a brother of the two hunters.

For more than forty years, the Evans brothers have been hunting bear in the Davis Mountains, and the Black and Mogollon mountain regions and this grizzly is the second they have killed.

The thrills of hunting the grizzly, according to G. W. Evans' story, by far eclipse all other kinds of hunts.

In the story, Evans tells of another bear killed, but it was so small when compared with the big kill that little space is devoted to it. In commenting on the hunt last night, Joe Evans, who makes his home in El Paso, said the big grizzly had been the object of many hunts but had always been successful in eluding his enemies.

Governor Dan Moody, of Texas, an ardent bear hunter, had been considering returning to El Paso soon and accompanying Joe Evans on a hunt for the killer of hundreds of cattle and sheep, but the hunt that started April 20 and ended April 28 with the killing of the big bear made that hunt unnecessary.

(But let G. W. Evans tell the story—Ed.)

We moved from the ranch to the head of Black Canyon, taking two days to make the trip. We left the hounds tied up the first day, taking only one along to look for signs. We found a grizzly track headed north about six miles from camp on the east side of the range. I took the hounds the next day and was to go down into the rough country where we saw the track. The other men took stands out on top at places where they thought the bear would come out if we got a start. The track we found the day before seemed to be old, but the hounds finally took it. They trailed it

OLD MAN GRIZZLY

into a rough canyon about half a mile north and hit a red-hot trail. I had about twenty hounds, most of them young. They had not been hunted with lately and were fresh and eager to run anything. Just as they went off under the first rim of this rough canyon, they hit the fresh trail of the bear where he came from a cow that he had killed about a half mile down the canyon just east of where I was. All the hounds except Little Brownie and one other took the back end of the trail that led down to the kill. I ran out to the edge of the bluff to listen, and heard Little Brownie and the other hound barking "bayed" right down under me. They had already come up on the bear and were not a hundred yards from me. The brush was so thick I could not see the bear at all. I waited there a few minutes and could hear him breaking the brush as he walked around with the hounds barking at him.

There were a lot of bluffs there just over the bear and it sounded to me as though he was coming up the hill and was going to pass west of me. I moved a few hundred yards west and when I got where I could listen I found the bear had run east and right under where I had moved from. All the hounds that had gone on the back trail were out of hearing. I found later that after they had reached the kill, they had scattered and were running deer and coyotes. The last time I heard Little Brownie, he was still baying the bear and going southeast exactly away from where the men were stationed. They never did know what happened. It was too rough to ride so I followed Little Brownie on foot and could see this big old bear track every once in a while. I finally lost the track, and the wind came up, so I lost out entirely.

I hunted Little Brownie all afternoon. I went back to my horse and made a big circle but did not find anything. Hounds began to come to me, but no Little Brownie. I went back to camp late that evening, with most of the hounds, and Little Brownie came in about ten o'clock.

While in the canyon where the cow was killed, I saw the track of another fair-sized bear. Three of Lee's hounds didn't come in, so, next day, Lee and A. L. Inman went to the Ladder Ranch to look for them, and the rest of us moved camp about five miles south and camped in the saddle between the head of Mimbres and Palomas creeks, right on top of the Continental Divide. We had a pretty camp and a good place for our horses. Lee and A. L. Inman found Lee's hounds at the Ladder Ranch and got back to our new camp late that evening.

The next day, we all decided to go down near the kill. I was to take Little Brownie and go down to the cow and get the trail straightened out. When I got down near the kill, Little Brownie struck a trail and I soon found that it was the little bear instead of the grizzly. The grizzly hadn't come back. Lee and A. L. Inman let the other hounds go when they heard Little Brownie, but it was a big, rough country and before they could get to him he had gone into a rough canyon behind a point and neither the men nor the hounds could hear him.

McGahey and Deming Inman had taken a stand at the head of the canyon that Little Brownie was going up. Most of the hounds that Lee and A. L. Inman had released had run off after a deer and were scattered all over the country, most of them going in the opposite direction to the bear. The bear came out in sight of Bud and Deming Inman and they shot at him about fifteen times. We all got together about where the shooting occurred and saw Little Brownie go out by himself where the bear had gone. A. L. Inman and I waited there to gather up the hounds and put them on the trail as soon as they came back to us. The other boys went out on top to work around to some deep saddles on top of the divide in the direction the bear was going. We waited there about an hour and finally gathered up eleven hounds. We had to go around the head of a rough canyon to get to the bear's trail. As soon as we got over there the hounds hit the trail and left in "high." We followed them but they crossed a rough canyon or two and

OLD MAN GRIZZLY

left us far behind. We went on in their direction though, and found them treed in about the third canyon and only about a mile east of our camp. We killed this bear, a brown male, and as Lee and the other boys were within hearing distance, we all soon got together. I guess Little Brownie already had the bear treed before the other hounds got there, or the bear would have been much farther off after having been shot at so many times.

The next morning we started south from camp and hadn't gone a mile until Little Brownie struck a trail, and we saw from the tracks that it was the old big grizzly, going south right down the Government trail. He went down the trail for about six miles, all of the hounds trailing. It was all we could do to stay within hearing, loping nearly all the time. They finally turned off east and followed near the main divide for about two miles, when they went off into the head of a very rough canyon and we heard them come up on the bear. Grizzlies don't run when the hounds come up on them.

All six of us were together on this rough point and we decided that Bud and I would go on foot, as it was too rough to ride, and see if we could get a shot at the bear. There were eight or ten hounds down there making a lot of noise. The brush was so thick one could see only a few yards ahead. The bear didn't stay there very long, but I think we got within fifty or a hundred yards of him before he ran. As soon as he ran, the hounds overtook him again and he must have turned on them, for all but Little Brownie and possibly one or two others came back in a bunch to me. I hurried to the edge of a big point that they had gone over and when I got where I could look out I heard Little Brownie off on a mountainside, and located him and the big bear going around the side of the mountain. Little Brownie was only a few feet from the bear's heels, and the bear was in a lope. There was only one other hound behind Little Brownie, a black hound, either Inman's

SLASH RANCH HOUNDS

Dobie, or Lee's Black Alice. The bear was headed south or southeast and going off into the north fork of the Animas.

It began to get pretty hot and I thought the bear might stop when he crossed the canyon, as there were lots of big bluffs there, with thick brush and a running stream of water. I hurried off the mountain thinking I would get a shot at the bear as he crossed the canyon. Bud and I had gotten separated in the first canyon the hounds had crossed. There were some big falls in the canyon and as Little Brownie was the only hound barking I soon lost hearing of him when I got near the water.

There were eleven hounds with me at this time, none of them trying to follow the bear. I did not know what had become of Little Brownie except that I knew he had quit or had crossed the canyon out of hearing. As he didn't show up, I figured he was still with the bear, so I sized up the country and picked out a saddle on the south side of the canyon that would be a likely place for the bear to come out. I climbed up to this saddle and found where the old bear had gone through, with Little Brownie's tracks right in his. The other hounds took up the trail there and followed it as it began to turn west and into still rougher country. As soon as I got well over onto the rim of the next canyon I could hear Little Brownie baying about a mile west of me. A few of the hounds went to him, but most of them came back. I could not get to him without crossing a country where I believed the bear could hear me, so I decided I would go off into the canyon and up to a point where I could climb out and come up on the bear from the opposite side. It took me about an hour to do this, and when I came up over the point where I thought the bear was, he had moved, but I was within about a hundred yards of him.

Several of the hounds went over to where he was but they didn't stay long. The brush was so thick I could not see the bear, although I was close and could tell where he was by the hounds. He kept moving, staying in one place for only a few minutes. It was about noon and getting awfully hot. I kept climbing around after the hounds and the bear, and I was so close to them the hounds with me would go to him every once in a while, but would not stay long.

The wind began to blow, and there were several minutes that I could not hear the hounds at all. I kept hunting around and could see the old bear's tracks. I knew he was giving out or was too hot to travel, and he seemed determined not to leave this mountain. It was about the roughest place in the country, with the brush so thick I could hardly crowd through it. I sat down on a rock at the edge of a point to rest, and had been there only a few minutes when I heard the hounds just below me. I moved over a little farther and could hear them plainly, only a short distance below me. I got down there a few minutes later, and there were three hounds with the bear this time—Black Alice, Dobie, and Little Brownie. As I came near, some of the other hounds went to them and began barking at the bear.

I slipped down towards them and kept getting closer. I could only see for a few feet because of the thick brush, but finally located the bear. He was lying down with his right side to me and I could see he was panting. When I was about fifteen or twenty feet from him, I shot at about where I thought his shoulder was, or a little behind. He made an awful noise and began to break the brush and bellow like a bull. I got a little closer and could see he was staggering badly. I shot him again in the neck and he died a few seconds later.

He was on a steep hillside but the brush was so thick he rolled only about thirty feet, breaking the brush as he rolled over it. Not a hound bit him, even after he was dead. I never saw such a bear as he was. I caught hold of a foot and could not turn him over.

I knew that if I did not get help the hide would be wasted, so I left the bear and went to a high point and shot three times. I sure was pleased when Lee answered me with answering shots.

SLASH RANCH HOUNDS

Lee finally got to within about three hundred yards of where I was, and we began to talk to each other and decided what to do about getting the hide out.

We decided to get Lee's horse as close to the bear as we could, skin the bear, and bring the skin out on the horse. We got back to the bear at three o'clock and got him skinned by five. We got the skin back to the horse and then worked our way off into the canyon where there was water, and there we stayed until morning. Then we loaded the skin and began to climb out toward the top of the mountain where we had left the boys and horses the day before. Lee walked and led his horse all the way out, but the huge skin was so heavy that the horse gave out carrying the load. If we had not had a horse near the scene of the kill we never could have gotten the skin out at all.

We got out on top about ten o'clock and the boys met us with some food and fresh horses. We got the skin to camp about three o'clock. When we went the next day to get some pictures of the bear's carcass we found that there was another grizzly on the same mountainside and found where the other bear had gone out. We decided, however, that, as our horses were pretty well tired out and our grain supply running low, we would pack up and move out toward home instead of sending for grain to continue the hunt.

The "little" bear were getting so thick that we could not go in any direction without striking a trail. When we moved out of camp we led Little Brownie to keep him off bear trails. He struck a trail even wearing a collar and chain.

CHAPTER XVI

FIVE LION HUNTS

HORSE-KILLING LIONS

In December, 1922, Lee and Lou C. came to Beaverhead for a hunt and visit. Their two daughters, Pauline and Mary Jo, were going to school in El Paso at the time and we planned to meet them at Socorro when they came home for Christmas vacation.

Although we got our mail only once a week, we were on a U. S. Forestry Service telephone line. This line was necessary for fire protection in the remote area in which we lived. While Lee was there I had a call from George Owsley, who, at that time, had the Bear Springs ranch just a few miles northwest of Magdalena. He was running both cattle and horses, and said that a lion had caught one of his brood mares, but that the mare had thrown him off somehow and was still alive but badly cut up.

As we were hunting lion at this time, we planned to start our trip to Socorro a few days early, take some hounds along, and check this reported lion sign. Lou C. went with us to Magdalena, where we left her at the Aragon Hotel while Lee and I took Bell, Ranger, and Blue out to Bear Springs, where we would be closer to the country in which we were to hunt. Neither of us had been in this area before.

Owsley was busy and couldn't go with us, but he had a couple of good horses for us to ride. We felt a little handicapped, as Brownie was sick when we left Beaverhead, and we had been using him for a start hound. In his absence, we used Bell to do the starting, although we didn't know what to expect of her. She was a very smart hound, and took the lead as soon as we rode from camp that morning, acting as though she had been doing this all the time.

It had been very cold the night before, and there was a high wind with a light fall of snow on the ground—ideal conditions for checking tracks. Bell worked well out in the lead, and barked several times in some good saddles and on favorable hogbacks, but the scent she was barking on was under the snow and no tracks were visible. We thought she was barking on lion sign and acting just like an old start hound, but all of the sign was old. We kept riding, going into the most likely places for lions and, about noon, when what little snow there was had melted, except in the shade, Bell worked off into a rough header and opened good.

When we got to her we were happy to see some fresh tracks of a very large lion, made since the snow of the night before. We soon reached an area that had so many lion tracks we couldn't tell one end of a trail from the other, indicating the presence of more than one lion, and that we were in the vicinity of a kill.

About the middle of the afternoon we came upon the kill, a full-grown mare, in the middle of a small mesa that had considerable scrub cedar on it, with much lion sign all around. Every lion hunter dreams of finding just such a setup, a big animal killed, with many feeds left on the carcass, and actively in use by the killer. If our time had not been limited we would have taken the hounds back to camp, and come straight to the kill the next morning, but knowing that we would have to meet the girls the next

FIVE LION HUNTS

day and go to Beaverhead, we let the hounds work until night, hoping to get on a track that would lead to a lion. They took many trails away from the kill, only to make a circle of a mile or two and wind up at the kill again. I was standing a couple of hundred yards from the kill, holding my pony, when I noticed a big lion track in a patch of snow, with no hound tracks around it. I called the hounds and put them on this track, which they readily took, but worked on very slowly.

They were twenty or thirty feet ahead of me and not more than three hundred yards from the kill, when Ranger darted in under a cedar and grabbed the biggest lion I have ever seen, right by the rear end. He bit so hard that he sunk his teeth through the skin and the lion went out of there so fast that Ranger was actually hung to him, with all four feet spread out setting back. It was in this position that the lion took him for a fast ride for a few yards across the mesa, in plain view. The race was on and lasted only a minute or two. There were some small bluffs just under the hill to the east and the hounds soon brought the big lion to bay on top of a rock. He was squirming, ringing his tail, with his back going up and down, and hissing and spitting. He was actually smarting from Ranger's bite.

This was on the dark side of the hill, where the sun already was down, and we decided to kill the lion at once, jerk his skin off, and go to camp. This we did, and, while skinning him, Lee and I estimated him to weigh over two hundred pounds, definitely the biggest one either of us had ever seen, and we have never seen one as big since. I had the skin mounted and presented it to Elliott Cowden, of Midland, Texas.

It was getting pretty dark by this time, so we loaded the skin, with the feet on, and headed for camp, about four miles away. We were up early the next morning and took the hounds back to the kill to see if anything had been back, but before we reached the kill, the hounds picked up the fresh trail of another lion and, after a short race, treed a big female. We killed and skinned her, went back to camp, loaded the hounds and returned to Magdalena, where we picked up Lou C. We then went on to Socorro to wait for the early morning train that would bring Pauline and Mary Jo from El Paso. We met the train about 4:00 A. M., and, with Lou C. and the girls, our saddles, three dogs, and the lion skins, Lee's old Cadillac was really loaded. We had the side-curtains up and plenty of blankets for protection against the zero weather, with no car-heater to break the piercing cold. We had a good hunt and had developed Bell into another start dog.

LION KITTENS

Many lasting friendships have been made during lion and bear hunts held on our ranches. Instances are friendships formed during the visits of Dr. M. W. Sherwood, of Scott & White Clinic, of Temple, Texas; and of John Hampton and Al Wilson, oil operators, of Wichita Falls, to Lee's ranch in the Mt. Taylor area. It was during one of these hunts, in 1926, that Hampton and Wilson became part owners with Lee in the Mt. Taylor ranch, John Hampton still being an active partner in this enterprise, known as the L Bar Cattle Company.

In 1925, John Hampton was interested in hunting mountain lions and visited Lee's Marquez ranch. John was so enthusiastic over this first lion hunt that, a year later, his partner, Al Wilson, came with Lee and his wife to Beaverhead for a hunt. My wife and Lee's wife being sisters, there were many fine exchanges of visits on the two ranches. Being ranch women, they were excellent cooks, and always put tempting meals before us. When we went out in hunting camp, they would always cook up a lot of fine food for us to take along, which made our cooking jobs easier.

With the help of Zane Smith to handle the horses, we moved our camp outfit to O Bar O ranger station, twenty miles northwest of Beaverhead headquarters. Garvin Smith, Zane's father, was

FIVE LION HUNTS

forest ranger for this district at the time, but he had moved away for the winter and gave us permission to use the ample facilities of the ranger station for this hunt. There was a house, running water, plenty of wood, and a fine barn and corral for the horses; but better still, the whole setup was close to the base of Elk Mountain, the area in which we wanted to hunt.

We had plenty of ranch-killed beef for ourselves, and burro meat for the hounds. We had some young hounds to be trained, part of them pups out of Bell and Brownie, and there is no better training than hunting bobcats. We found plenty of cats around the O Bar O, and spent the first two days trailing them. I think we killed three.

On our third night in camp, we decided that the next day we would keep the hounds close in, and under no circumstances would they be permitted to trail a cat before we reached the summit of Elk Mountain, elevation 9,780 feet, where we wanted to check for lion sign. We were favored with six inches of new snow that night, and we knew that if we didn't waste time running cats we would have time to cross the mountain. If a lion had passed along since the fresh snow, we would have just what any lion hunter would wish for—a lion track in the snow, good hounds to take the trail, and good horses to carry us.

Having spent two days in trailing and treeing cats, the hounds were really cat-minded, and it was not easy to keep them down as we passed the many fresh cat tracks on our way up the mountain. We held firm, however, and were amply rewarded by finding where a full-grown lion had crossed our trail, headed north, just as we reached the top of main Elk. The hounds were away in a hurry, and were really making the music an old hunter loves to hear.

The hounds piled off on the north side of Elk Mountain, where the going was too rough for a horse. The day was still, and we could hear every bark. When they were under the turn of the

SLASH RANCH HOUNDS

mountain they headed toward the west, which was fine for us, as there is a blazed trail running east and west along the top of the mountain. We would ride at a fast gait along the trail for a while, then move over to the edge and listen. Each time we could hear the hounds going strong, and about even with, or a little ahead of, us.

We kept this up for about three or four miles, and then the hounds crossed back over the top just ahead of us. Not long after that they treed just under the crest on the south side of the mountain, where the going was much better than on the north side. We rode to where they were and, looking around, found two freshly killed bucks close together. Al was the guest, so he shot the lion, which was a mother, suckling young.

The problem then was to find the den with the young ones. Knowing that the extremely rough terrain all along the north side of Elk Mountain, over which the hounds had come, would be ideal for a den, Zane and I started out on foot to follow the back trail looking for it. We didn't believe the hounds would take the back end of the trail of a lion they had just caught, but in this case we were wrong. They went back on the trail just as they had come over. Lee and Al kept the horses on top, going back over the same trail by which we had come.

We found that walking in the snow, which was knee-deep on the north side, was slow going, even though the going and coming of eight hounds had broken out a pretty good trail. The hounds ran ahead of us and were soon out of hearing. We went on, and after two or three miles, we heard a hound bay. We were both certain we had heard it, but something seemed to cut off the sound, and we couldn't hear anything. We kept plowing on through the snow, following the fresh trail the hounds had made, and again we heard a bark, but no farther away; then, again, the sound was gone. We were completely mystified in hearing just the one hound out of eight, and this only at intervals.

FIVE LION HUNTS

We finally learned what was happening. The hounds had found the den of kittens in a big cave, and they were all in there barking and making lots of noise, but could be heard only after we reached the mouth of the cave. Brownie would come out of the cave and bark occasionally, then go back in. He repeated this performance until we got there. Lee and Al had heard him too, and were at the den with the horses about the time Zane and I reached there. We always believed that Brownie came out of that cave at regular intervals and barked so that we could find where the hounds had the kittens bayed back in the cave. It was just another unusual thing for a hound to do.

In the cave we found three male lion kittens that were able to get in cracks on some ledges, out of reach of the hounds. We decided to take them alive. They were about the size of wildcats, and dealt us plenty of misery before it was over. If one is equipped with a good supply of rope and sash cord, tying a grown lion that is treed in a reasonably low tree with plenty of limbs, is not too difficult; but trying to handle a bunch of kittens is a good way to get scratched.

We started out on the hunt with a limited supply of good soft-shelled pecans. These soon were rationed and we were supposed to know just how many pecans each of us carried out with him while riding. When we were in the cave and had gotten hold of two of the kittens some one suggested that if Al would take off his coveralls, which were very large, we could put a lion kitten in each leg. Al removed his coveralls, but was slow in passing them to us. The reason was that he had a lot of extra pecans in his coveralls pockets and was transferring them to pockets in his outer clothes. We got a laugh out of that, and Al laughed with us. He had been holding out on us.

We sent the kittens to the zoo in El Paso.

SLASH RANCH HOUNDS

A FAMILY HUNT

We were making a regular summer branding work on the Slash Ranch in June, 1931. We had three camps, the D Bar, Cooney, and Horse Camp, where there were cabins with cookstoves, corrals, horse pastures, etc. These camps were well distributed, and, with the range that could be reached from headquarters, we had to move camp only four times to cover the entire ranch.

For branding works in summer and gathering works in the fall we had a "wagon cook," but in summer, when all the children were out of school, these works were made with the three or four permanent ranch hands aided by Joe and his three boys, my three boys, and sometimes Lee and his two girls, the cook being the only extra help needed.

The custom with cow outfits is to have fresh meat in camp at all times, therefore it is necessary to butcher a calf or yearling about once a week. The hounds enjoyed these general works as wagon cooks are generous with meat and other scraps, so they were never left behind. Hounds and cattle don't mix, so the hounds were kept tied until the riders had gone, then turned loose by the cook so they could run around.

We had moved to Horse Camp, and on the roundup drive near Indian Creek we found a calf and an antelope that had been killed by a lion. Hunting with hounds in hot weather is not practical but we felt this deserved checking, so Lee and I were up at 2:00 A. M. headed for Indian Creek with the hounds to see if there was a lion around the kills.

Daylight comes early in June, and Indian Creek was five miles east of camp, but we reached there just as day was breaking. The antelope kill was the fresher of the two and we planned to go there first, but a quarter of a mile short of the kill the hounds broke away at full speed with heads in the air. They went northeast toward Cooney Mountain with Lee and I in hot pursuit,

FIVE LION HUNTS

through open country where a mountain pony could make good time.

When the hounds started up Cooney Mountain they must have been crowding the lion, for, instead of going on to the top, he made a circle to the right. This change in direction suited us fine as we couldn't stay up with the hounds on the upgrade. We were crossing the mesas between Indian Creek and Cooney Prairie, going south through scattered pine when it got light enough to see the hounds. They were still running with noses up, indicating they were following by body scent in the air and not the trail on the ground. Lee and I realized the lion was still out on his nightly prowl when the hounds picked up the scent, so it really was a jumped race from the start. We knew also if we could stay close enough we would soon see him running ahead of the hounds, and, sure enough, that is what happened. It was a big male, really stretched out, trying to reach the breaks on Indian Creek. It was a wild race, and we stayed in sight until the hounds overtook the lion just when he made a long spring into a pine tree. I have seen lions tree from across a canyon, but this was the only time I was actually in the race when one treed.

Lee and I thought this would be a good chance for our families to see a lion up a tree, so I stayed at the tree while he went back to camp after them. I didn't think they could possibly have had time to get there when I heard the rocks rolling and they had arrived. Beulah, with two-year-old Jim up in front of her; Lou C. and the little Evanses mounted on good ponies and riding hard with Lee showing them the way. The children wanted to see a race, so I threw a chunk at the lion and out he came. He was in a tree close to the breaks of Indian Creek, and in a few long jumps reached the edge. I have never seen such a wild ride as those youngsters made as they piled off into Indian Creek Canyon behind the hounds, and, they, too, were close enough to see him take the next tree. Deming Inman, who was about the same age as our boys, was with us, and he had a pistol. This was the only firearm in the crowd, as we had not expected to hunt and had not taken our rifles on the roundup.

After the lion was shot out of the tree with Deming's pistol they were sitting around on their horses and I noticed Beulah feeding Jim. Lou C. had carried a tin cup filled with crumbled-up biscuit and covered with milk gravy. Jim was just past two years old so he probably is the youngest Evans to have seen a lion in a tree. He still remembers it and especially when the lion opened his mouth wide and made a loud noise as he snuffed at us.

When Jim was eight he shot a bobcat out of a tree, but at twenty-two, and after having many opportunities, he has never shot anything else. He says he had rather look at wild animals than shoot them.

ONE MORE CHANCE

I remember one hunt for which I find no recorded date, but I do have pictures. I was in Albuquerque visiting with my family when my friend Kirkpatrick called from El Paso to tell me that Roy Pratt, president of Del Monte Packing Company, of San Francisco, and one of his sales managers, Fred Austin, of Houston, Texas, were in El Paso and wanted to go to Beaverhead for a couple of days. Kirk wanted to know if I could meet them at the ranch.

We did some fast planning over the phone, and arranged for Kirk to come by Tom Jones' ranch, on Taylor Creek, on their way to Beaverhead, to see if Tom could bring his hounds and meet us at the old Kemp place early next morning. I was to drive from Albuquerque to the ranch to meet Kirk, Roy, and Fred. We would send horses out to the Kemp place, and take the hounds in a pickup to meet Tom; then hunt the Kemp Points back toward Black Mountain.

Everything worked fine. It took Kirk about six hours to drive from El Paso to the ranch, which is about the time it took me to

FIVE LION HUNTS

drive from Albuquerque. We had supper that night in the bunkhouse, played cards, talked hunting, and planned to be up early next morning for the Beaver Creek ride. The road down Beaver Creek was so rough that the boys, Scotty and Chet, with the horses, made as good time as we did in the pickup, but by hauling the hounds the eight miles distance they would be in better hunting condition than if they had followed behind the horses.

Tom was waiting when we arrived, and we mounted and started up Trap Corral Canyon, where the hounds hit a fresh lion trail. They went west, up the bed of the canyon, and soon left us behind, as it is pretty slow going on horseback. Two or three miles farther on they left the canyon, and when we got out where the riding was better we overtook them. They were not doing so well now and, although we had seen the fresh track of a lion coming up the canyon where they first started, we discovered they were now on the back-track of a lion of the same size.

We figured the same lion had made a two-way trip in the canyon but the hounds had failed to find where the track had turned. Such a mistake was easy to make, especially if the lion had climbed or jumped up a high place just when leaving the bottom. With the other scent still there, even though it is the back-track, it is perfectly natural for the hounds to go right on with the trail. A fresh pack, especially when mixed with another pack, is more likely to make this mistake than well seasoned hounds.

We were a little bothered and were wondering just how to get on the right trail, when Tom discovered that Boob, one of his old hounds, was missing. We were now on a flat, piñon-covered mesa near a high peak, so before going back into the deep, rough canyon, to try to find the right track, we climbed to the top of the peak to listen. When we reached the top we heard Boob barking "treed" just north of us. He hadn't been fooled as had the others, but stayed on the right track and had treed a big male lion all by himself. We were all together now with a lion up a tree and it was only 8:00 A. M. (See Illustration 17.)

We got pictures and then jumped him out for another race. Roy thought this a foolish thing to do but Tom told him it was customary to give the lion one more chance. Roy was a good sport and thought if this was regular practice it was all right with him. The lion made a very long leap, and hit the ground on the downhill side, which gave him a little start on the hounds. They piled off the steep hillside after him, leaving a cloud of dust. Roy said to me, showing some concern, "Will we ever see him again?" Before I could answer they had him up another tree. After the lion was killed we returned to the ranch early.

The guests decided they could ride until noon the next day, and then drive back to El Paso. We rode north from the ranch next morning, and enjoyed a lively cat race in an area easier to ride over, and Roy, especially, seemed to enjoy riding at a fast pace.

The following Christmas I received a fine saddle made by S. D. Meyers, of El Paso, and on a silver plate on the back side of the cantle was inscribed:

Tom Jones, Lee Wilson, J. W. Kirkpatrick, Roy Pratt, and Fred Austin
To Dub Evans, Beaverhead, New Mexico
Christmas, 1934.

The inscription on the saddle therefore establishes the date which had somehow been omitted from my tally record.

FASTEST HUNT ON RECORD

My friend, Colonel R. L. "Ray" Harrison, of Albuquerque, loves to hunt, but on each of several occasions when he had come to Beaverhead, he would be called away on some urgent business. He said, "Looks like my business won't permit me to finish a hunt in peace, but if you ever run across a fresh kill where we might get a lion quickly, I will come if you call me."

FIVE LION HUNTS

Some time later I found lion sign in the Kemp Points, which is only two hours' ride from Beaverhead headquarters. I went back several times during the next three or four days, trying to locate a kill or something definite to start from. About the fourth day I found a deer covered up and it looked fresh enough for the lion to come back to. I went to the ranch and called Ray, telling him what I had found, and suggesting that he drive to the ranch that night, so we could make an early start next morning. He said it would be impossible for him to leave Albuquerque before the next day, but he would try to get to the ranch around noon. I didn't think much of this plan but told him to come on.

Next morning I left early to take the hounds to the kill, leaving Scotty at the ranch to wait for Ray, with instructions to bring him to a certain high peak in the Kemp Points. Nothing had been at the kill since I was there, and I was afraid Ray would waste his trip, but, knowing I would have several hours before Scotty and Ray could get there, I started out to see what I could find. I hunted until noon, going to all the best places, but had no luck. I then went to the peak where Scotty was to meet me, and sat on a rock to eat lunch and wait. I had finished eating when I noticed a young hound smelling right on top of a rock near by, and wiggling his tail just a little. The old hounds were tired and lying around in the shade. I called Brownie, and put my finger on the rock so he would check it. He pressed his nose against the top of the rock, wiggled a little, and then began coming alive all over. Then he threw his head up and howled, long and well drawn out. We had a lion trail, cold but better than anything we had had for a long time. Soon all the hounds began taking the trail. It was too rocky to see any kind of a track so I had to take a chance as to whether they were on the right end or the back-track.

It does seem that hounds can follow the back-track when the trail is real cold with greater ease than they follow the right way of the same trail. I have sometimes thought the reason for this was that the lion had on his feet the scent of a kill which would be somewhere behind, thereby making it easier for the hounds to follow.

As the hounds worked the trail from the flat-topped mesa over to the north slope where there was more brush and the ground was somewhat cooler, the trail was definitely better. At that moment Scotty and Ray rode into the scene. I told Ray he might be in luck, as this trail, which the hounds had been working less than thirty minutes, was the best they had smelled in the several days I had been hunting. We didn't wait long, probably ten minutes, until we heard them jump and tree on the same hillside.

We rode down the hill to find a nice male lion up a pine tree. Ray certainly was in luck this time. He shot the lion and I gutted him and began to feed the hounds. The underbrush was real thick but I missed three hounds. We loaded the lion on Scotty's horse and started him toward the ranch while Ray and I looked for the missing hounds. The wind was coming up and making so much noise in the pines we couldn't hear anything. We went through one saddle and up to the top of another point and when we stopped to listen we could hear the three hounds giving chase to something. I told Ray that the chances were good they were after another lion, but I was bothered because they were running so fast. I thought it might be something else. We rode after them, and soon there was a lull—after a fast race, a good sign that something has treed.

We kept going in the direction we had last heard the hounds, wishing the wind would die down so we could hear better. Then I heard the short bark of dog looking at something. We rode up and there were the three young hounds with a female lion up a tree.

Ray Harrison is the only man I know to leave Albuquerque,

FIVE LION HUNTS

drive two hundred miles, ride for a couple of hours, and kill two adult lions in time to get back to Albuquerque the same day. This is what he planned to do but when we reached the ranch and finished a fine evening meal, I persuaded Ray to spend the night and return home the next morning.

CHAPTER XVII

OLD FIVE-TOE TOM

The following letter from Judge C. M. Botts to his son, Robert, tells, graphically, the story of a lion hunt which he made with us in May of 1932.—G. W. E.

DEAR BOB:

At last here is the account of the lion hunt which I have been promising to send you. In fact, since I first made this promise, I have been on a second hunt and Mr. Evans is urging me to go on another.

Dub had warned me in advance that I should get some practice in horseback riding before we went on one of those hunts. Although I had not been on a horse for over fifteen years, I believed that, because of former long experience on horseback, I would be all right after the first few days of soreness wore off. He warned me especially that my knees would give me great pain. All of this I brushed off with the feeling that he was not dealing with an Eastern tenderfoot, but with a man who had been raised up among horses, and was totally unlike the guests to whom he was accustomed. How very painfully was I disillusioned.

OLD FIVE-TOE TOM

All day Wednesday was consumed in getting out to Lee Evans' ranch in the Mt. Taylor country, but early Thursday morning, Lee, Dub, and I were astride our horses, with the pack at our heels, on the way to a nearby canyon. We probably had gone a hundred yards from the ranch when Dub and Lee started on that confounded little cow-puncher jog trot, and, of course, I had to keep up with them. It seemed to me that I had never been aboard such a rough-traveling steed; and by the time we got back to the ranch that night I was barely able to navigate.

It would be impossible to describe to you the wonderful scenery which unfolds before you in these mountains; and even the pictures we took portray only a very small fraction of the great panorama of nature at its best.

We rode up and down canyon sides where it would seem almost impossible for a goat to go. We went across beautiful flat mesas and through splendid parks of pine, and frequently could ride right up to the edge of things and look out, as it seemed, across the whole world. This was especially true down in the Beaverhead country, where I had my second hunt. And when you stand on the rim of the Middle Fork of the Gila you could readily believe that the lines of Bob Service might have been written from the very spot upon which Scottie and I were standing, when he wrote:

Have you gazed on naked grandeur where there's nothing else to gaze on,
Set pieces and drop-curtain scenes galore,
Big mountains heaved to heaven, which the blinding sunsets blazon,
Black canyons where the rapids rip and roar?

And the cabin over in the Mogollons, where we had to lie out one night on my second hunt, is across from the Horse Camp area of the Middle Fork of the Gila, and is one of the most isolated spots in the country. From the high rims of some of these canyons we could look down and see bald eagles circling far below us which will give you some conception of the heights of the mountains and the depths of the canyons.

In Beaverhead country the deer are very plentiful—you see so many of them that they become commonplace—and we sometimes saw as many as 250 antelope in one day's ride—many times there were one hundred in a herd.

On the first two days of our hunt in the Mt. Taylor country we found no lion sign whatever, although each day we had a chase after bobcats. Both times the quarry took refuge in inaccessible places. The evening of the second day found us at a cow camp some fifteen miles from Lee's ranch, from which, on the morning of the third day, we went off into Guadalupe Canyon; just before getting down into the canyon, we found an old lion marker under a big pine tree. We could see the lion's tracks in the snow, and Lee and Dub estimated that the trail was about a week old. They based their opinion on the fact that a recent snow had fallen in the area.

To my amazement, the hounds picked up the trail and carried it for some distance off the mountain and down the canyon; but it was too old, and the boys had to call the hounds off.

The fifth day we started back on a long swing toward Lee's place and late in the afternoon picked up a fresher trail, which we ran until late in the evening. We called the hounds off and went back to Lee's for the night. The next morning, that is the morning of the sixth day of the hunt, which was the second of February, we were out long before daylight, and by sunup we were back where we had left off the night before, and the hounds were away on the trail. They finally ran it to a loss and Lee and I took the horses and rimmed out to the top of a high, level mesa while Dub went on foot with the hounds on a wide cast to see if he could pick up the trail. By the time Lee and I got to the top we heard the hounds running and soon had them located below us. Fortunately, the trail led right along the foot of the cliff on top of which we were located, so that we could ride out on a point on the rim and watch the hounds until they passed us, when we would gallop on ahead to another point of vantage and again take in the show. To say that this was a thrilling experience is putting it too mildly.

After doing this several times, we rode up to a point where I saw a number of big pine trees growing up from below the foot of the cliff. I suggested to Lee that this would be a good place to stop, because this looked like a spot where the lion would be likely to do a little prowling around and it would be interesting to watch the hounds work their way through. Just as we rode up, Lee pointed to a tree below us and there was our lion. The hounds were there by that time raising Old Ned, trying to climb the pine and daring the lion to come down. You doubtless wonder what my feelings were as I rode up on that old boy.

Lee and Dub had promised me that if we found a lion I might try my luck at bringing him down, and, during all of those six days I had been rehearsing that thought in my mind determining that if such an opportunity presented itself I would not lose it by getting a case of buck-ague, but would keep cool and unexcited. So I dismounted, took off my heavy sheepskin coat, unlimbered my kodak and crawled down and along the side of the cliff until I was in front of the lion and just about on the level with him. I was distant from him at that time about thirty feet. I adjusted my focus and shutter, took careful aim, and snapped the picture, which is not very plain, as I had to shoot directly into the light. I made further adjustments and was just ready to snap the second picture when the old boy opened his mouth so wide it looked like I could stick my head in it; and at that moment I snapped again. Then I folded up my camera, took my gun and asked Dub if I should try for a shot at the eye. Frankly, his eyes looked so big at that moment that I felt sure I couldn't miss that mark.

He said he thought it would be better to shoot him a little above the eye—so I did. The lion crumpled up like a wet rag and tumbled to the ground. I don't think he so much as quivered after

SLASH RANCH HOUNDS

I shot him. The hounds, of course, had hold of him by the time he hit the ground and wooled him all over the landscape. We clambered off down the cliff as quickly as possible, got the hounds off and took some pictures of the dead lion. In at the killing was Old Red, one of the greatest hounds I think that ever lived. His right ear is shorter than his left, the end of the ear having been torn off in some previous encounter.

After we had taken more pictures, and removed the lion's entrails, the three of us, with a great deal of grunting and sweating, got him to the foot of the cliff. Dub and Lee went to the top, tied a couple of lariats together, and let one end down, which I tied around the lion's neck; they then hauled him to the top, where we loaded him on a horse. Then we rode back in to the ranch. The next day, with the lion over the fender of Dub's car, we drove back to Albuquerque; and frankly, it seemed that we had a lot of running around town to do after we got there.

Of course, I wouldn't admit that I was trying to show off, but really the lion was very heavy and we did not think it was necessary to remove it from the front of the car while we were driving around over town.

This lion had been depredating in the country for several years. He was about the size of the two large lions in the city zoo. His right foot had a projecting pad on the left side of the foot which had a horn-like appearance, like another toe—in fact, he was given the name of Old Five-toe Tom. About two or three years ago they found where he had killed a full-grown horse. The killing of old Five-toe on Lee's ranch was really an exciting and enjoyable adventure.

On the second hunt down in the Beaverhead country, we didn't get our lion, though we saw some beautiful hound work while we were trailing one for two days. On Sunday, Dub suggested that we get on our horses and "prowl around a little." It seemed rather strange, now as I look back upon it, that our "prowl" went in a perfectly straight line to a point where we had left the trail the night before. We had no more than reached the rim of the canyon than Old Brownie found a marker and took the trail with the other hounds following down into and across the canyon. We spent the balance of the day following the hounds through all sorts of country until night overtook us and found us too far from camp to get back. As luck would have it, we came to a cabin where we found some chuck and shelter from a drizzling rain which had started to fall. The next morning we started back to camp finding nothing of interest on the way except the wonderful scenery. (The remote location of this cabin has been previously mentioned.)

This has been a great experience. After living in lion country for a quarter of a century and never having gone on a hunt, I had the opportunity to make, and did make, two hunts within a period of thirty days. I get almost as much kick out of looking back over those days as I did when I was actually going through them; and of all the pleasures thus derived, one of the greatest lay in the fact that, during all those days, I did not hear a locomotive whistle or a honk of an automobile, nor the jangle of a telephone bell; that I did not receive a single telegram or see a single newspaper; that I was not called upon by a single neurotic woman who believed that the economic depression, as to her, could be cured by a judgment for alimony; and that everything was so quiet and peaceful just fightin' wildcats and mountain lions.

Yesterday Dub was in the office insisting that I go with him on the tenth of this month to help him and the hounds make an inspection of his little back yard of some 150,000 acres; and a few days ago Lee told me he had recently seen the track of a big lion just a short distance from where I killed mine, and thought we ought to do something about it. But, one thing is sure, if I do go again, I am not going to crack my knee ahead of time, especially

SLASH RANCH HOUNDS

my left knee; and I am going to take, in the way of firearms, nothing short of a cannon.

I wish you could have been with me through it all.

Your Pal,
Dad

CHAPTER XVIII

TWO STOCK-KILLING BEAR

Our Beaverhead Slash Ranch was an ideal prowling ground for bear in the early summer, and, occasionally, when natural feed, such as berries, piñons, and grubs are scarce, a stock-killing bear will show up. When this happens, the only way to stop the depredations is to kill the bear. Sometimes this develops into a very difficult task.

We Evans boys had been raised in bear country and had been taught by our father never to kill a bear in the spring or summer unless the bear was a stock killer. His reason was that a summertime bear was no good—if he had any grease on him it would not be any good, and neither would the meat or the skin. In the fall, however, if the mast was plentiful, the same bear, left to live, would be a fine trophy, yield a lot of fine cooking oil, and some good meat.

When we moved to New Mexico in 1919, there was no closed season and many bear were killed during the summer months. The sportsmen and the Game Department wanted to have a law calling bear game animals and putting them on the protected list, but there was much opposition from livestock people, some of whom felt that all bear were predators. I never felt that way and helped to get a law passed to protect bear, but with a proviso that bear could be killed any time they were killing livestock. There was some conflict for a while. The stockmen found that when a bear started killing stock too much damage was done before a permit to take the killer could be secured from the Game Department. In this state, however, the Game Department officials are practical men and have always co-operated in stopping any sort of depredation by predatory animals as quickly as possible.

In all the years that Evans Brothers have raised cattle on the Beaverhead ranch, only a few times have we suffered from stock-killing bear.

One incident concerns the outstanding work of a well-trained hound. The time was June, 1935, and Joe Evans and his family, from El Paso, were spending the summer with us at the Beaverhead headquarters. He and I took the hounds and started for Horse Camp to do some riding and to look over the western part of the range in general. Chet McCauley was camped at Horse Camp at the time. It was our custom to send out sufficient supplies at one time to last at least a month, thus avoiding too frequent trips over the twenty-mile pack route from headquarters. Consequently, we had not seen Chet for some time, and had not had a report from that end of the range since Joe had been visiting us.

Our neighbor, Tom Jones, who lived on Taylor Creek, and who was with us on the "Old Shot-tail" race, had some good hounds and he never missed a chance to ride with us. Tom was a good hunter, good company, and pretty hard to beat in a friendly pitch or domino game. We sent him word that we were going to Horse Camp for a few days and asked him to join us. Joe and I started out, going west from the ranch, up Wolf Hollow on the Black Mountain Forest Service lookout trail until we reached the head of Gillett Canyon. The drainage of Wolf Hollow is into the

TWO STOCK-KILLING BEAR

East Fork of the Gila, and Gillett Canyon runs into Indian Creek on the west, then into Middle Fork.

After we crossed the divide and headed down Gillett Canyon all the hounds, except Little Brownie, were behind our horses. He always traveled ahead, and was the official checker for bear or lion sign. We had gone only about a mile down the canyon when we heard a commotion just ahead and a little out of the canyon bottom on the left. At this point the canyon was not deep, and had heavy pine and spruce timber in the bottom, and to the south, which was on our left. Cooney Prairie, a nice, grass-covered mesa, was on our right.

We hurried forward, and so did all the hounds that were following us. Brownie was sitting under a big spruce tree looking up at a very large, brownish-looking bear. There was a nice bed under this same tree, where the bear must have been asleep when Brownie came upon him. He probably ran in and nipped the bear and the bear went up the same tree he was bedded under.

Joe said, "That is the shortest bear race on record." He was pretty excited, and thought the bear should be killed, but I told him we never killed a bear out of season until we knew he was a stock killer. Joe argued that the bear couldn't be in such fine condition at that time of the year unless he was eating stock. The bear was unusually thick and heavy-set, built much like a good Angus bull. I told Joe that there was no objection in trying to get the bear to come down so we could have a nice race, as we had some young hounds that needed training anyway.

We threw sticks and rocks at the bear but couldn't get him to come down. Joe said, "I will shoot the bark off the tree right over him, and he should come down." I warned him not to hit the bear. He shot, and the bear shook his head. On looking closely, it was easy to see a hole in one of the bear's ears where the bullet had gone through. Still he didn't come down, nor would he climb higher in the tree. He was standing on a horizontal limb about twenty feet from the ground and seemed satisfied to stay there. I thought we had better get away from there before Joe killed the bear. I told him to stay at the tree and scold the hounds and I would ride down the canyon and call them. This we did, and soon had them away from the tree. Joe then came on and overtook me.

About a mile or two down Gillett Canyon, and at the southwest corner of Cooney Prairie, is a storage dam across the canyon bottom, creating a watering place for cattle, known as Gillett tank. The day was very hot and the hounds went out into the water, swimming, lapping the cool water, and having a good time. One peculiar characteristic of a trail hound is that when it gets real hot, it seems necessary for him to cool off before he can smell a trail. We watered our horses and discovered many bear tracks around the edge of the water.

Joe still wanted to see what had happened to the big bear we had left treed, so, with the hounds freshened up after lying around in the cool water, we decided to go back to the tree. When we arrived there the bear was gone. The hounds soon took up the trail, which led off to the south toward Black Mountain. The whole Black Mountain area is ideal summer range for bear, and this trail led us into the dense thickets, especially on the north side, where it seemed all rocks were freshly turned over and all the bark torn off the fallen logs. The hounds began to scatter everywhere. It was about noon, and hot as only June days can get at high altitudes, and we decided it was best to call in the hounds and go to camp before we lost the whole pack. Brownie was the only one that didn't want to come in—he never seemed ready to leave either a bear or a lion trail. We got the hounds together and went on into camp.

We had sent my son, Bob, and Joe's son, Jodie, with our beds and chuck around the mountains, over an old wagon road on the north side, via Houghton Canyon and Cooney Prairie. They reached camp about the same time we did, and Chet was there

TWO STOCK-KILLING BEAR

also. The first thing Chet said was that he was glad to see us and the hounds too, as he had seen a big bear catch a yearling steer the day before. He said the bear had broken the steer down in the back and, of course, would have killed the steer if Chet had not run him off. Chet could not kill the bear as he was unarmed. He so described the bear that we knew he was the same one we had treed. He said the steer was still alive, but that he was broken down in the back and could not stand up.

After dinner of good ranch chuck, with hot biscuits and plenty of coffee, the boys took a pack mule over to where the crippled steer was. They killed and quartered the steer and brought the meat in for the hounds. They had been gone only a short time when we saw Tom Jones riding into camp carrying a fresh bear hide. He had had a most unusual experience. Having left his place on Taylor Creek that morning, his trail to Horse Camp was through Black Mountain, a few miles south of the trail which Joe and I had followed. Just as he reached the edge of the heavy timber, traveling west off Black Mountain, he heard a calf bawl as if in great distress. Looking up, he saw the calf coming out of the brush at a full run with a rangy-built black bear in hot pursuit.

This was the opportunity of a lifetime, and a break for an Evans Brothers calf. Tom and his hounds took after the bear, and, of course, to defend himself, the bear left the calf. Tom had a .30-30 saddle carbine that he usually carried and it wasn't long until he got a shot which killed the bear. Of course Joe said, "I told you we should have killed that other bear." I agreed with him then, but it was too late. Anyway we did not catch the bear in the act as Tom had been lucky enough to do.

We were up early the next morning and went back into the Black Mountain area near where we had left the big bear trail the day before. The hounds were kept in close and not permitted to take any trail until we found what we thought was the trail of the bear we had seen the day before. It was most difficult to keep them in with so much fresh bear sign all around. Before the summer rains, and after a wet winter and lots of freezes, the ground puffs up and makes the surface ideal for tracking. One could hardly look down without seeing a bear track.

Tom, Joe, the three cowboys, and I had before us what seemed like an impossible task—we were looking for just one bear track among tracks that were too numerous to count. Our plan was for all the other men and hounds to stay pretty well behind and I would work out in front with Brownie, checking all tracks, hoping for the one we wanted.

Luck was with us and we found what we thought to be the track of the killer bear. I put Brownie on his trail, and after he opened up it was impossible to keep the other hounds back. They were keen, fresh, and eager to run, and were soon on another bear trail. This particular area was good riding and it was possible to stay close to the hounds. We stopped them after finding they were on the wrong trail, and Brownie soon picked up the right one. It wasn't long after that until it was easy to tell by the tone of Brownie's voice that the hounds had the right track. We were greatly relieved when we got the bear up and he soon headed for the Middle Fork.

After this trail led out of Black Mountain and began to cross the surrounding mesas, we had no more trouble, as the hounds were making good time on the trail of a fast-moving bear. It was probably around 10:00 A. M. and getting hotter by the minute when we got the trail straightened out. Not good for the dogs, but no better for a bear carrying some fat. There are some rough canyons between Black Mountain and the Gila, and this is the course the bear took. I think the hounds must have overtaken the bear about where Crystal Lake Canyon joins Indian Creek, where he must have spent some time in the running water trying to cool off. We couldn't stay up with them any longer and finally lost the sound of them. However, we kept working down Indian Creek

TWO STOCK-KILLING BEAR

toward the Middle Fork and found they had treed the bear in a big spruce tree on Indian Creek about two miles directly east of Horse Camp. When we killed this bear he had the bullet hole in his ear where Joe had shot him, trying to make him come down out of the tree.

I have heard of bloodhounds staying on the scent of a certain person, and passing through and over the scent of many others without losing the right trail. I have also had lots of experience in trailing wild cattle with a good trail hound that would follow one trail through many other cattle tracks; but this was the first time I needed to track one particular bear through the fresh sign and tracks of many other bear; and I take great pleasure in recording this very fine hound work.

We suffered no more losses from bear that year, although there must have been two or three dozen bear which stayed on our fully stocked range all the rest of the summer. I would not like to live on, and operate, a mountain ranch without a good pack of hounds. Not only are my hounds a great source of pleasure to me and my friends, but this is one of many instances when they have been of actual value to the ranch.

CHAPTER XIX

"TAKE YOUR TIME, BUT HURRY"

BY HOXIE THOMPSON

The following letter, written in September, 1935, by Hoxie H. Thompson, of Trinity, Texas, to his son Hoxie H., Jr., who was attending Davidson College, at Davidson, N. C., tells the story of a lion hunt better than I can tell it.—G. W. E.

DEAR SON:

I am sending you, under separate cover, a small package of "jerky." This jerky is the lion hunter's food, and when he leaves camp each man puts some of it in his pocket, and he always expects to stay on the lion's trail until he loses the trail or captures the lion. You can go for several days on a pocket full of jerky and about three drinks of water per day. It was positively amazing to me how long these fellows could go without water.

In eating jerky, you should not try to bite or cut it, but just take a piece and pull off a string which you can chew until it disappears. Really, it is made from the very best beef of a young steer, dried and cured immediately.

This trip is the outstanding hunting trip or any other trip that

"TAKE YOUR TIME, BUT HURRY"

I have ever made. My opportunity to make the trip was purely accidental, as I found out after going to El Paso. It seems that Mr. Kirkpatrick and the Evans Brothers, at a camp meeting during the past summer, agreed upon a family party for the first part of September. As I had told Mr. Kirkpatrick several times that I was very anxious to make one of these hunts, he asked if it would be all right to bring me along. They told him it would be, so really I had the benefit of the entire party trying to give me the opportunity to kill a lion.

I arrived at El Paso Tuesday afternoon about five o'clock, my train being nine hours late because of a washout. Mr. Kirkpatrick met me at the train and gave me some little instructions about necessary preparations for getting off the next morning at five o'clock. He called for me at the hotel at that hour, and we had breakfast with one of the Evans men at his home; leaving immediately for the Evans headquarters ranch at Beaverhead, known as the Slash Ranch. Looking at the map of New Mexico you will see the Elephant Butte Dam where we turned west for about sixty miles, arriving at the Slash Ranch about four-thirty in the afternoon, having stopped at the home of Graves Evans at two o'clock, where he and his wife had prepared a wonderful chicken dinner.

We were up early Thursday morning, September fifth, and each man was furnished with his saddle horse for the day, out of a bunch of more than fifty horses. All the camp equipment was loaded into a wagon with four mules attached. As soon as everything was packed and horses were saddled, we left with the following men:

Mr. G. W. "Dub" Evans, who was the "Generalissimo" of the party; J. W. Kirkpatrick, whom you know, and who had been on these trips several times; Rube Evans, who lives in El Paso, and who was the lifesaver for me the day I got my lion, as he met me on the opposite side of the canyon on his horse, without which it would have been impossible for me to have gotten up on the other side of the canyon; Lee Evans, who really could handle a bunch of hounds—and you could hear him call these hounds two miles across the mountain; Bill Cowden, a brother-in-law of the Evans men and a brother of Gene Cowden, who, you remember, owns the ranch adjoining Mr. Hughes' ranch at Kerrville; Paul Evans, who lives in the Davis Mountains near Valentine, and who is a real hunter himself, with his dogs; Graves Evans, who lives on his ranch near Winston, and with whom we stopped for dinner the first day; Reeder Webb, from Odessa, Texas, sheriff of Ector County; Eli Jones, who has been with the Evans men at various times, and is certainly a wonderful man to be with on a camp, especially at meal times, as he is a real "flapjack" cook; Tom Jones, who owns a ranch near Beaverhead, also a great lover of dogs and likewise a lover of hunting; and Joe Evans, Jr., and G. W. Evans, III, who looked after the horses. How these boys could ride. They would be in the saddle before daylight, and get out and have all the horses back before you knew they were gone; they rode at a run whether it was daylight or dark. One other young fellow whom they called "Chet," was the teamster for a part of the time.

One thing I want to say for this entire party, and that is that it was the most agreeable and cleanest bunch of men that I have ever been thrown with for that length of time. I regard this Evans family as distinctively outstanding. There are eight brothers and one brother-in-law, Bill Cowden, all living, and not one of them ever touched liquor in any form. As you will note, we had five of these brothers on this trip, and I believe only one of them even uses tobacco, and he smokes cigarettes occasionally. During the entire week in camp there was no unclean language or dirty jokes, and, believe me, we had plenty of fun.

These men have been reared on the range in the West, and it is very remarkable that they conduct themselves in such an upright manner. I would give the credit to the mother, and I am

"TAKE YOUR TIME, BUT HURRY"

sure that she is a wonderful woman. Of course, in cases of this kind, the dad can do his part, but I always feel that a mother really deserves the credit for the best influence over her son.

I told Dub Evans that I would like very much next summer to come up there with you while he is rounding up his cattle and spend some time with them and help them in this work, as I know you would enjoy this more than any other kind of vacation. If you will lay to it and get yourself in shape so that you can graduate in 1937 without having to go to summer school next summer, I will try to arrange for a trip to this ranch with you, and, believe me, this is worth some good, hard work on your part.

Included in this outfit were twenty-two hounds, all blooded hounds, and one Airedale. We had fifty-two saddle horses. However, the reason for those extra horses was that they were taking them over to Horse Camp to be left in the pasture there. It was about twenty-five miles from Beaverhead to Horse Camp, where we had our camp for seven days. Leaving Beaverhead Thursday they took the hounds in a run for about a mile in order to keep them together; and on this first mile I found out that I had one of the best horses in the outfit, as he always wanted to stay in the lead, especially when the going was fast.

We had quite a bear chase the first day, following his trail for about three or four hours, but were never able to jump him. We arrived in camp about five o'clock in the afternoon, and I realized what it was to be sore from horseback riding, as we had covered more than forty miles of very rugged mountain territory, and a good part of this time we were going in "high gear." My knees felt as if they had tenpenny nails driven through each one. However, after getting off the horse and stretching around for awhile, I was able to stand up fairly well.

The first night the bed seemed very hard, as we were sleeping in tents and had our bedrolls on the ground. However, on the second night, I was so tired that I did not know how the bed felt, and was dead to the world until time to be up at four o'clock the next morning. The third night the soreness from the top of my head to the end of my big toe was so complete that I was almost numb, and I felt like it was immaterial whether I awoke the next morning or not, but after a good night's sleep the soreness seemed to begin to disappear, and from then on I was in good shape.

Mr. Kirkpatrick, with Dub and some of the other men, had a wonderful lion chase, and came in with a young lion and a bobcat. They reported that they were sure there was an old lion with two cubs, and that we would be able to get the trail on this old lion the next day. On the following morning (Saturday) we got over into the same part of the country, and the hounds started the trail and carried it across the Gila River for about five or six miles until three o'clock in the afternoon, when we finally called them in, thinking that we might start again in the morning. We were back early the next morning, but the trail was cold and the hounds did not have much luck in picking it up, so we decided to spend part of the day fishing. Mr. Kirkpatrick had several lines with some hooks and flies, and we cut poles along the river. In about three hours we caught twenty-five mountain trout, which were cleaned and carried into camp, and, believe me, we had a wonderful meal that night.

On Monday we made a hard day's hunt, but were unable to pick up any trails. We did strike a good trail in the canyon, but the hounds must have followed the back-end of the trail, because when they got to the top of the rim they found where the lion had spent the night and could not follow it any farther. It is often possible to get a good trail down in the canyons but when you get to the top of the rim, where the sunshine and wind can hit the grass and rocks, the hounds are unable to follow the tracks. On Tuesday, the seventh day out, we got back into the same territory and the hounds were soon on a hot trail, as the old mother

"TAKE YOUR TIME, BUT HURRY"

lion and her other cub had finally come back into that country to see what had become of the other member of the family. I was riding with Eli Jones when we heard the hounds and we crawled out on a high point where we could locate them down in the canyon. We soon discovered Lee Evans, Tom Jones, and Graves Evans standing out on another high point waiting to see which way the hounds would come out of the canyon.

Lee called Eli and told him that he thought the hounds would go out on the other side, and, if so, to get around on another point where he thought we could get down into the canyon, and to make it snappy. It was a good four-mile ride for us to round one of the headers and get out on a point where we could get into the canyon and we made this four miles in "high." We got down as far as the horses could go, when Lee called and said for me to shed all excess baggage and try to get down into the canyon on foot with a rifle.

In the meantime, Dub and several of the other men had already gotten across the canyon on another point. When he saw that I was coming down on foot, Dub got out on a high point across the canyon and proceeded to direct me so that I could slide down to the river. After quite a bit of sliding and slipping I was able to get to the bottom, although I had slipped once onto a big cactus plant and was punctured with cactus needles on my left arm and hand. Dub met me at the bottom of the canyon, and said that he would take my gun and that I would have to climb three or four hundred feet where they had a horse waiting. I told him that I just possibly could not climb two feet.

"Oh, yes, you can, take your time, but you will have to hurry." He said the hounds had a lion up a tree and had been holding him there for more than an hour, and he was afraid that the lion was going to decide to leave. He took my gun and I proceeded to crawl for about four or five hundred feet up the side of the mountain where Rube Evans had his horse, and I finally reached him. I got on the horse and Dub caught hold of the horse's tail and we climbed on up the mountainside within about three hundred feet of where the lion was treed. Then we had to get off and do some more climbing over the rocks.

We finally got up to where the lion could be seen, and several of the other men were there and told us it was a tremendous big lion. Dub looked over the rocks and turned to me and told me it was a male lion, and it was one of the biggest ones he had seen, all of which did not help my condition much. When we finally got over the rocks where we could see him lying out on a limb, he looked big as a horse, but I was so weak and out of breath that I could hardly hold the gun to my shoulder, much less do any shooting.

Finally, Dub tried to hold me up so as to help me get my breath and at the same time steady my nerves. I will admit that seeing a big lion up a tree for the first time was somewhat exciting. The first shot was a clean miss and the lion went out of the tree, but those hounds were right on him and they had him up another tree in less than a half mile. When we discovered the lion in the second tree, it was right over our heads, and I was very much opposed to trying to shoot it myself, as I was afraid that I would miss again; but they insisted that I go ahead and shoot, as, even if I did miss, the hounds would put it up another tree. When I looked along the gun barrel all I could see were those two big old eyes and they seemed to be riveted on the gun barrel and to know what it was all about. This shot went right between the eyes, and that was the end of my lion hunt.

The men were able to get hold of the lion before the hounds had an opportunity to do much chewing, so were able to get a very fine skin in perfect condition; but instead of being a male lion, it turned out to be a female, and, of course, the mother of the young lion which was killed four days previously.

We returned to camp after going off into the canyon and up

"TAKE YOUR TIME, BUT HURRY"

again; and the next morning broke camp and returned to Beaverhead. Mr. Kirkpatrick and I returned to El Paso in his car that afternoon. I thought that I was "stove up" from horseback riding, but after getting into the car and starting back to El Paso, I found that I was really sore and unable to do more than slide out of the car seat. This soreness wore off very rapidly after a good hot bath, and I returned home determined to have another trip as soon as I could get the invitation and make the proper arrangements. However, on my next trip out, I am going to try to do a little training, especially in some real rough horseback riding before the hunt.

Your devoted,
Dad

CHAPTER XX

"HOUND VITAMINS"

BY HOXIE THOMPSON

The following story of a lion hunt made with J. W. Kirkpatrick and H. H. Thompson in April, 1940, is told in Mr. Thompson's words.—G. W. E.

J. W. Kirkpatrick and I left El Paso shortly before noon on Tuesday and drove to the Graves Evans ranch, near Winston, New Mexico. After arriving at the ranch and playing a few games of dominoes we drove over some of the ranch property with Graves and his two young boys, aged ten and twelve years. We rounded up a good big herd of sheep, put them in a corral and hung up a lighted lantern on one of the fence posts. This lighted lantern serves as a watchman for the sheep during the night, as the wolves will not come into the corral as long as there is a light near.

The evening meal was one of those for which the Evans families are famous.

After lunch the next day we left for Dub Evans' Horse Camp ranch, where we were to start hunting the following day. This is

"HOUND VITAMINS"

shown on the United States forestry map as Double Springs, but to all of us who have known this place for some time, it is Horse Camp; in fact it has been known as Horse Camp since the early days, when this country was first settled by the Spaniards. Horse Camp is in the Mogollon Mountains and the Gila National Forest, being located about six miles north of the Gila River. This is now the home of Mr. and Mrs. G. W. Evans. They have recently added to the original old log house, and have made a very comfortable home of six bedrooms with two baths, and they were building also a separate camp house.

This is one of the finest game countries for deer, wild turkey, lions, and bear; for scenery, it is not excelled in any part of the United States and is one place where nature is in its original state. Between the Black Springs post office and Horse Camp, as Kirk and I drove in on Wednesday afternoon, we saw a large number of deer and antelope; and we saw them on each trip in and out of Horse Camp.

When we reached Horse Camp, Mr. and Mrs. Lee Evans were there, with Lee's hounds, having come down the day before for this hunt. We were given one of the usual famous welcomes, with everything planned and arranged for our comfort, happiness and pleasure, and I wondered if the Evans families are not entitled to be at the top of the list of those who can make a fellow feel entirely at home.

The five of us were out early Thursday morning with nine hounds, and mounted on good horses of the husky Spanish type. These horses, for many generations back, have been bred and raised in these mountains; which is absolutely necessary, for you depend upon your horse and know that the horse can get over the ground better and safer than you can.

The hounds, one of the best packs that Lee and Dub have ever owned, were as follows:

"Pancho Villa" is one of the lead hounds; the only trouble with him is that he rarely barks on the trail; but the other hounds can tell by his movements when he is right and they make plenty of noise.

"Queenie" and "Brownie," two very dependable hounds.

"Neeley," one of the old hounds, and when opened up you know that he is right on the lion's trail.

"Rough," another very dependable hound; he and Neeley could be depended upon to follow the lion's trail, no matter how hard the going was, and when they came to the worst places either Neeley or Rough would be the first to take the leap. The others would follow if they could.

"Hoxie," a little red bloodhound, which was given to me by Lee Simmons, former manager of the state penitentiary, and which I gave to Dub. He developed into one of the finest hounds in the pack, and they call him the "double checker." He has a very peculiar voice, and even I was able to tell he had hit the trail when he gave his three tones. The entire pack has complete confidence in "Hoxie."

In addition to the above there were three other older and very dependable hounds to carry the trail on through when it got too cold for the younger ones. It was remarkable how Lee and Dub could put the hounds right when they got balled up on a trail out in the open spaces where the sun and wind had weakened the scent of the animal, which is so pronounced in the canyons and shady places.

Next morning, which was Thursday, just as day was breaking, we started out for that section where the last mountain lion sign had been seen; but before we were half way the hounds took up a hot wildcat trail at the foot of Skunk Mountain, and started out fast and furious. We followed them for several miles, until we were on the east rim of Indian Creek with no place near where we could get down into the canyon. We sat and watched those hounds follow the tracks of the cat, over the rocks and through

"HOUND VITAMINS"

the crevices, until finally they were on the west side of the canyon. Watching them follow the trail and its meanderings was like having a front-row seat in the balcony of a theatre. We could see each hound and hear every bark until they got into such rough country they couldn't follow the cat any longer, and we were forced to call them off and go back to the house.

That afternoon, Dub, Lee, Kirk, and I took .22 rifles, got into Dub's car, and went prairie dog shooting on his ranch, which was quite interesting and enjoyable; with each fellow trying to prove his marksmanship was superior to the others. While out shooting prairie dogs we saw several droves of antelope and Dub ran his car beside some of them so I could make moving pictures. When antelope are running their best they are covering territory pretty fast.

Friday morning, after breakfast, we were again on our way before four-thirty, headed for the panther country. It was not long before we got on a cold trail, which was followed through Green Fly Canyon and worked back into Cassidy Canyon, where it was lost, so we headed back through Green Fly and into a third canyon called Jordan Canyon. All these canyons are very steep and can be crossed only in certain places; especially is this true of Cassidy and Jordan. Green Fly is a smaller canyon and connects Jordan before joining the Middle Fork of the Gila River.

While we didn't get the lion that day, Kirk and I got our systems filled with "hound vitamins," which Kirk insists is the greatest cure for what ails you.

Saturday morning we were out again at four o'clock and again picked up the trail over in Cassidy and worked it back toward Jordan. About noontime we found a buck which the lion had killed the day before and had dragged into a very good hiding place high up on the side of the canyon. Later we saw where the lion had hidden behind a small bush and exactly where he had jumped on the deer as he made the kill. Evidently the lion cuts the deer's throat with a downward sweep of his mighty claws.

You might think that when you had found a kill where the lion had been eating, it would be a simple matter to follow the lion's trail, but just the reverse is true, especially if there is more than one lion and they make return trips to the kill. In this particular case we were soon convinced that this was a female lion and that she had her kitten, or kittens, over in Cassidy Canyon, a distance of about five miles from where the kill was made. After finding the kill on Saturday and following the back trail over into Cassidy, we did not get back to Horse Camp till about dark.

Kirk said we would have a lion before ten o'clock Sunday morning and it would be a female with some kittens. Kirk's guess was correct concerning the kind of lion, but we failed to make the killing on Sunday, nor did Kirk share the kill. Kirk's bad knee got so bad at this time that he could not ride, so he left us Sunday night and went home. We hunted unsuccessfully all day Sunday and returned to camp late that evening with a very badly worn-out bunch of hounds, men, and horses; it was the sixth continuous day of hunting through these roughs and it was unusually hard on all concerned. But Tuesday morning we were out again at four o'clock and over in Cassidy about six. The hounds again struck the panther's trail and followed it over to the mouth of Cassidy where it joins the Middle Fork of the Gila River, a very deep and beautiful canyon. At four o'clock Tuesday afternoon Dub, G. W., III, and I were sitting high on the rim of Cassidy, and Lee had worked his way down into the canyon with the hounds, where they had again opened on the trail.

Looking across at the very steep bank on the other side, I asked Dub if one could get along that side of the canyon under the bluff. He replied that he had been across there once on his horse, but that it was very rough. However, within the next thirty minutes he was riding that same side of the canyon for the second

"HOUND VITAMINS"

time and leading a horse for Lee. G. W., III, and I heard the hounds again barking on the trail. I asked him how we could get to them if they should happen to jump this lion; and he pointed to a very steep point and said that we could get down into the canyon there. I told him that he might get down there, but that I knew I couldn't. It was only a few minutes until we heard the hounds jump the lion, and they ran it for less than thirty seconds before the lion took to the tree, and as soon as they called me to come down I knew that I had to follow G. W., III, over this so-called deer trail, which proved to be no trail at all—it was just a slide—and that is where I had to have confidence in my horse.

It required about thirty minutes for us to round some of the headers to the canyon and slide down to the bottom. During all this time we did not hear the hounds and were very much afraid the lion was gone. However, when we reached the bottom of the canyon Dub was waiting and the lion was in the top of the tallest pine tree it could find. As the sun had already gotten down behind the mountains, we did not have any too much light in the canyon, but Dub told me not to be at all nervous, and that he could show me the lion up in the tree. He said to shoot at it just as if I was going to shoot a prairie dog. I asked him if it was a female lion and if she had any kittens.

He said, "Yes, but go ahead and kill her, as the old male lion will look after the kittens."

The hounds were under the tree waiting. Old Rough had been making many trips back and forth from the tree to a place on the side of the cliff, where at least one kitten had taken refuge. We think there was only one kitten.

Fortunately, I was able to hit the lion in a vital spot with the first shot, and the hunt was ended. If the lion could have stayed out of the way thirty minutes longer we would have missed her altogether, as it was the last day we could stay for the hunt.

As soon as we got the lion I asked Dub if we were going to

SLASH RANCH HOUNDS

skin her down there in the canyon, as I did not see any chance of getting her out of there.

He said, "No, it is getting too late"; also that we would need to take some pictures of the lion, and that G. W., III, could bring it out on his horse.

Dub had worked his way down into the canyon with his rifle and I knew that he had to get back to his horse on foot. I asked him if I should take his gun; but he said no, that he would take the gun, G. W., III, would take the lion and that I would do well to look after myself, as it was going to be a worse job getting out than it was getting in. However, in this case he was somewhat mistaken. It was worse on the horse but easier on me, as I did not get a single bruise or scratch coming out, although I had gotten plenty going down. It was eight-thirty when we got back into Horse Camp, and I can truthfully say that it was the most interesting experience that I have ever had on any kind of a hunting trip.

CHAPTER XXI

A NINE-FOOT LION

Still another one of our hunts was "written up" by Joseph Kornfield (?) and published in the Wichita, Kansas, Beacon. The story appeared under the headline, "Harvey Blair Kills Nine-foot Lion," and is quoted in part below.—G. W. E.

Into the last stand of the Old West, early in December, 1937, went Harvey H. Blair, prominent Wichita sportsman and oil operator, accompanied by Roy Shoeb, of Augusta, to hunt for mountain lions.

The biggest reward of the hunt was a large lion skin measuring nine feet from tip to tip. The kill was made on the old Slash Ranch, eighty-five miles south of the town of Magdalena, New Mexico, among the foothills on the east slope of the Rockies.

Five chases were necessary before the big cat was spotted and treed for the kill.

At an elevation of nearly two miles (*sic*) above sea level, the scene of the hunt was in the fastnesses of the Black Range and the Mogollon (called "Mugayown") Mountains.

Inspiring is this Mogollon Mountain country. Like spires, the silver spruce and long-leaf pine, three feet in diameter, shoot up nearly one hundred feet into the rare air. The mountain lion, hunters explain, is a member of the cat family like the tiger, panther, etc. It inhabits mountainous and foothill regions from timberline down to around four thousand feet. The elevation at which they are found depends on the season, since they follow the migrations of the deer which are their prey.

A lion will kill on an average of one deer per week. The lion springs from a tree or bluff onto the back of the deer, ripping downward with murderous claws. It prefers to make its kill on the north side of a mountain or in a canyon where it is hidden in the shade. Mountain lions have tremendous strength and have been known to carry their prey for considerable distances from where the kill was made in order to find plenty of leaves and grass with which to cover the carcass. (Cowboys on the Slash Ranch recall an instance where a lion jumped over a rail fence carrying a sow snatched from a pen.) The lion returns again and again to the hidden carcass for further gorging. Because the carcass is so well hidden beneath its camouflage of brush and pine needles, it is rare that a man ever finds one, but the hounds always nose them out.

Blair and Shoeb were guests for two weeks at Slash Ranch, one of the best known ranches in the West. Owned by the Evans family, it covers more than 310,000 acres. Blair described the Evanses as "the most gracious hosts in the world." He explained that these men neither smoke, drink, nor swear, but are "he men" in every sense of the word. They never take any game out of season and are known for their efforts on behalf of game conservation. Although best known for their mountain lion hunting prowess, the Evans brothers have also shown their skill as bear hunters. During the past ten years, the brothers have led hunts on which a total of forty-four bear and eighty-six mountain lions were killed.

A NINE-FOOT LION

On a lion hunt, the hunting party rises at five o'clock. The men are armed with .30-30 rifles. Although lobo wolves are now extinct in the Mogollon country, the coyote remains a nuisance and the rifles are as much for them as for the actual game sought. Two packs of hounds accompany the party, some veterans of four or five years, others young hounds taken along for training. One pack runs for two days, making thirty-five to seventy-five miles per day. The speed at which the pack travels causes the horses to strike up a good pace in order to keep within hearing of the hounds. It is remarkable that it is possible to do this, considering the rugged topography of the country.

CHAPTER XXII

BEAR AND ANTELOPE HUNTS

Captain A. T. McDannald, of Houston, Texas, is a big independent oil operator, and also has some fine ranches. In 1940, one of these was the Adobe Ranch in New Mexico, about fifty miles from Horse Camp, just south of the Magdalena-Horse Camp road.

The Adobe Ranch supports one of the largest antelope herds in the state, and each year, when there was a special season on antelope, Cap would invite from twenty to thirty of his friends from Houston and elsewhere to the Adobe as his guests for an antelope hunt. Early in September, 1940, I had a long distance call from Cap, who said he wanted to arrange for a bear hunt during the four-day antelope season, because, when the hunters got their antelope the first day, as about half of them usually do, there is not much else to occupy their time for the next three days while the others are getting theirs. After the first day it is much harder to get good shots, as the antelope get pretty wild and work back into rougher country.

Cap said when the first ten or fifteen of his guests got their antelope he wanted to bring them to my place to hunt bear with the hounds. I tried to tell him that bear hunting wasn't like that,

BEAR AND ANTELOPE HUNTS

and that the only way to have a successful bear hunt would be for a small party of good riders to come to Horse Camp and spend the night, leaving at daylight with the hounds and a cowboy guide for each hunter. Even by doing this it might take several days to catch even one bear.

Cap said they couldn't do that, that they wanted to stay at the Adobe where they were all set up with cooks and comfortable quarters, and drive over after breakfast, reaching Horse Camp around 9:00 or 10:00 A. M., hunt bear for a few hours and return to the Adobe. He has a way of getting things done so I told him I would do what I could to help out.

In preparation I asked Jack Hooker, of Silver City, to come with his pack of bear hounds for the hunt, and had a couple of extra hands come over from our Montosa Ranch. On September 29, we were ready when some of the hunters drove over from Adobe Ranch, saying Cap would come to Horse Camp next day with any that wanted to hunt bear. This was rather indefinite, but I thought there would be at least ten who would want horses. As we had seen some bear sign toward Cassidy Spring our plan was for Jack Hooker and me to leave about daylight with the hounds. G. W., III, and Jodie Evans would stay in camp and have at least twelve horses saddled and ready when the Adobe party arrived. The boys were to accompany the hunters to Cassidy Spring and wait there. I told G. W., III, to stay well separated from the party, and on high ground when they reached Cassidy, and to listen for a signal from me. With these instructions Jack and I took off as scheduled.

Fast riding was impossible, as there had been an unusual amount of rain and the ground was so soft a horse would sink to his ankles. Before we even reached Cassidy Spring, Rough picked up a trail. With Jack's four hounds, two I had borrowed from Johnnie St. John, a Government hunter, and five of mine, we really had a pack. Mixed packs don't always work well together, but the trail was fresh and the morning real damp and cool, and it wasn't long until the eleven hounds were working together on the feeding trail of a bear. We saw tracks in the mud and knew it was a big bear. The trail led through oak thickets and we saw the tops broken where the bear had pulled the oaks over to get at the plentiful supply of acorns. The saplings were not big enough for a bear to climb, being about as high as a man's head on horseback, and it was plain to see what had happened.

Any feeding trail is slow because the animal goes round and round over the same ground. It wasn't long, however, until the trail straightened out, leading toward Black Mountain, the summit of which was about six miles to the east. Once the bear quit feeding and led a straight course, the hounds traveled too fast for us to stay close, because of the deep mud. A good fast trot was about the best we could get out of the horses, and the hounds were soon out of hearing.

We had followed about two miles when we heard hounds barking "treed" off to our left in a header of Sam Martin Canyon. We thought everything was working out fine, but when we reached the tree, instead of a bear we found a bobcat. Making a hasty check we discovered only five of the hounds at the tree with all the old hounds absent. I shot the cat at once and scolded the hounds so they would leave it and go to Jack, who was calling them.

As soon as we left the tree the hounds took off ahead, going at once to the bear trail. They soon left us far behind, but this put us on the course of the other hounds. We were now certain they had gone over the top and far away from Cassidy, where the guests were to stop. When we reached the Forest Service fire trail from Black Mountain lookout to Horse Camp the going was better, and we didn't stop to listen much until we reached the lookout tower on top of the mountain. I climbed the tower to listen, but before I was hardly started up, Jack said he could hear the hounds far to

BEAR AND ANTELOPE HUNTS

the east in Trap Corral Canyon. We listened a while to see if they were moving or staying in one place. We decided the bear had stopped and that we would ride east down the divide to a low saddle between Trap Corral and Jordan canyons, a favorite passageway for bear. I would stop there while Jack rode on east until he reached a point even with the hounds, where he would go off into Trap Corral, being sure to approach from the east. We had no desire to shoot the bear, and we knew it was too far away to be reached by Cap's party that day.

Cassidy Spring was some ten miles, maybe farther, from where the hounds were baying the bear, but just about between the bear and the Middle Fork. In this area, if a bear is followed long enough he will finally go to the Middle Fork because of the natural refuge it provides. We figured if this bear did move we might head him back over the mountain toward Cassidy. Jack approached the hounds from the east as planned, and found the bear was not treed, but stopped in a tangle of fallen logs. He was plenty big and able to defend himself, but with that many hounds around he had to back up against something to protect his rear. The bear had rested a while so, when Jack rode up, he broke to run. I was listening and, noting they went back up Trap Corral, I moved west also so as to stay about even with them.

By the time they reached the Crystal Lake saddle at the head of Trap Corral, it was getting hot and the bear had whipped back a lot of the hounds. I rode down into the saddle, losing my advantage of high ground and good listening, to put some of the hounds back on the trail they had quit. The bear, with three or four of the lead hounds, had already passed through and was returning near the course he had followed on the way over.

Some of the hounds with me now would follow the trail but would come back as soon as they got far ahead. This was good for me as the soft ground had tired my horse to a slow pace. I followed the trail as indicated by the hounds, and soon climbed out of Crystal Lake Canyon, working farther south and straight toward Cassidy Spring.

I couldn't imagine what had become of Jack. He was a good bear hunter and, although he had never been in this immediate area before, he was at home when following his pack in any mountains in the state. I had to give my pony plenty of time climbing out of Crystal Lake Canyon, but when I got on top and started downhill he did much better. The trail went off into a steep header of Sam Martin Canyon, high up on the west slope of Black Mountain; and about two miles down the canyon I rode right up to the hounds with the old bear up a large spruce tree. He was standing on a horizontal limb about twenty feet up and seemed pretty well satisfied to stay there. We were three or four miles from Cassidy and I had little hope that G. W., III, could hear even a shot at that distance. I rode all around the tree talking to the bear, while more hounds kept coming all the time, and they, too, were making lots of fuss.

The bear seemed pretty well settled, so I climbed to higher ground and fired several shots, but received no answer. After a while Jack came. He said his pony just about quit on him so he unsaddled and let him rest awhile before coming on. He agreed to stay at the tree to keep the bear up while I went to Cassidy to see if any hunters had arrived. My horse was so tired that when I reached a little park across the last canyon from Cassidy, I yelled; and G. W., III, answered immediately.

I asked if he had anyone with him and he said, "Yes." I told him the hounds had a bear treed and for him to bring the party across to where I was. There was a little opening just east of Cassidy Spring and the ground there was flat. I thought of Coxey's Army as twelve mounted men dashed into sight, and about midway across the little flat, a horse hit a soft place, bogged to his belly, and rolled over.

Jodie was off in a minute, and told the hunter to take his horse

BEAR AND ANTELOPE HUNTS

and go on while he got the horse up. When they reached me I told them the news, and we hurried as fast as we could through the brush and rocks with the horses bogging to their knees. The bear hadn't moved, and any old-time bear hunter will be wondering if he would remain treed while so many mounted men approached. He must have had enough running, for he didn't move when we rode up. The time of day was about noon.

One of Cap's party had a movie camera and was anxious to get a picture, but clouds had built up and it was real black toward the west. U. K. (Kub) Barker, who was cooking for this occasion, had provided all the riders with lunches so we ate while waiting for the sun to come out. After a hard downpour of hail and rain, accompanied by severe lightning, the sun appeared and pictures were taken.

The big bear was finally shot by several of the hunters, who lined up like a firing squad and fired all at once on my count of three. We picked the strongest horse in the bunch, loaded the bear whole, and, walking, led him toward the ranch. I told Cap of the cat we had shot that morning which would be near our trail into camp. He suggested that we pick it up, too, to have for pictures. This party of fourteen was the largest I had ever seen at a treed bear in my life. And to have ten men travel fifty miles over wet mountain roads, get a bear which they all saw together, return to camp, and make the fifty-mile return trip in time for an early supper was almost unbelievable.

Captain McDannald's guests on this bear hunt were: George E. Peddy, R. H. Stork, Jr., Paul B. Hunter, E. F. Hall, V. A. Brady, Gene Farren, Roy W. Smith, Cleaver McDannald, and R. M. McDannald. Once again Cap was ambitious but his effort paid off.

Several hunts have been made on our ranch by the Phillips Petroleum people, of Bartlesville, Oklahoma. These men enjoyed both deer and antelope hunts as well as fishing trips. The same party came each time and was made up of K. S. "Boots" Adams, president of the company; George Oberfell, vice president; Arthur Hughes, in charge of sales; and many of their district agents. Sometimes they would bring distinguished guests, a few of which were John Ringling North, of Ringling Brothers Circus; Tom Cooper and Moss Patterson, of Oklahoma Transportation Company; Paul Tibbets, of Greyhound Bus Lines; Dr. McBride, of Oklahoma City, and many others.

Usually the Comer brothers, Jack, of Santa Fe, and Brad, of Albuquerque, would make all arrangements in New Mexico. Billy Parker, in charge of aviation for the Company, would leave the home office with Boots Adams, and some of the other officers, and go anywhere in the United States where there were guests who were to come on the trip. Often he had gathered up each of the guests in one of the big Company-owned planes, then would fly to Albuquerque, where the plane would remain until the hunt was over. Jack and Brad Comer would provide a truck for baggage and cars for the party to drive to Horse Camp.

In October of 1943, Jack and Brad made reservations for the party for one of its biggest hunts, but something happened at the last minute and the big party couldn't come. However, Jack and Brad knew I had made preparations for them so they came anyway and with them was Bill Black, of Santa Fe, and Carl Shappiro, of the Northern Oil Co., Duluth, Minn.

Jack and Bill both got their antelope the first day and were eager to hunt bear while the other boys bagged their antelope. Jack and I started down Indian Creek with my bear hounds, Ranger and Hoxie. We had two younger hounds along but didn't expect much help from them. Benito acted as guide for Bill, and they were instructed to work around in front of us on the east side of Indian Creek, so in case the hounds jumped a bear which they couldn't stop, Bill could get in position for a shot at the bear ahead of them.

BEAR AND ANTELOPE HUNTS

Indian Creek is very rough, but not as rough as parts of the Middle Fork, so every bear that is jumped in Indian breaks for the Middle Fork, Benito knew the country well and took a stand where a jumped bear would be most likely to pass. The hounds soon found a feeding bear trail along the hillside on the east side of Indian. Jack and I rode out to the top so we, too, could be between the hounds and the Middle Fork, and as soon as we were out on top where riding was good we went at a gallop along the mesa that extends up to the top rim of Indian.

We went about a half mile then rode out on the very edge to listen. We didn't wait long to hear that the hounds had jumped, and, as we expected, were coming at a fast clip in our direction. In less time than it takes to tell it we saw a brown bear coming toward us, not more than two hundred yards from the top rim and traveling in a lope, but across a canyon from us. The hounds were coming fast, with Ranger in the lead and closing the gap between bear and hounds. They were on the opposite side of a pretty wide side canyon and at least three hundred yards away from us. Jack asked if he should shoot but I advised waiting to see what would happen when the hounds overtook the bear. I hoped he would tree.

Just then we heard shots to our left which had to be Bill as there was no one else in the area. I told Jack to cut loose, as we were closer to the bear than was Bill, and chances of soon treeing this bear were spoiled anyway. The bear turned back at Jack's first shot, but the second shot downed it and it rolled over a time or two into the shadows of the steep side canyon and was out of sight between us and the hounds. The hounds were soon there and baying the bear. I called out then to locate Bill and Benito and they answered from about halfway down a long point, in a little saddle that led into Indian Creek from the east.

I asked Bill what he shot at, and he said, "A bear." I asked what color, feeling certain he was shooting at the same bear although it was entirely too far.

He replied, "Black."

Benito had located a bear lying under some big rocks across the side canyon, and on the same point the brown bear was on, and Bill had shot at it without having seen the brown one. Bill said the black bear was wounded but had gone out of sight toward the bottom of Indian Creek Canyon, and that Benito had taken Bill's gun and was looking for the bear.

Jack and I thought the brown one was done for, as the hounds were still baying in the narrow bottom of the side canyon. We rode down the point to where Bill was, and at about the time we reached him, Benito began to shoot in the bottom of Indian. He was really bombarding, and when the shooting was over he called to us that the bear was dead.

Still thinking the brown bear was safely ours, we went with Bill off into Indian to where Benito was. When Benito found the bear, he was still up but badly wounded. Benito was riding a young horse and was afraid to dismount to shoot, so he rode as close to the bear as he could and fired from his horse. The shadows were heavy and Bill's rifle had a scope sight through which it was difficult to see in the darkness, which was why it took so many shots to finish the bear.

He was a big male and we thought it best to help hang him up before leaving. We gutted and hung him as quickly as possible and then realized we could hear nothing of the hounds. Jack and I rode out of the canyon we had come down, listening all the time. When we reached the top we heard the hounds a long way off to the north which was up Indian Creek and back toward camp. We decided Jack's shot must have creased the bear and he had recovered, and we really rode to get closer to the hounds. Every time we stopped we could hear them baying the bear but they seemed to be traveling all the time.

BEAR AND ANTELOPE HUNTS

We finally got ahead of them, and heard them coming down a boxed-up side canyon into Indian Creek. There was a little bench about fifty feet high above the bottom bluff. They were on top of the bottom run, with Ranger in front of the bear, traveling and looking back, Hoxie close behind the bear. Jack was off his horse with his gun in his hand when they came in sight, and shot the bear, which rolled off the bluff and fell almost at our feet.

We had two male bear, a brown and a black, killed before noon, and had never been more than five miles away from Horse Camp at any time during the day. The antelope hunters had filled out and there was a pretty happy party of hunters around the dinner table at Horse Camp that night.

The only wound we could find on the brown bear from Jack's first shot was a hole through his left front ankle. The leg was not broken but would give way when the weight was on it. A broken rock from the ricochet must have struck the side of his head enough to knock him down, for the foot wound was too slight to do much damage.

CHAPTER XXIII

BLANCHE

In January, 1941, State Game Warden Elliott S. Barker introduced me to Mr. Edwin R. Closs, of Sparta, New Jersey, who was eager to do some lion hunting. I told Mr. Closs that Mr. John Haire, of Fort Dodge, Iowa, had arranged for a hunting trip early in February, and there would not be time for another hunt before then.

Mr. Closs suggested that I take him with me to Horse Camp, where he could do some riding and take some pictures while waiting for Mr. Haire to finish his hunt.

We had been out at Montosa Ranch ever since the close of deer season the previous November, leaving Saturnino Chavez as caretaker at Horse Camp, to feed the hounds. One of our best female hounds at the time was Blanche, whose two male pups, Ranger and Crook, were about five months old when we returned to Horse Camp the last of January. Having been absent from Horse Camp for two months, I did not know where there might be lion sign, so I told Mr. Closs that my first duty would be to make some rides with the hounds along, to check the surrounding coun-

BLANCHE

try. He wanted to go along, taking his moving picture camera just to see if anything showed up.

My main pack now consisted of a black-and-tan, named Neeley, full brother to Blanche; Rough, a blue tick out of Blanche; a red hound named Hoxie, which was a purebred bloodhound sent to me by Hoxie Thompson; and another red hound named John, an outstanding hound out of one of my bitches and a red hound from Lee Brothers of Tucson. The four last named were true on a trail but when not hunting regularly and being real keen, might run a coyote or fox.

Mr. Closs and I went southeast from camp the first morning. He was riding a mule and I a good mountain pony. We had reached the drainage of Jordan Canyon, which empties into the Middle Fork, at a point about three miles south of the summit of Black Mountain. Riding down the west prong of the canyon, we had to stop to fix Mr. Closs' saddle which was about to slip off over his mule's head. About the time we had the saddle off, I heard the hounds around a bend and hurried around the point to find a dead deer right in the bottom of the canyon. It appeared to have been killed by coyotes just a little while earlier and they probably were eating on the deer when the hounds rounded the bend. The temptation was too great and all of the hounds but Hoxie ran after the coyotes.

We rode on in the same general direction, looking for lion sign. We still had Hoxie, and had gone only about a mile to the divide between Cassidy and Jordan canyons when I saw a lion track. I dismounted to show it to Hoxie. He was a little timid but I followed the track only a short distance before I saw him working on it, but not opening. I got out of the way and he passed, showing more interest, but still silent. I got back on my horse and followed Hoxie closely, as he was silent and we didn't want to lose sight of him. Luck was with us for we jumped the lion within a quarter of a mile. When the lion got up, Hoxie opened and howled loud and fast, but not for long, as the lion soon treed in a pine in the middle of a small park. I told Mr. Closs to get some pictures while the lion was in the tree with the hound beneath, and be ready for a fine running picture on the ground when I made the lion jump out. He did just as I suggested and should have gotten some fine moving pictures but I have never seen them.

By the time the lion treed again some of the other hounds had come back and it wasn't long until they were all there. We needed meat for the hounds and as it would be a week before Mr. Haire would arrive, I told Mr. Closs to shoot the lion, which he did. We got more action pictures of the hounds wooling the lion and of me feeding the hounds the liver, heart, etc. It was a female and not heavy, probably a hundred pounds, and we loaded it on my horse and returned to camp that evening without seeing any more sign.

Next day we went east up toward Black Mountain. When we climbed above eight thousand feet, the snow was too deep on the north hillsides for good riding so we circled back to the north toward the head of Indian Creek. We found no lion sign but did tree a bobcat, which Mr. Closs shot with a .22 pistol after taking some close-up pictures. The hounds were getting a pretty good work-out and were settling down.

We were expecting Mr. Haire to arrive the next day, and, as the roads to Magdalena were bad, G. W., III, went there to meet him. Mr. Haire was to leave his car at our Montosa ranch and come to Horse Camp in the pickup.

In the morning, we went south down the west rim of Indian Creek to the Middle Fork. After going off the top rim, we found some lion sign on the hillside and benches. We worked all the way down to the river finding some old sign most everywhere. We left our mounts about halfway down and walked to the river, checking some rough country on the way. The snow was all gone in this area, except in the shade on north slopes. We rounded a

BLANCHE

bend in a side canyon near the river bottom and walked right up on a big bunch of turkey gobblers. By the time they took off, climbing and flying up over some high rocks, Mr. Closs had his camera on them and buzzing.

We had located more lion sign and were killing time until Mr. Haire arrived, so, the following day, Mr. Closs and I went back to the Middle Fork, where we got a lion up after a thrilling race, through some of the roughest country a pack ever followed a lion. We followed this lion on the west side of Indian Creek from the top rim down through the high spiral rocks almost to the river bottom. There we came to a place in the bluffs where no hound could pass and where their barking indicated they were neither bayed nor giving chase but, rather, that they were bothered. We worked our way over to where they were, trying to climb up through a gap between two high rocks. Mr. Closs, with his camera, was right with me but neither of us was armed. We were expecting Mr. Haire that night and had agreed to shoot nothing else until he arrived.

I was the first to climb up and peep over the gap where the hounds indicated the lion had passed. I saw the lion below me in a kind of a sink in the rocks, down about fifteen feet and seemingly with no possible exit except back through the very narrow opening where we were. Mr. Closs was just behind me and I told him I could see the lion and to squeeze in beside me and be ready for a most unusual picture. As soon as this was done he began letting his camera buzz with the lion looking up at us and most as nervous as we were. I told him to hold it on the lion while I dropped a rock and that there would be action. I also told him that the lion might have to come out over us and if so to hold the camera on the lion as long as he could, then duck down, covering his face with his arms, and let the lion go over our backs.

As soon as I dropped the rock the lion began to move, looking up all the time for an escape route. Without much hesitation she started to scale the wall of sheer rock about thirty feet high and not more than fifteen feet across from us. If Mr. Closs did keep his camera on her, he has one of the most unusual wild animal pictures in existence.

We could go no farther and, feeling we had the picture of a lifetime, climbed back down the way we had come. We returned to camp but G. W., III, and Mr. Haire didn't get in until late, as they had trouble on the road.

We talked a lot that night about the excitement of the day and were eager to go back into that country next day. This we did but after completely circling the area where we had seen the lion we failed to find where she had come out. Later developments indicated she was still in there.

Having seen the signs of young lions on our previous trips into the area, and failing to get a fresh trail of the lion we had seen the day before, we decided to go back to the place where the hounds had picked up the trail originally. We put them on the back track and followed it to where the lion had left her young before we got after her. This was interesting and it worked. The back track led across one header and up a mountainside to a break in the bluffs near the top of a high pinnacle at about the same level as the main top rims of the Middle Fork.

Just after the hounds passed through a cut which led into the shady side where there was timber and snow, they jumped two young males. Luckily the pack split and soon treed both of them not far apart. Neither of the hunters seemed eager to kill lion kittens no bigger than a bobcat but both had come a long way at great expense for just a single trophy. They finally decided to kill one each. Mr. Closs would have one to go with his female and Mr. Haire would have one to go with the female he hoped to get.

We had a full day by the time we reached camp but decided that if we returned next day to the spot where we jumped the young lions, sooner or later we would get the track of the old

BLANCHE

one. It was too rough for horses, but the hounds were "lion minded" now and we had only to start up the side of this pinnacle to have them go right on up. They opened as soon as they got near the top. The old lion had been back in the night and they were on her fresh trail.

Now for the reason for this chapter. As I stated earlier Blanche had run loose around Horse Camp all winter with her two pups, Ranger and Crook. The caretaker, Saturnino, said she would take the pups off at times and be gone for two or three days. The country is so big and rough and the distance we cover on horses in one day so great that we usually wait until hounds are about eight months old before we take them out with the pack. If started too young they are inclined to stay with the horses where the going is easier. For this reason we had been leaving Ranger and Crook in the pen.

On our way to the river the day we got the fresh trail of the old lion, we were overtaken about four miles from the ranch by Ranger and Crook, who had finally dug out of the pen and trailed us up. We were glad to see them and decided if they wanted to go that badly we would let them. They paid no attention to us, but stayed with the pack, close to Blanche. We soon heard new voices in the pack and when they came off the mountain, where we could see them, both of the pups not only were working, but were right up in the lead.

The river was about three feet deep and the icy water was very swift, not easy to cross on a horse and really tough for hounds. We stopped at the river, wondering if the lion had crossed. The hounds were coming fast, straight down toward the water. Just ahead of them was a big rock, connected with the hill on one side, with a drop of seven or eight feet straight off into the water on the other. The hounds soon covered this rock indicating the lion had turned around a few times on top of it. Without hesitating, little five-months-old Crook bailed off into the water, going out of sight, but he came up swimming and headed straight across, without a bobble. He picked up the trail immediately, followed it across the bottom, and had started up the hill on the other side before any other hound got there. They all had to swim the river but none of them jumped from the rock into the water as Crook did.

The water was about thirty feet wide and we think the lion jumped all the way across from the top of the rock. We could go no farther on horses so picked a good place to watch and listen, hoping they would jump and tree the lion before going out of the Middle Fork. We didn't want to try to get horses up the frozen hillside, which would be necessary to get out of the Middle Fork going south. They did jump about halfway up but didn't tree until they reached the very top rim. We waited until the hounds had the tree definitely located, then John Haire and I started the difficult climb to reach them.

We finally made it, but circled the tree some so as to keep the lion up, for we knew if she jumped out her next stop would be over the top. Both of the pups were under the tree baying like veterans and I feel very certain Blanche had shown them other varmints before this. After John killed the lion and she finally stopped rolling we had to hold onto her all the way down so the skin would be worth saving after reaching bottom. John, too, now had a female and a kitten, as did Mr. Closs.

John was anxious to try for a cat with bow and arrow. Mr. Closs was so enthralled with the Gila Wilderness area that he wanted to finish out his two weeks at Horse Camp, while John and I took the hounds back to Montosa to hunt bobcats. The Montosa ranch is mostly a woodland type with scattered pines; a nice country to ride over and bobcats are plentiful. The only way a cat can escape good hounds there is to climb a tree, as there are no cracks to crawl into. We had fine luck. John got three cats—shot out of trees with bow and arrow. We might have had more but

BLANCHE

he ran out of arrows and some of them are probably still sticking in pine limbs too high to climb for.

We were amazed and thrilled at the speed and accuracy of Ranger and Crook after cats. Blanche had done the best job of training that I have yet seen. Both developed into good bear and lion hounds, but Crook died at the age of two years. Ranger soon became my lead hound but got poison and died while in his prime.

We left Blanche at Horse Camp again later with two pups for her to train, but this time it didn't turn out so well. She went away with the pups and did not return. Next year she turned up at Sam Means' ranch west of Silver City.

Sam told me that Kenneth Hollman, a prospector, found Blanche and the two pups with a lion treed somewhere in the Mogollon Mountains, probably forty or fifty miles from Horse Camp. Hollman killed the lion and took Blanche and one pup to his camp. The other pup was wild and wouldn't follow them, and the one that followed, soon left.

As Mr. Hollman had no use for Blanche, he let George Seismore have her. Sam had gone to Seismore's to get a hound named Freckles, when he saw Blanche and was very much impressed with her looks and actions, so Mr. Seismore let him take her home with him. He later mated her to Freckles and produced Beave, a blue tick.

It was some time before I knew about all this, and when Sam was telling me about it he asked if I had a hound that he could borrow to train Beave and another pup or two. He said Blanche and Freckles were too old and slow to hunt much. I let him have Bell, a black-and-tan bitch, and he soon caught a lion or two. He then bred Beave to Bell and she had four pups, and when he sent her back to me he also sent Blue along.

Blue is a wonderful hound. He is a little off type; his ears are too short, and his head a little thick, but otherwise he is exceptionally good—muzzle strong, good eyes, stands up well on his feet, and has the kind of voice that makes the hair stand up on your neck and a thrill go down your spine. He has great endurance, is absolutely true, with courage enough to tree a bear or lion, even alone and in strange mountains.

At Lee's suggestion, I bred him to one of Lee's females, Yellow Bell, and out of this we now have four young hounds about eighteen months old.* Two black-and-tan males, named Don and Brownie, and two females, one a blue tick named Bugle Ann and the other a black-and-tan named Betty. These four young hounds show a lot of promise but there is little chance of training them on lion, as it is rare now to find a lion trail within reach of Horse Camp. It makes one feel sad to go to a favorite hogback or saddle, checking for markers or scrapes, find none, and go back six months later to learn nothing has been there since the first visit. At the present rate of extermination this great American cat will soon be extinct.

---

* The pedigree of these hounds is as follows: Alice and Redbone were mated to produce Bell and Brownie. These litter mates were mated and produced Little Brownie and others, including Albert Pickens' hound, Sam. Another litter from Bell and Brownie produced Al. We mated Brownie Wyn, a registered bloodhound, with Al, getting Boots, which, mated with Drum, an Inman hound, produced Neeley and Blanche. Boots was also mated with Little Brownie, producing Alice. A mating of Alice and Yankee Dan gave us Queenie, which we mated with a full brother of Little Brownie, producing Yellow Bell.

CHAPTER XXIV

NO BAG LIMIT ON LOOKING

Bear and mountain lions are remarkable connoisseurs of natural beauty. The habitat of each, it seems to me, is most usually found in mountain areas where the scenery is truly spectacular. And not only do they choose to live in such beauty spots, but generally make their last stand there. I recall a certain tree in the great mountain range of southern New Mexico not so much because the hounds brought to bay there a bear or a lion, but because it was one of the most beautiful spots it has been my privilege to view.

All wild animals have a characteristic beauty, but none can compare with a bear in prime condition during the fall, or a mountain lion during the winter months. Bear have some protection now by law and, since this animal plays such an important part in the wildlife picture, I repeat, I hope it is never exterminated. But it is different with mountain lion. This picturesque animal is extensively hunted both by the predatory animal control branch of the U. S. Fish and Wildlife Service and by hunters of the State Game Department. In addition, of course, are those who hunt for sport, most often experts who maintain packs of lion hounds.

SLASH RANCH HOUNDS

The records might show that more lions are being taken now than ever before—but this does not mean there are more mountain lions. It means simply that they are more extensively sought and run down. The paid hunters, both federal and state, have excellent hounds along with equipment such as trucks and trailers, and they can move their camp from one mountain range to another in a matter of hours, where, formerly, weeks were required. Communication also is greatly improved. The U. S. Forest Service maintains telephone systems into all mountain areas of the state for the purpose of fire protection, but all permanent ranches throughout the area also are on these lines. Thus, if lion sign is seen, the word is soon telephoned around and it is not long before a hunter is on his trail.

It might seem foolish for a stockman to raise the question, but I feel that the mountain lion, one of the most beautiful of America's big game animals, is, under present hunting methods, on the road leading to early extinction. Again I repeat, I would not like to see this happen. Certainly I will not be guilty of killing the last one.

But in this day even the wildest beauty, the more remote views and panoramas, no longer are reserved for the bear and the mountain lion—or even those who follow lion and bear hounds on the hunt. More and more the American people are rimming out over the West in their search for natural beauty. Millions find what they are looking for in the spectacular national parks and monuments; other millions content themselves with the varied facilities available in the national forests, or state forests and parks. It all depends upon the degree of beauty one is looking for—and the kind. But whatever it is, it can be found in abundance in America's West, and particularly in New Mexico.

Unquestionably the most interesting, and unique among the beauty seekers, is a group called the Trail Riders of the Wilderness, men and women from all parts of the country who, regardless of

NO BAG LIMIT ON LOOKING

age and station in life, find common ground in unspoiled, uncrowded, roadless country and the enjoyment and fellowship that goes with exploring it in organized parties. Riding under the sponsorship of The American Forestry Association, these expeditions for beauty and enjoyment also have the Federal Government's sanction, for both the U. S. Forest Service and the National Park Service participate.

Most of these trail trips, which, by the way, were first organized around 1933, are in national forest wilderness areas or the back country of national parks and monuments. By "wilderness area" is meant an area 100,000 acres or more maintained in its natural state—that is, no roads, no buildings, no development of any kind. If you want to enjoy it you must park your car somewhere in the foothills and walk or swing onto a good mountain horse. Nor is it country for week-end vacationists, for to really benefit by the wilderness you must dwell awhile in its fastness, under wilderness conditions. That is what the Trail Riders of the Wilderness do, spending from twelve to fourteen days away from the road's end in expeditions ranging from twenty to twenty-five people.

Beginning in 1935, I was privileged to handle Trail Rider parties in the Gila Wilderness for seven consecutive years. They were wonderful people from all walks of life, from practically every nook and corner of the country—men and women who rode long and hard trails just to look, to gaze and absorb beauty in its wildest form. And it never failed to impress me that they came away as fully satisfied with their "bag"—natural beauty—as the hunter is with his. In a way, perhaps, more so.

Hunters and fishermen keep taking from the land and the waters until there is nothing left to take. But Trail Riders leave everything as they found it for those who follow—the next rider or bunch of riders. That is why there is "no bag limit on looking."

And that is why this kind of wilderness use should be encouraged and expanded. There are a number of areas in New Mexico that justify this type of expedition, and the people of the state should do everything possible to attract these wilderness riders. Not only do they bring additional revenue to New Mexico, but each completely satisfied Trail Rider is a real ambassador of good will for the state.

In view of the fact that most of the hunts I have made were in the Gila Wilderness and over much of the same ground covered by the Trail Riders, it occurred to me that the wilderness people have enough in common with the hunters to warrant a place in this book. And when I approached Erle Kauffman, at Washington, D. C., on the idea he responded by practically writing this chapter for me.

Erle Kauffman is the editor and writer who, until a few years ago, was the guiding hand of the Trail Riders of the Wilderness. It was he who originated the idea, developed it, and, until 1949, organized each of the expeditions—sixty or more in all, I believe. And though he personally lead expeditions breaking new ground throughout the West—in the Cascades of Oregon and Washington, in the Sierras of California, in the Wind River country of Wyoming, and in the Rockies of Colorado, Idaho, and Montana— the trails of the Gila rate first in his books. Not only did he lead the pioneering expedition for the Trail Riders in the Gila country in 1935, but he returned with the expeditions of 1936 and 1938. Like many wilderness people, his regard and affection for this great area was, and remains, boundless.

Thus when I asked Mr. Kauffman, who, up to 1950, was editor of *American Forests,* the official magazine of the American Forestry Association, to look back on the Gila trails of the thirties, as well as the Trail Riders who rode them, the response was enthusiastic.

"This business of re-discovering the wilderness is always pleasant," he wrote, "but when you draw a line around the Gila and say, in effect, 'This is it!', it is simply too much to resist.

NO BAG LIMIT ON LOOKING

Better than fifteen years have passed since we broke trail in the Gila for the Trail Riders, and I have not looked down into the West or Middle Fork canyons for more than a decade. Yet my impressions of that country are so great it is easy to re-live each mile we covered, each canyon we explored, each twilight when we filed silently out of camp in search of lion sign, or the print of a bear paw, or the sight of wild turkey flashing and thundering out through the timber. I did not appreciate then, as I do now, the part big game played in the enlightenment and enjoyment of Trail Riders. I'll never forget, for instance, the hush that always settled over the string of riders coming down the rough, rocky trail from Mogollon Baldy to Turkeyfeather Creek when you would turn in your saddle and say, 'Watch out for sign, folks, this is lion country.'

"We invariably would ride for two or three miles in a state of excitement and high expectancy, as though we feared, or hoped, that a great, tawny puma would spring at us from every concealed rock or overhanging branch. One of the riders, whose name I cannot recall, told me afterwards that these three hushed miles, where there was no sound save the metallic clink of horseshoes against rock, were the most enjoyed of the entire fourteen-day expedition, mainly because of the electrifying atmosphere they created. It is the excitement, simulated or otherwise, of never knowing what a turn in the trail will bring.

"In fact, I still receive letters reciting the story—and it will be told around campfires whenever Trail Riders gather—of the young physician from New Jersey who went camera hunting for a bear, and actually found one. Remember?—It happened on Iron Creek Mesa just before the party disbanded at Willow Creek in 1936?

"Half the pack string and practically all the saddle animals broke away the previous night and headed toward Beaverhead Ranch. While the boys were trying to round them up—or enough to move us out—this young doctor tucked his movie camera under his arm and headed up the trail. There was but one thing on his mind—a last effort to film a bear for the folks back home.

"There are now a dozen versions of what happened after that, but the one I like best goes something like this:

"Fellow riders overtook the excited doctor about three hours later on the trail, breathless and carrying a boot in each hand. What had happened? With the light of sweet victory in his eyes, he related how he had stopped by a small stream to cool and rest his feet. 'I had just pulled off my boots,' he explained, 'when I happened to look up into the face of a black bear, a huge, ugly-looking critter. Guess I should have been frightened, but I wasn't. All I could think of was what a great picture that bear would make standing there, not twenty feet away, staring me in the eye. I reached for my camera but before I could bring him in focus he was hightailing it through the underbrush. I went after him and for ten minutes we played hide-and-seek. Finally he was out in the open and, man alive, what a picture I got!'

"'But why are you carrying your boots?' someone had asked.

"'Boots!' was the incredulous rely. 'Good Lord, did I chase that bear in my stocking feet?'

"Ranger Henry Woodrow, when I told him that story one night at Prior cabin, enjoyed it tremendously, and declared he knew the bear personally, a little runt of a fellow who came to the stream occasionally to drink.

"No, there is no bag limit on looking, as you so often said—and no hunter has had a more spine-tingling experience than the New Jersey doctor—Dr. Charles Oderr, of Westfield—who came to the Gila country for its fantastically beautiful scenery and ended up on a dramatic bear hunt with a camera. But then they sort of go together—wild life and wild beauty.

"Another favorite game story of the Gila springs from a mountain lion you or one of the boys killed on the rock slides back in

NO BAG LIMIT ON LOOKING

1939. As it was told to me, the riders talked the cooks into roasting a quarter and after a liberal sampling, some of the more vociferous howled from every canyon they came upon.

"These are the episodes Trail Riders like to tell around their campfires—and they grow richer with each new telling. But, as you so well know, the purpose and spirit of trail riding goes far beyond the dramatic incident. The idea was born around 1930, a product of too much road building and too little wilderness preservation. Priceless areas like the Gila and the Pecos, just north of Santa Fe, were beginning to vanish under the pressure of roadbuilders and exploitation. To halt this trend in the national forests, at least, the Secretary of Agriculture placed primary wilderness areas under lock and key. Today, something like fourteen million acres are so protected.

"With this accomplishment came the pertinent question of how the average American citizen was to enjoy these areas—how he could cash in, so to speak, on the wilderness that had been saved for him. Not everyone, by any stretch of the imagination, could go to the wilderness, saddle up Old Paint, throw a decent pack and head up the long trail. Without know-how and experience it was much too hazardous. To buy experience in individual guides and packers was, for most people, much too expensive.

"Thus, organized trail riding on a non-profit basis as a service to wilderness enthusiasts developed from an idea into the Trail Riders of the Wilderness. And it has been tremendously successful. I suppose two thousand or more men and women have participated in the expeditions, and that these have influenced additional thousands to the wilderness cause by recitals of their experiences. The important thing is that perhaps not more than a handful of these people would have set foot in wilderness country had it not been for the kind of trips you helped develop.

"But back in 1935 when we gathered at Silver City for the first Gila expedition, trail riding was in its swaddling clothes.

SLASH RANCH HOUNDS

Not many people knew then that the American wilderness had not perished in the tracks of the last covered wagon. I would have given a great deal to have peeped into the minds and hearts of those fine people we accompanied out of Silver City on the first Gila expedition—to have shared their inner thoughts and feelings as we moved by Sapillo Creek, Gila Hot Springs, Grudgings and the Cliff Dwellings, and on into the Middle Fork and West Fork of the Gila River. Veritable Edens of color, ruggedness, and unspoiled beauty, these great canyons must have played heavily upon each rider's emotions.

"I once put the question to Dwight Taylor, the eminent Washington, D. C., attorney, who was a member of that first party. 'They were overpowering,' Dwight replied, 'but not to be compared with the emotional upheaval when you stand on the summit of Mogollon Baldy and look back over a maze of mountains and mesas and canyons. It is then you suddenly come to realize the magnitude of your accomplishment—that for fourteen amazing days you actually have been living in a half million acre wilderness under true wilderness conditions, slightly modified, of course, by such conveniences of the modern world as ready-made sleeping bags, flashlights, and canned butter. For anyone geared to sidewalks and beautyrest mattresses, this is indeed quite a transition. The remarkable thing is that you do not realize it until you look back. That is the magic of trail riding.'

"It should be interesting to trace through that pioneering expedition for it set the stage for all trips that followed. From Grudgings and its fascinating history, as I recall, we explored Little Bear Canyon and the narrow floor of the Middle Fork before bedding down at Prior. If my memory is good, it was raining and cold at Prior and we were not at all unhappy over the descent the following morning into the canyon of the West Fork, at Jenks. Here was the heart of the Gila, as intriguing a spot as you will find anywhere in these United States. It was here, too, that our good friend Elliott Barker, state game commissioner, paid us a visit, accompanied, as always, by some of the best big game stories in the Southwest.

"From Jenks began the three-thousand-foot climb to Mogollon Baldy with its vast panoramas—and then to Turkeyfeather Creek, a rough descent, including the three hushed miles we watched for lion sign, at your suggestion. From Turkeyfeather it was but a short ride over Iron Creek Mesa to Willow Creek and trail's end.

"To mention all the splendid wilderness people who made that pioneering ride in the Gila is not practical, but certainly it should be recorded that two members of the expedition, Marion Mair, of Oneonta, New York, and Margaret Loughran Bruns, of Long Island, New York, went on to become top-ranking Trail Riders in the United States—ratings being based on the number of expeditions and miles ridden. And because they played such an important part in pioneering expeditions in other wilderness areas during the years that were to follow, mention also should be made of A. H. Hutchinson, of Chicago; Lillian Judd, of Waterbury, Connecticut; Mrs. L. F. Gates, of Wilmette, Illinois; and Dwight and Helen Taylor, of Washington, D. C. All won their spurs on the trails of the Gila Wilderness.

"From 1936 on, minor changes were made in the route Trail Riders followed in the Gila, and for several years your Beaverhead and Horse Camp ranches were used as expedition headquarters. I particularly remember when we operated out of Horse Camp, for that was the year such newspaper notables as Erwin Canham, editor of the *Christian Science Monitor;* Doris Fleeson, the well-known columnist; and John O'Donnell, star reporter for the *New York News* turned Trail Riders, and with great success.

"But the ultimate goal of every group was the bald summit of Mogollon, the magnet that attracted Trail Riders from the moment they swung into the saddle. Jessie Saunders, of San Francisco, who rode with three Gila expeditions and then wrote a

25,000-word manuscript on her experiences, had a lot to say about this ascent. I vividly recall some of her descriptions—'Aspen trees even a large man could not reach around,' and 'Magnificent Douglas firs towering like redwoods toward the sky.' On top she could look 'South into Old Mexico, west into Arizona; to the north and east New Mexico spread out on all sides.'

"But most of all Jessie was impressed by the Eden of wildflowers on Mogollon's higher reaches, and collected innumerable specimens—Canadian aster, penstemon, wild geranium, larkspur, mallow, cinquefoil, harebell, to sample a few.

"Others wrote at length and interestingly on the Gila, of course, while several, like Lloyd R. Koenig, of Webster Grove, Missouri, developed an extensive photographic collection.

"But writing and photography and rock and wildflower collections are but by-products of the main business of trail riding. No richly booted dudes from foothill guest ranches, no experimenters with emotions or time, the Gila Trail Riders knew what they were about. They knew that eyes trained to interpret stock market reports are endowed with new clarity by penetrating wilderness vastness, by seeking the movement of antelope or deer or mountain lion or bear at twilight. They knew that mental reservoirs drained by the problems of everyday living are quickly refilled at the spring of natural beauty. And they knew that fellowship born under wilderness skies is a treasure of great value.

"Glorified nature lovers? Not by any means. It might be said that the trail rider is a symbol of everyman's search for knowledge and contentment. But you and I also know him or her as a slightly romantic individual responding to an inherent urge to explore and to adventure, well salted with the age-old desire for understanding, for a good time, and for good fellowship. The thing that sets the trail rider apart from others is that he recognizes this urge and does something about it.

"Come upon them before they get into levis and boots and you

NO BAG LIMIT ON LOOKING

find hard-working clerks and bankers, teachers and industrialists, nurses and engineers, salesmen and physicians. You find plain, everyday Americans with domestic duties and income taxes—the same old problems that bother you and me. But there is a difference. Once the wilderness is ahead, once a boot is thrust into a stirrup, the chattels of the past vanish. So do the years. Pioneers are on the move again.

"Yet there is not a seasoned explorer among them. Few, in fact, have ever been away from the sound of a locomotive whistle or an automobile horn. But they go, sometimes timidly, sometimes boldly, facing the hazards, the hardships, and the inconveniences of wilderness travel and wilderness living with the same zest, the same urge, which characterized their nineteenth-century, covered-wagon ancestors.

"This possibly over-dramatizes the situation—though I am not too sure. But to play safe, let's put it another way. The American wilderness is being rediscovered. The partnership of man and horse, interrupted by the roadbuilders and the machine makers at the turn of the century, is again in ascension. And, what is more to the point, the multitudinous blessings of wilderness living, like rain upon a parched earth, are once again being bestowed upon a pressure-weary people.

"And since there is no bag limit on looking, the Gila, the Pecos, and other wilderness areas in New Mexico should continue to bestow their blessings."

CHAPTER XXV

OLD BROWNIE

The following, written by the late J. W. Kirkpatrick of El Paso, who is often mentioned in this book and who was one of Old Brownie's friends and admirers, is a tribute to Old Brownie, called by Kirk "one of the greatest hunting hounds of all time."

"O Lord of humans, make my master as faithful to his fellow man as I have been to him. Grant that he may be as devoted to his family as I have been to him and them. May he be as open faced and undeceptive as I have been. Give him a face as cheerful in its expression as has been my wagging tail; a spirit of gratitude as unto my licking tongue. Fill him with patience as I have been patient, waiting for him to come to me. Fill him with my watchfulness, my courage, and my readiness to give even life for him or his. Keep him always young and endowed with the spirit of play, as I have been. Make him as good a man as I have been a dog. In short, make him worthy of me, his dog."

www.ingramcontent.com/pod-product-compliance
Lightning Source LLC
Chambersburg PA
CBHW071703160426
43195CB00012B/1557